Nicole L'Hirondelle
August 2008

Praise for the Authentic Canadian Real Estate System from Canadian investors:

"If you want a predictable real estate future, you must design it in advance. I know of no other real estate expert and educator who is as competent as Don Campbell. His research is unmatched and his results predictable."
—Gordon D. Wusyk, Founder and CEO of Predictable Futures Inc.

"Seventeen months after joining and starting the ACRE system, I now own 141 units! I learned more from the author in this time about character, business, investing, money flow and personal goal setting than I have in my entire career. Don R. Campbell is a mentor and an inspiration, who provides something unique and extremely helpful."
—Ernst Marsig, Investor and Business Owner, Y2 Marketing

"I have thought about buying real estate for income for 30 years. The ACRE Quickstart program has changed my mindset from *thinking* about it to *doing* it—and believing that it is not just possible, but necessary."
—Joan Watson

"Using the ACRE System, I bought 154 positive cash flow properties, all while working a full-time job. I now own over 350 properties."
—Arlen Dahlin

"My journey began when I signed up for the ACRE Quickstart program. Since then I have bought four properties (two by myself and two as joint ventures) and sold one, helping pay off all my debt—all in less than 14 months. Last August I got married to the love of my life and we paid for our wedding—a very fancy one! I owe my success to what I have learned from Don Campbell and the network I have established through him."
—Ali Ardakani, Momentous Consulting

"My involvement in REIN and the Quickstart ACRE system since 1995 has significantly changed my life. Following your strategies, I have been able to create a lifestyle that has given me peace of mind in terms of financial security. In fact, I took a big jump in terms of lifestyle by taking a job I've always wanted—National Ski Team Coach. Not only does REIN positively affect my real estate, but it has had a huge overall impact on my life, providing me the freedom and confidence to attain my life goals."

—Murray Cluff

"We've been implementing the various techniques in the system, with flawless results. Quite simply, this system is a must for all existing and prospective landlords. By implementing this system, you will increase your bottom line while significantly reducing your time commitment and headaches.

—Brent Beagle

"As a novice, I appreciate the opportunity to get the real, no-hype, nuts and bolts on real estate investing. After taking us step by step through the process, I am already feeling confident about putting it into action."

—Nicola Battista

"I can't imagine a better educational investment than being a member of the REIN group. The value of what we are learning doesn't become evident until the rubber hits the road. It gives one the confidence to get into the deals and know we have someone to call when we need help."

—Garet Bonn

"I joined REIN and, using their ACRE Quickstart techniques and doing due diligence on my part, I was able to buy five investment properties in one month. Their extensive support; helpful forms, *Insider Reports*, and networking opportunities have given me the confidence and momentum to start my future full-steam ahead."

—Brian Simpson

"This is extremely motivating. I am always amazed by how exciting it is to be with and meet others with the same objectives. A five out of five!"

—Angie Wu

"The best business decision I ever made was in joining the group (out of all the training I've done). I owe you a lot … you've changed our lives. Thanks so much for your continual commitment to the group and the inspiration you give to me and my family."

—Madeleine Ficaccio

"Great information, I have spent thousands of dollars on other courses but this is the first one that I feel I can get started on with real action."

—Patrick Plummer

"It has allowed me to increase my net worth exponentially. The very valuable information helps me to manage my properties with ease and fosters a great business relationship with my tenants."

—Audrey Sloan

"This real estate business has not been easy. And many times my wife could not understand why I persisted. But from the ACRE Quickstart program I discovered the very towns that I live and invest in are number one! Now my capabilities are unlimited. Your system has taught me the true power of a network and cooperating with like-minded people."

—Jules McKenzie

"A real kick for overcoming analysis paralysis. ACRE Quickstart is an excellent program to make someone take action. It provides one with the tools and skills along with a 'go to it' attitude."

—Brian Soucie

"Finally, I am not scared of real estate. I realized that I can do it because this program gives me a focus and logical system to follow."

—Duska Bazdar

"I have received insights into the art of creating deals that are simply mind-boggling."

—Eldon Siemens

"A workable system with a lot of the uncertainty and guesswork removed. I like the balance between the money-making aspects and the necessary balancing-of-life aspects."

—David Platt

"After only three months, I learned more than all the years investing previously. Finally and certainly not the least important is the support and help I have received from the members I have connected with in the group. The willingness to help, the openness with knowledge and the integrity with their ventures has changed my view of the way it works. It has been quite inspirational!"

—Ken Wilson

"We really appreciate the opportunity to be part of such a fantastic organization. I will be eternally grateful for the skills I have learned which will enable me to succeed in real estate and raise my children at the same time."

—Julie Hoffman

"Without the ACRE Quickstart system and REIN™, I would not be a full-time real estate investor. This freedom could never be equaled in my mind. It's great!"

—Celeste Chaytors

"After joining the Real Estate Investment Network, our lives have completely changed and we are on the path to success. With the guidance of several members, we sold the house we were currently living in and turned it into four properties. One of these properties is the beautiful house we now live in and thoroughly love. The REIN system is so simple and easy to follow. All you have to do is take action and amazing things happen."

—Jeff Dick & Debbie Jeannotte

REAL ESTATE INVESTING IN CANADA

Also by Don R. Campbell with Barry McGuire, Peter Kinch, and Russell Westcott

97 Tips for Canadian Real Estate Investors
51 Success Stories from Canadian Real Estate Investors

REAL ESTATE INVESTING IN CANADA

HOW TO CREATE WEALTH WITH THE ACRE SYSTEM

Foreword by Les Hewitt, co-author of the bestseller *The Power of Focus*

DON R. CAMPBELL

PRESIDENT OF THE REAL ESTATE INVESTMENT NETWORK

WILEY

John Wiley & Sons Canada, Ltd.

National Library of Canada Cataloguing in Publication Data

Campbell, Don R.
                            Real estate investing in Canada : creating wealth with the ACRE
System / Don R. Campbell.

Includes index.
ISBN-13 978-0-470-83588-3
ISBN-10 0-470-83588-5

1. Real estate investment—Canada. 2. Residential real estate—Canada.   I. Title.

HD316.C318 2005   332.63'24'0971   C2005-900853-9

Production Credits:
Cover and interior design: Mike Chan
Printer: Friesens

John Wiley & Sons Canada Ltd
6045 Freemont Blvd.
Mississauga, Ontario
L5R 4J3

Printed in Canada

10 9 8 7 6

CONTENTS

FOREWORD

In this stormy age of corporate greed, shady mismanagement and out-of-control egos, Don Campbell has forged a reputation as a man of integrity, with solid unwavering values and a vision to help people who want to create financial success. He is a straight shooter. I like people who tell it the way it is—no smoke screens, no guessing games, no hype.

What you'll find in this special book is a simple step-by-step system for creating amazing results in Canadian real estate. Whether you are thinking of buying your first home or your 50th investment property, you will find this book to be a valuable resource. How do I know? Quite simply, it's working for my son and me.

My son Andrew recently finished university. Like many young people he's ambitious and wants independence versus being stuck in a dead-end job. Slowly climbing the corporate ladder is definitely not for him! Reading inspirational books has ignited a spark in him. He and a few like-minded friends attended one of Don Campbell's Real Estate Investment Workshops. They were impressed by two factors:

1. The integrity of the program.
2. Strategies and examples designed specifically for the Canadian market.

That initial spark quickly became a blowtorch! Within a year my son and his friends had purchased one million dollars worth of residential real estate. Each of their properties is fully rented and has positive cash flow. They achieved all of this while studying full-time at university. How? Simply by following the systems that you'll discover in this book. Now my son and his team of friends are looking forward to financial independence by age 35! Andrew says: "This program is simple and it puts you into action quickly. I was impressed with the fact that Don's long-term focus is entirely on real estate and teaching people how to work the plan. Unlike others, he's not trying to sell you a bunch of products at the back of the room, then disappear, leaving you stranded."

Take it from me, Don Campbell walks his talk. Currently he owns more than 200 properties and continues to invest using the systems he presents in this book. In addition to his own success, his main purpose is to change people's financial lives for the better. As you'll come to know, his greatest joy is the stories he hears from excited clients who have made their dreams come true.

The sad reality is that only 3 percent of Canadians ever get to fulfill their greatest hopes and dreams. The vast majority never achieves that elusive commodity called financial freedom, although many talk about it. The ultimate form of regret comes from not living life to the fullest, settling for just getting by when so much more is possible.

This book provides a proven plan for Canadians from all walks of life, a plan that really works. I have personally witnessed the results.

Les Hewitt
co-author of the bestselling series
The Power of Focus

ACKNOWLEDGEMENTS

Successful real estate investing is a collaborative effort, and so is this book. I am blessed with having many quality people in my personal and business life, and without them this book would never have been created. I thank everyone who has been a part of my success, including:

My team, without whom none of the success over the last 12 years would have been realized, especially Deb Butler, Sonya Oblak, Donna Sylvestre, Sue Hamilton, Barry Friesen and Russell Westcott. Thank you all for your insights and support. Every day it is my pleasure to be able to work with you.

The members of the Real Estate Investment Network™, who have chosen to take control of their financial lives. Their commitment to what they undertake is astonishing, especially in view of the fleeting attention spans that are prevalent in our society today. Thank you, members, for your wonderful success stories; they are the rocket fuel that powers me.

The folks at John Wiley & Sons, notably my patient and understanding editor, Don Loney, whom I count on as a friend and sounding board. His guidance and encouragement helped turn this book from an exciting idea to a purposeful reality.

Alan Jacques, Tim Johnson and Barry McGuire: a home cannot be built without a strong foundation, and neither can a successful investment system. The foundation for this book was laid many years ago by Alan, Tim and Barry. Thank you for providing such a strong footing on which we have been able to change so many people's lives.

My friends and family for their love, support, and understanding during the creative process. I appreciate you all so much. A special thank you for the life foundation my mother and father, Ginger and Jack Campbell, built for me. You taught me long ago to focus my energy outwards on making people happy and successful and your hard work is paying off. Thank you.

My lovely wife of 17 years, Connie (LB) Campbell, without whom this journey would not have been as fun or successful. Your encouragement, insights, love and amazing cuisine are always appreciated but never acknowledged enough. Thanks for bringing balance to my life and helping me appreciate every day. If I had to do it all again, I would hope it would be with you at my side.

INTRODUCTION

A CANADIAN SYSTEM FOR CANADIAN INVESTORS

Oh no, not another real estate book! As someone interested in Canadian real estate, you've probably been very disappointed by the lack of information that focuses on our Canadian market. There are huge differences between our real estate market laws and those in the United States. Yet it seems that everywhere we look, all we have are U.S.-based books and programs.

The good news is the situation has changed. This book, 12 years in the making, has been developed by successful Canadian investors for fellow Canadians. Whether you want to buy your first property or your 100th, this book will provide you with a proven step-by-step *Canadian* system. You will discover the exact steps to take to ensure you are investing safely and securely. This book focuses on turning your real estate dreams into realities—one property at a time.

How do I know it will work for you? Simple. What you'll discover in this book has already allowed Canadians from all walks of life to invest in more than 10,000 properties with a total value that exceeds $1 billion—real estate purchased using the step-by-step strategies and secrets you're about to discover in this book. These investors didn't start with a huge load of cash or an IQ of 160. The people who have already proven the success of this system are average Canadians creating above-average results.

Over the last 12 years, I have been investing in real estate and teaching thousands of other investors. If you have a compelling reason why you want to create wealth using real estate as part of your portfolio and you have determination, all you need to do is follow each step of this proven system, and your success will follow.

In this book, you'll discover how to cut through all the hype that surrounds the real estate market, so that you can focus on one thing and one thing only—finally making your real estate dreams come true. You'll discover, as thousands of other Canadians already have, that real estate investing can be simple, fun and very financially rewarding. Whether your goal is to buy one property or more than 100 properties, the steps you'll discover in this book will take you there. Allow the system to take you wherever you want to go financially. It is my earnest hope that you will have a real estate success story to share with us.

CHANGE YOUR RESULTS BY CHANGING YOUR ACTIONS

This book provides you with the ability and the tools to cut through all the hype, the theories, the sales pitches and all of the other baloney that surrounds real estate investing. In this book, I destroy some long-standing myths about real estate investing. I ask you to look at "what's behind the curtain?" in every real estate transaction.

You will discover a real estate system that is based on fundamentals, not emotions. Why is this so important? Simply put, the results from emotional investing are the same as eating too much sugar: you feel good for a very short time but then you crash. On the other hand, the results from investing based on true economic fundamentals, as you'll discover, are similar to eating well for a lifetime. You'll feel good for a long time, avoiding the major highs and crashes that emotional investing delivers. And most important, fundamental investing gives you results, which last for a long time with no regrets or ill effects.

I'm sure you've witnessed the major stock market swings—you may have even been caught in some. Uninformed investors in the real estate market are not immune to swings, either. But you will discover how to avoid any major swings—how to use fundamentals to tell you when to get in and when to get out. The ups and downs of the real estate market are predictable if you look at fundamentals. I'm not talking about market timing; I'm talking about inevitable real estate cycles.

The great news is that those "sugar crashes" of emotional investing are about to end for those who read and apply this book by following the proven Authentic Canadian Real Estate™ (ACRE) system. From now on, you'll have the ability and tools to cut through the hype and analyze any sales pitch and, most important, to identify exactly when and where to invest and how to identify if you're near the peak or not. This is not a get-rich-quick book; it is all about creating long-term wealth and making a real financial difference in your life.

If successful real estate investing is something you've always wanted to do, or have been doing for a while, the systems in this book will make you a better, more confident and much more successful investor. Combined with the special on-line updates you can receive, this book is a true road map to Canadian real estate success.

I must warn you: some of the content will be controversial; some may even upset certain people in the industry. But my commitment is to inform you of what is working in today's Canadian real estate market, not old theories or re-hashed strategies.

How do I know the strategies work? It's simple; these are the same strategies for buying investment real estate across the country that my clients and I continue to use today.

In addition to access to market research, throughout this book you'll be given direct access to additional resources, analysis tools and research. These support tools are exclusive to registered readers of this book and are designed with one simple purpose in mind: to provide you with the confidence and knowledge to take this proven system and put it into action. It's no longer time to dream of what may come—it's time to make a real difference in your life.

SOPHISTICATED INVESTOR ACTION STEP

Special Bonus—Free CD

The real estate market is constantly changing, and strategies that worked a few years ago may not work today. That's why this book, and the ongoing updates made available to you, are so important. Our real estate market research is continually updated, and as a registered reader of this book, you can tap into our most recent research for free. Simply visit www.reincanada.com today and register your copy of this book. By doing so, you will automatically receive a free CD, which will update you on the latest strategies. Plus, you'll continue to receive ongoing research updates regarding market changes. Register by visiting www.reincanada.com and clicking on the "Register My Book" icon.

Don't be shy with this book: write in it, highlight sections, fill in the blanks, dog-ear the pages you feel are most important to you so you don't lose track of them. And be sure to complete the exercises and checklists right on the pages. There are too many books sitting on people's shelves that look brand new, obviously never having been put into action. Make this book a workbook and an idea book—a book of action!

With this in mind, here's your first action step: Take a pen right now and on the first page inscribe your name. That's the first step in making the systems in this book your own—and putting them into your life. Over the 12 years I've been teaching Canadian real estate investors the truth about the markets, I have found that those who participated the most and took the most notes and completed the most exercises were always the people who became the most successful.

I like to remind investors of the often-quoted definition of insanity for investors: "Doing the same thing over and over again, expecting different results." So, if you truly want to create different and more successful results, the first step you must take is to change your actions—starting with this book.

You will find that each section provides you with a clearly laid-out action plan, to which you can refer for each property you're analyzing. Remember: if you continue to do the same thing, you will continue to get the same results.

 **KEY INSIGHT**

You must change your actions to change your results.

The actions you take with this system not only affect your financial situation, but that of many others in your life—your family, friends as well as people you'll never know. Imagine if your grandfather had created an extra $1 million of wealth in his lifetime for his family. Now imagine what kind of impact that would have had on your life. Starting today, you're in a position to have this type of impact on those people around you. The time to make a difference is *now*.

So turn the page to discover how you can follow a simple system that has allowed thousands of Canadians to invest in close to one billion dollars of real estate right in their own backyards. You too can start doing the same.

YOUR REAL ESTATE SUCCESS ROAD MAP

If you don't know where you're going, you'll never get there.
Anon.

The above statement is especially true with real estate. Often, when I ask someone what their real estate goal is, I hear, "I want to get rich!" or "I want to make a million dollars." Well, as you'll discover in this book, these goals are a sure-fire recipe for failure.

First, you must define where you want real estate investment to take you financially. Be specific about how this success looks:

- **How will you be spending your time?**
- **What exactly will your financial picture look like?**
- **Will you continue to work in your field or will you live off the cash flow from your properties?**

As with any successful journey, you need to know where you're going in order to get there. And that destination needs to be very specific.

The next step is to set a realistic time frame in which to achieve this success. Ask yourself:

- **How long do I realistically believe it will take me to get there?**
- **What buffer time do I have in case of unforseen detours?**
- **Will I be disappointed if I get to my financial destination later than expected?**
- **How will I feel if I get there earlier than expected?**

The key is to be realistic and remember that proper real estate investing is not a get-rich-quick scheme, but a long-term wealth-creation strategy.

Third, your financial journey cannot be a success unless you have a clear road map showing you exactly how to get to your destination by the safest and most direct route. That's exactly what this book will do for you—show you the road to take, the trouble spots to avoid and the highlights to watch for.

Finally, with all of the above in hand, no journey could ever come to a successful conclusion unless you actually take the first steps and make a commitment to see your journey through to the finish.

ACRES OF WEALTH:
YOUR REAL ESTATE SUCCESS ROAD MAP

ACRES is an acronym for the Authentic Canadian Real Estate System—a system that has provided to thousands of investors the exact steps to success. The ACRE system you're about to discover in this book will take you to whatever financial destination you choose. It could be that you wish to own one or two rental properties to increase your income and wealth, or you may want to use real estate as your major ticket to financial freedom. You choose the destination and the ACRE system will take you there. But you must take that very important first step.

Many of us know a colleague, relative or acquaintance who has clearly defined his or her personal financial goals, spent thousands of dollars on learning how to get there (through seminars, books and tape sets) and then, in the end, decided to do nothing with his or her new knowledge. Richard McTavish—the individual you are about to meet—is exactly that kind of person. He knows where he wants to be financially, but has not been able to get himself there.

Richard McTavish is one of those people who has planned his life away. He is 41 years old and lives in the suburbs of his hometown. He is married and has two small children; his family is the love of his life. He has always wanted to provide them with more than he experienced while growing up, and to that end Richard has been a voracious reader of financial success books his whole life. In fact, his bookshelf is overflowing with self-help classics by Napoleon Hill, George C. Clason, Les Hewitt, Robert Kiyosaki, David Chilton and many more. He's read them all.

He has also attended so many seminars on wealth creation and get-rich-quick strategies that he's lost count. He's on everyone's mailing list as a "buyer" of information. He started with real estate (only to find that all of the information was U.S.-based); next it was high-tech stocks (well, we all saw what happened to that bubble); high-tech stocks were followed by stock options, and most recently he thought about getting into currency trading. All of these ideas provided him with an initial rush of excitement. Some even yielded a few months of success, but in the end, none of them provided him with the means to reach his financial goals. These strategies have worked for many, but not for Richard.

Every time he attended another event or spent a few thousand dollars at another "free" workshop, his wife Emma would shudder. She knew he'd come back excited about this new strategy, only to have real life prove that it didn't work in *his* life. Emma also knew that the inevitable result would be a larger credit-card bill, a spurt of excitement, a little profit (maybe) and then nothing.

That's why, for 15 years, Richard has continued to commute every single day to a job that's comfortable but not very challenging. He earns a decent wage and has the golden handcuffs of a benefits package provided by his employer. However, just over three years ago, Richard was jolted out of his comfort zone. His friends and co-workers began losing their jobs through layoffs and the insult called "redundancy." These colleagues had been working at their job for over 10 years in some cases. He saw the stock market steal thousands of dollars from his supposedly secure retirement fund. He noticed that every time there was a bit of bad news or a negative headline in the newspaper, his RRSPs would drop in value. Life was not fun.

Adding to the family's financial pressure, Emma's hours at work were cut in half and her benefits taken away after her company was bought out. Meanwhile, their kids, ten-year-old Sam and seven-year-old Alison, were acquiring new and more expensive interests (hockey equipment and dance recital outfits don't come cheap!) and his mother-in-law was facing a long-term stay in the hospital. His financial picture wasn't looking very pretty. Maybe their comfortable existence wasn't so comfortable after all. Even Emma, usually upbeat, was expressing concern, so Richard knew he had to take a hard look at where they were headed as a family. The financial wall was looming in the distance and Richard knew if he didn't change something, they would hit that wall, and hit it hard.

One Sunday afternoon, when his kids were at their friends' houses and Emma was visiting her mom at the hospital, Richard decided to go for a walk. He thought, "I'm 41 years old. Because of my insurance policy, I'm worth more dead than alive! I guess I better start getting serious. There are three other lives depending on me to make a better living."

Across the street from the house they rented was a beautiful park with a pond. His thinking spot was a bench overlooking the lily pads and the geese. It was so secluded that Richard could only faintly hear the voices of others playing in the park. He wandered over and sat down in his spot, as he had done many times before. But this time it felt different.

Emma had recently voiced concerns about their finances, and Richard knew for a certainty that when Emma started to voice concern, it meant she had held it in for a long time. His wife is the most positive person he knows, so he definitely heeds her comments and takes them to heart. That's why this time, sitting on his favourite bench, Richard knew it was time to be brutally honest with himself and take a hard, critical look at his life.

As the breeze brought a hint of autumn coolness, Richard thought of the many times he had come to this bench just to sit and think. Often, he would find himself here either full of excitement for a new venture, or feeling low because the venture hadn't turned out the way he had wanted it to. This was his bench of transition.

He had heard at some seminar, many years ago, that it was important to inventory his financial achievements by taking stock of what was real in his life and compare it to what he wanted to achieve. This would provide him with a clear, if not pretty, picture of how well he'd done so far—and how much further he had to go.

After working through this thought process, what he discovered shocked him. The difference between what he had actually accomplished and what he had wanted to achieve was vast. He was finding out why most people avoided doing this exercise: honesty sometimes can be a difficult pill to swallow.

He started to look back at his many money-making schemes and what they had brought him in the end, and he noticed a pattern. Everything he went for had an element of excitement, a chance to win big in a short time, an emotional pitch that was almost impossible to resist. However, despite all of these big opportunities, here he sat wondering why he was barely achieving mediocrity.

The Secret of Mediocrity—Lack of Control

It became very clear to Richard why his life *felt* so mediocre—*it was*. As he reflected, he began to get a little embarrassed; he clearly saw that both his short- and long-term financial well-being were completely controlled by someone else. The short-term money—his job—was controlled by his superiors in the stagnating company for which he worked. They could end his job at any time as they had done for many of his buddies. He couldn't increase his job income without begging for a raise, and that wasn't going to happen given the state of the company's finances.

For the long term, the meagre investments in his RRSP and bank mutual funds were controlled by the gyrations of the stock market. He understood that the markets were not really driven by long-term economics but rather by herd mentality and investor emotions. He'd invested in RRSPs to get the tax receipt, just like everyone else, and his returns were dismal.

Even his home wasn't his own. Because he rented, he could be asked to move at any time. And to top it all off, because he was renting he was once again missing out on any increases in real estate values.

In other words, not one major financial decision was under his control. This realization made him feel angry that he had allowed others to have so much control over his future. Even though his wife had been patient with all of his investment ideas, he had to face the fact that all his get-rich-quick schemes had turned into next to nothing.

Richard could see his current road map was taking him nowhere, and he didn't like it! Well, he thought, at least he was taking a week's holiday to a place that *he* had decided on. He chuckled when he thought that at least this was one decision that he did get to make.

• • • •

Richard and I met on the airplane that was carrying him back from his annual end-of-summer family escape from real life (oops, I mean holiday) to their favourite discount beach resort. He could only stay for a week because his boss wouldn't let him get away for any longer. He was travelling home alone; his family stayed at the resort to enjoy a second week of fun and relaxation.

The stress of having to leave early had destroyed any relaxation gains Richard had made during his week on the beach. The scene as the family dropped him off at the airport played through his mind over and over again during the flight. He could still see the sadness on the kids' faces and the look of concern on his wife's. And even though he was returning from a vacation, I could see that he wasn't a very happy person; he had a tired and sad look about him—not what you'd expect from someone who had just enjoyed a holiday.

I was returning home from making a special presentation to 200 successful real estate investors. I was still riding that special high you get when you hang out with positive and successful people. Speaking to and meeting groups of enthusiastic action takers is one of the pure joys I have in my life, and I grab that chance whenever I can.

Soon after we took off, I pulled out the notes from my presentation, planning to complete my regular post-event debriefing so that I could focus on my family as soon as I landed. (I feel it's critically important to continually improve in everything you do, no matter how successful you are; that's why I take the time to make notes.) I couldn't help but notice that Richard, who was sitting beside me, was reading over my shoulder, trying to decide whether to make an introduction. Then he said, "Hi, my name is Richard McTavish. I see you're involved in real estate. Man, I wish I had got in before the current real estate boom."

With that opening statement he unknowingly took his first step on what would prove to be his true financial journey. It would be a three-year journey that would take him from having zero control over his financial life to being a financial success in real estate, well on his way to achieving the dream, instead of just dreaming.

This also marks the beginning of your own personal journey to real estate success. The secrets and strategies that Richard discovered over the ensuing three years are exactly what you'll discover in this book. No matter what your dream or what your current financial picture looks like (good, bad or amazing), you can use the ACRE system to turn your financial life dream into a reality, just like Richard did.

Throughout the book, you'll hear from the same experts who led Richard out of the investment wilderness. These veteran investors and other key people came to influence Richard's life, and all of them played a role in his success. In just the same way that these experts helped Richard, their strategies and secrets to personal success will propel you to become a confident and wealthy investor.

The FLIGHT from Nowhere

2

People are always blaming their circumstances for what they are. I don't believe in circumstances. The people who get on in this world are the people who get up and look for the circumstances they want, and if they can't find them, make them.

—George Bernard Shaw

"Hi, My Name Is Rich—Although I'm Not"

"Hi, my name is Richard McTavish. I see you're involved in real estate. Man, I wish I had got in before the current real estate boom," he said just loud enough for me to hear. I had heard similar sentiments of regret many times over the years, from many people, most of whom just continued making such excuses and creating reasons why they didn't act. However, this time when I looked up, I saw a spark in Richard's eye—a spark of determination.

"Hi, my name is Don Campbell. Yes, I'm involved in real estate. Very observant of you to notice."

"My name is Richard. Some people call me Rich, although I'm not rich, yet," he said wryly, as if he had repeated this line a thousand times before. I knew there was a lot of work to do, starting with turning around the negative attitude he had about himself.

I asked him why he felt he'd missed the boom, although I already knew his answer. It was the same answer everyone gives who doesn't understand real estate investing.

"Well, isn't it obvious?" he chortled. "Prices have skyrocketed everywhere in the last 10 years. They just can't go any higher!"

"And what makes you believe they're at the top?" I asked.

"Everyone I talk to is saying so. I read it in the media and hear it on talk radio every day. Prices are at all-time highs, interest rates are beginning to increase and people can't afford to pay the ridiculously high prices for a starter home—the boom is over! So once again I missed the boat right when I finally decided to take control of my financial future. That's just my luck."

Then the floodgates opened. Obviously, Richard had decided to dump all of his life circumstances on someone and I just happened to be the lucky one.

"And that's not all!" he said. "I just completed an inventory of my financial situation and have found that *all* of my major decisions are made by someone else—RRSP, job, income, house—everything! I've taken so many courses, read so many books—heck, I *know* what it takes to be successful. But still I sit here, 41 years old, missing out on another real estate boom. Do you have any secrets I can use?"

He was fishing for secrets or shortcuts because that's what he had done all his life—looked for an easy fix to a not-so-easy situation. Then I asked the critical question: "These people who have told you that the boom is over, do any of them own any real estate for investment?"

"Well, yes, a few of them do own their own homes, but now that I think about it, none of them own any investment real estate." I could see a light bulb turning on above his head, and it wasn't the "fasten your seat belt" light.

"Richard, I find that whenever I ask that question of someone in your position the answer is invariably the same as yours, so don't feel bad! We are all surrounded by people wanting to share their opinions on *anything* and *everything*, whether they have any real knowledge on the subject or not. The key is to fight your way through these uninformed opinions and get yourself to the facts as quickly as possible. We have lots of time on this flight; are you interested in hearing a short story about how to turn a raving success into an absolute failure?"

Richard nodded his agreement, and I launched into a story I was told many years ago by a sage advisor.

The Downfall of the Hotdog Vendor

"I'm sure you've seen those roadside hotdog vendors, with their brightly coloured umbrellas covering their well-used barbeques. Bob Grant was a very successful owner of some of these stands and they provided him with his livelihood.

"He was very hard of hearing so he didn't own a radio, nor did he watch TV. He had trouble with his eyes, so he didn't spend much time reading newspapers. His life was consumed with the intricacies of running his hotdog stands, and he did it better than anyone.

"Bob had staked out the perfect high-traffic locations. He put signs by the side of the road telling all passersby, on foot and in vehicles, how good the hotdogs were. He even offered a guarantee that his dog would be the best dog you ever ate or your money back. People loved his secret sauce.

"He stood on the side of the road calling out, 'Buy a dog, mister?' Because he was so actively selling, people bought. Every day, he had lineups of regulars who brought their friends. He was incredibly successful in his selected niche. He increased his bun and meat orders on a regular basis. He bought more barbeques to keep up with the demand. His growth was amazing.

"Then, one day, his son came home from college to help him out, and that's when his business started to change. After a few weeks of watching his Dad's business, he took him aside and said, 'Dad, haven't you heard the news? There is a recession going on. The unemployment rate is skyrocketing and energy prices are through the roof. People can't afford to eat out any more like they used to.'

"His father thought, 'Well, my son has been to college. He reads the newspaper and listens to the radio. I guess he ought to know.'

"So, despite the obvious demand for his dogs, Bob reduced his meat and bun orders. He took down his advertising signs and no longer bothered to stand on the side of the road asking for the sale. Not surprisingly, his hotdog sales fell almost overnight.

"'Wow, you're right, son!' Bob proudly said to his son. 'We are most certainly in the middle of a great recession. Thanks for warning me or else I wouldn't have known because my business seemed to be growing at such a fast pace!'

"Bob's son didn't purposely try to hurt his Dad's business; he just gave his father advice based on what he had heard was happening through the media and his friends from college. The mistake he made was applying general overall strategies to a smaller specific market, and this misinformation became the downfall of his Dad's business.

"He didn't know the hotdog business like his Dad did, he didn't understand how unique and well thought of his Dad's business was in the community, and he definitely didn't understand that, although there was a general recession, the town in which his Dad lived and operated was booming, no matter what the national averages were saying!"

THE CURSE OF GENERALITIES

Richard's face revealed sadness mixed with anger. I said, "I admit the story is a bit depressing, but it's also a great lesson. Bob's son took generalized information and applied it directly to his father's small and specific market. This has been a sure-fire recipe for disaster throughout history.

"Generalities are a killer for *all* investors, no matter what they've put their money in. During a downturn in a stock market, there are still stocks that skyrocket upwards, and during a slowdown in the national real estate market, there are always pockets that have their best years ever. If you imagine trying to comment on trends in Toronto real estate by applying statistics from St. John's, I think you'll get the picture.

"And that's why, Richard, you must *always, always* check your sources of information. Make sure two key components are in place:

1. **The information is relevant to your specific market.**
2. **The source has extensive experience in the investment vehicle you are looking at.**

"Ask yourself, do they *really* know what they're talking about? Do they have experience in the areas of which they are speaking? Are they spouting generalities from something they read, or do they have knowledge about a specific market?

"I think in many cases, you'll find people making grand, sweeping comments—generalities. Just as I'm sure your friends have done with you when they discouraged you from real estate opportunities.

"Even more sad and depressing than the hotdog story is the story of people like you, Rich, all across this country, who allow their dreams and enthusiasm to be squashed by misinformed friends, family and co-workers. The good news is, once you cut through all of that outside noise, you can and often do create results you hadn't even dreamed of before."

I could see that Rich's mind was at work. "Don, you know what? When I look back at all of the opportunities I've been presented with over the last 10 years, I shudder to think about all of the money I've missed out on because I listened to naysayers you call the 'misinformed.' I know that I have been easily distracted by 'the next big thing', but it makes me angry that I allowed myself to be dissuaded by others' opinions. I guess that's why my job, my retirement and my overall financial security are held in someone else's hands."

"Wow!" I thought, "Richard is proving to be a quick study." So I asked him, "Would you like to know a secret to cutting through all of that baloney?"

He just about jumped out of his seat and said, "Absolutely!"

"The key is simply to ask, at every opportunity that arises, 'What's behind the curtain?' Yes, it sounds simple, but it is extremely powerful. Think of the movie, *The Wizard of Oz*. The truth was revealed to Dorothy, the Tin Man, the Lion and the Scarecrow when her dog Toto ripped open the curtain revealing that the so-called wizard was really just a man from Kansas named Oscar—not the powerful entity that everyone believed he was. That is how misinformation works; it hides behind general ideas and opinions that are peddled as fact.

"Your job as an investor is to continually rip open the curtain, revealing the truth behind any hype and misinformation. If anyone offers you advice, always ask yourself, What's behind the curtain? Here are some key questions to ask of those who dispense advice. You should write them down:

- **Do they really know what they're talking about, or are they trying to influence me into buying or investing in something?**
- **Do they have a financial incentive to get me to take an action based on the information they're giving me?**
- **Do they have experience in the market or are they just part of the cult of opinion?**

"Richard, to fully understand and assess an opportunity, keep asking yourself those four magic words until you get to the real answer. It is only after you cut through the first line of prepared answers that you'll start to get to the real truth. You must make sure that any decisions you make are based on reality and are not someone else's perceptions or opinions."

THE FINANCIAL AND EMOTIONAL COST OF MISSED OPPORTUNITIES

It was quite obvious that Richard's mind was churning at this point because he was writing as fast as he could. So I added, "Why don't you take a few minutes right now to make a list of 10 situations in which you acted (or didn't act) on information and it ended up costing you either time, money or happiness? For instance, it could be when your friends told you that you were crazy to invest in real estate 10 years ago, or when your financial advisor told you it was too risky to take your retirement funds into your own hands, or when a so-called success trainer introduced you to an investment condo seller, without revealing that he was taking a commission for doing so and it turned into a very poor investment. It could even be a fearful family member who held you back from taking a small risk because of his or her own lack of confidence."

After almost half an hour of writing, Richard turned to me and in quite a sheepish voice said, "Don, I had no idea. Why hadn't I heard of this exercise before? I think I might need a lot more paper to list *all* of the times I've been led down the garden path. I've got 10 situations here, but sadly there are a lot more!"

But Richard wasn't quite finished this important exercise. I took out my calculator and said, "Okay, Richard, you're not done quite yet. Of the occurrences you wrote down, circle the five that have the largest financial component to them. Now, knowing that you won't be 100 percent accurate, write down your estimate of how much wealth you missed out on for each of these occurrences. Ask yourself, 'If I had followed through on this, or avoided this manipulation, roughly how much could I have made?'"

When others have done this exercise, they've discovered they've literally missed out on millions of dollars of wealth by allowing themselves to be badly influenced. Of course, it was next to impossible to estimate the true values of many of these missed opportunities, so I told him to be somewhat conservative and pick a number that felt realistic. I'm sure if it wasn't for the whine of the jet engines, I could have heard his brain churning. It was obvious that Richard was already seeing how powerful an influence friends, co-workers and media are on the decisions we make in our lives.

He looked up from his exercise, astonished. I took a quick look at his numbers and thought he had grossly underestimated them. But he was already shocked, so I didn't want to add insult to injury. We added up his figures just as the flight attendants came up the aisle with dinner. Richard's eyes were as wide as saucers and I'm sure he didn't even hear the flight attendant ask "Chicken or fish, sir?" He nodded and was presented a plastic tray. He sat there, all the while staring at the total dollar figure on his sheet. I knew I had just witnessed another financial awakening.

SOPHISTICATED INVESTOR ACTION STEP

This is the first step to understanding exactly how powerful the four magic words "What's behind the curtain?" really are. Remember, exercises in books may not be something you usually do, but I urge you to change your actions to change your results. Take a few minutes right now to list just five times in your life that someone else's advice led you astray and estimate, conservatively, how much that bad advice cost you.

1. _____
2. _____
3. _____
4. _____
5. _____

After our airplane lunch, I leaned over to Richard and said, "How do you feel right now?"

Predictably, he said, "Frustrated, pissed-off and in need of a beer. But I'm also feeling *very* motivated not to allow that to happen to me again. I'm tired of others having control over my job, my finances, my *future* … over me!"

At this point I made a decision that would change both of our lives. I said to him, "Richard, it sounds like you're motivated and tired of playing games. How would you like to discover a system that thousands of Canadians have used to safely and securely invest in close to one billion dollars of real estate?"

"Absolutely, tell me more!" he replied.

I said, "There's not much more we can do on this flight. However, if you're truly committed, call my office on Friday morning at eight o'clock to say you're ready and I'll show you the exact steps to take to become a very successful real estate investor—so successful, in fact, that the numbers listed on the sheet in front of you will no longer upset you. Does Friday afternoon work for you? We could meet at my office."

"Yes, but can't you tell me more now?"

"I can tell you one thing: proper real estate investing is not a get-rich-quick scheme. If done right, it's all about creating long-term wealth—wealth that not only will improve your financial situation, but also that of your family and favourite charities." I looked him squarely in the eye and asked, "Do you have the patience to create long-term wealth? Because I'm going to need a full three-year commitment from you, and if you're not willing to commit to that, we won't be able to work together."

"Three years is a long time," Richard said slowly. "I've heard of people making fortunes in much shorter times than that."

"Let me explain. There's a problem that's occurring right across North America called 'investor impatience.' Most people have heard the story of some guy who knows some lady who's the cousin of a guy who made a fortune in real estate in six months and now lives on an island in the Caribbean. Well, sure this can happen, but only in very rare cases. What you don't hear about in these rare cases are the years of sweat, toil and preparation these people put in before they're successful. You'll also note that the story is often about someone you don't know, or can't contact, which makes it very likely an urban legend.

"When the majority of people hear these stories, they believe that everyone else is getting rich quickly. The reality is, 99 percent don't make it big fast. It takes some effort and it takes time, but the payoffs are enormous if you have the commitment and patience. Today's society is trained to expect everything to happen quickly, and because of this, most people don't have the attention span or focus to follow anything through to the end.

"That's why you see so many people run from one get-rich-quick scheme to another. I'm sure you can think of a couple of people in your life who are like that.

"Take a look around and see the hundreds of seminars and late-night pitchmen offering the quick and easy solution to just about any problem: weight-loss, cash flow, wealth, health—you name it. They always pitch a simple solution. However, in real life quick and easy is not the answer. If it were, everyone would already be healthy, wealthy and wise. The good news is that committed and simple works every time, if you have the patience. That's where the three-year commitment comes in.

"Rich, you're 41 years old, so you have over 40 years of habits you need to break. And breaking them won't happen overnight. But you've already taken the first step with the exercise you've just completed during this flight. If you're willing to stay focused for just three years, I am willing to sit down and meet with you regularly and show you the *exact* steps to take so your financial dreams come true through real estate. If you don't think you can deliver three years of focus, then now's the time to tell me."

Rich looked at me inquisitively and asked, "So, what's behind the curtain? What's in it for you?"

After I stopped laughing, I congratulated him on his astuteness for asking that question and then said, "I wasn't going to tell you the answer to that question until I heard whether you were committed or not. I truly didn't want to influence your decision. However, now that you've asked, yes, I am going to get something out of this as well. I am writing a book for Canadian investors that will show them how to invest right here in Canada, and by starting you from scratch and taking you through the whole process it will provide me with a wonderful story for the book."

He was nodding as I was talking and I could see that he was ready to say, "Yes, I'll do it!" However, before he got to that point I added one thing. "Don't commit to me now; think it over for a couple of days. A three-year commitment can be a long time for people who don't understand wealth creation. Here's my card; call me on Friday at eight to confirm that you'll be coming in for that meeting. If I don't hear from you, I'll assume you're not interested."

Rich leaned over and said, "Thanks for opening my eyes. I'll think over your offer and call you on Friday."

"Rich, it was my pleasure. The flight went by so fast and you were a very enjoyable companion. Thank you." I shook his hand for what would prove to be the first time of many.

As he deplaned, in his hand was the "missed opportunity" exercise he had just completed and on his face was a look of determination. His financial awakening had begun; the spark had been fanned.

KEY INSIGHT

- Listen to facts, not conjecture.
- Don't transfer market generalities to specific markets.
- Take a realistic look at what inaction has cost you.
- Long-term wealth creation is more doable and sustainable than get-rich-quick schemes.
- Patience and focus are critical in real estate investing.

People who soar are those who refuse to sit back, sigh and wish things would change. They neither complain of their lot nor passively dream of some distant ship coming in. Rather, they visualize in their minds that they are not quitters; they will not allow life's circumstances to push them down and hold them under.

—Charles Swindoll

It was 7:55 a.m. on Friday when Deb, my incredibly talented assistant, rang through to my office saying that Richard was on the phone, a bit ahead of time. That's a good sign, I thought.

"Hi, Richard. How was your week back at the office?"

Not surprisingly, he answered, "I couldn't concentrate at all. All I could think about was your 'What's behind the curtain?' idea. It even worked when a company that advertises free workshops called me on Tuesday to ask if I was interested in attending another session. Usually I would have jumped at the chance to go and listen to a bunch of experts, but this time I sat back and asked myself, 'What's behind the curtain?' It was then that I realized that among the guest speakers, one was selling condominium investments and another was selling a stock market trading system."

"So, did you go?" I inquired.

"Sure I did, but this time with a different purpose in mind. I wanted to see it from 'behind the curtain.' I wanted to see how the speakers positioned their product and influenced the audience. And let me tell you, what an experience that was!"

"You'll have to tell me all about it this afternoon. Can you come in at three?"

"Great, I'll see you then."

When Richard arrived I showed him into my office and went to grab us some coffee. When I re-entered my office, I noticed that Richard had his notepad and pen ready to go and I thought, this guy's keen. "So Rich, tell me about that seminar you went to this week. Did you find out what's behind their curtain?"

"Well, these guys pitching real estate made it look like these were the ultimate investments, with no downside risk. They even told these people that a certain town (in which they had just sold a previous project) was past the boom and now this new town (where today's project is located) is the place to invest, and if you don't hurry and run to the back of the room to buy into it, you're going to miss out. The properties sounded good, but I decided that I would just take the information and check into it further, rather than make an emotional decision.

"At the event, I noticed only one person stood up to ask some due diligence questions. He was told that if he needed all of that additional information, he might miss out because the properties were selling so fast. You know, I've seen this before; emotionally charged people rushed to the back to buy $90,000 properties in a shorter time than it takes most people to pick a restaurant for dinner. I wanted to jump up and tell everyone to 'look behind the curtain' first, but of course I didn't. I just left, feeling I had learned something. Watching how this event was structured really was interesting. It is true; you don't get something for nothing."

"Wow, Rich, that's quite a shift in just a few days. Now you can see why emotional investing leads to so many investors creating average or below-average results. They base major decisions on someone else's numbers and someone else's homework. By giving up responsibility for their actions to someone else, they invariably give up power in their life. They also create an excuse if the investment goes poorly; they can blame someone else for not providing them with accurate information. Which, by the way, is the quickest way to stay broke—giving your power to someone else. Just so you know, many of these properties that are pitched like this can be good, quality investments. However, you'll never know unless you ask the critical questions. I think you're starting to see why the four magic words are so powerful."

"I sure am," Rich said with conviction.

It was obvious that he was ready to get started, so I threw out the question, "Hey Richard, how would you like to spend the next three years becoming a confident and successful real estate investor?"

"Well, I think you know what my answer is going to be. I wouldn't be talking to you unless I was ready. But before I answer, I have one more question: What is real estate really going to give me?"

"Richard, I'm going to introduce you to the ACRE system. You'll learn how it will help you evaluate locations, banks, realtors, properties and your own motivation, so that real estate investing will become quite easy. I must warn you, though," I continued, "unlike most other real estate programs, when you get started on the ACRE system, you will initially take slow and measured steps. It may even feel too slow compared to what you're used to. That's perfectly normal. The first 17 months of the ACRE system will be about building the foundation for wealth and purchasing only a few properties for your portfolio. Speed during this initial period is not an issue. Use this time to perfect your strategy, practising it until it becomes second nature. And, if you do this right, the system should become so automatic that it becomes boring!

"Which leads me to an important point—do not use real estate investing to pump excitement into your life. Make your investing systematic and boring so you can go out and find excitement in other areas of your life. Investing should not be filled with excitement; if it is, you're doing something horribly wrong. Do you think Warren Buffett goes out and invests just for excitement? I don't think so!"

Real Estate Investing Must NOT Be a Source of Excitement in Your Life!

Richard nodded in agreement. You could see he was ready to get going, but setting the stage about this not being a get-rich-quick scheme was critical. I continued, "Then, after the first 17 months or so, you'll be ready to take your action to the next level. You'll have practised and perfected all the steps in the ACRE system and they'll seem like second nature. At that point you'll be able to look at a property and, in less than five minutes, decide what kind of potential it has and whether it fits into your portfolio or not. Do you like the sound of that?"

"Absolutely!" Richard exclaimed. "But you haven't answered my question yet: what is real estate going to give me?"

"That answer comes not from me but from you, and it's the foundation from which all successful real estate investing is built. To build this foundation, you've got some very important homework for the weekend."

"All right! I get to look at properties already. That should be fun!"

"No, this weekend is not about looking at properties; it's about building your foundation and answering the question: what do you really want real estate to provide for you?"

• • • •

The first step in being a successful real estate investor is to clearly understand that the motivation for investing in real estate is not about money. Yes, that sounds strange, but the truth is, if you focus on chasing money you will be stuck on that treadmill for the rest of your life. However, if you focus on creating a clear vision of exactly what real estate is going to provide you, a destination, you will be driven to success.

Typically, this is what I hear when I ask a group of 300 beginning real estate investors what they want real estate to provide them:

- 30 percent say, "I want to make $1,000,000."
- 30 percent say, "I want to make enough money to quit my job."
- 20 percent say, "I want to own 10 properties."
- 19 percent have any number of other responses.
- Less than 1 percent knows exactly what they want and how they're going to get it.

Those first three responses are the most common answers I hear. They're generic and none are very compelling: boring, boring, boring!

For instance, I know that a million dollars, even though it is still considered a lot of money, doesn't buy much freedom anymore. Quitting your job may be a worthy goal, but what if you love what you do? Why 10 properties? Is this a magic number or is it an opinion based on what others may have told you? The worst part is that these boring goals are the exact same goals these investors have had for years, and they're no closer to achieving them than when they started. The biggest mistake these investors make is having goals that are too general and not the least bit personal.

A truly compelling goal, destination or vision is the foundation of your real estate success. With it, you'll be able to choose a clear pathway; without it, you'll be wandering in the dark. Your vision must be the first thing you think of when you get up in the morning and the last thing you picture before you go to sleep. It will keep you going when the inevitable bumps in the road appear; it will drive you forward even if others in your life are questioning what you're doing. It will be a lighthouse leading you to safety through every storm and it will allow you to be a champion in your real estate practice.

Canadian Gold Medalist Kyle Shewfelt had the goal of being an Olympic gymnastics champion from the age of nine. He told me how he thought of this goal every day when he woke up and again before he went to bed. He visualized standing on the podium; he continually kept his goal in the front of his mind. His clear vision was so compelling and so exciting that it pushed him through the rough times and kept him focused during the good times. He became Canada's first gymnastics gold medalist at the 2004 Olympics because his vision was so motivating, and he didn't allow others to distract him from it.

ARMAND'S HARLEY-DAVIDSON VISION

A well-defined vision will give you purpose and it will make you feel alive. I can say, without hesitation, that the majority of my successful real estate clients have a compelling vision. Take the remarkable story of Armand from Vancouver, for instance.

Armand has been a client and friend of mine for many years. He's a music fanatic and motorcycle enthusiast. He enjoyed having fun every day of his life, his enthusiasm was right off the scale and everyone who met him walked away feeling energized. Every day was an exciting adventure for him.

Although he was an active investor, he didn't speak much about real estate; he was always talking with passion about his hobbies and exploits. This was during the previous boom in the Vancouver market. In 1994, we started to tell our clients that it was time to start selling, since the economic fundamentals were showing that the market was nearing its peak and it was time to get out. The ACRE system was saying sell, and we were selling into one of the hottest markets on record. As predicted, the market ended up peaking in 1995 with an average house price of $307,700.

In April 1995, Armand took me aside at one of the monthly workshops we hold for our clients. He had waited until close to midnight when everyone had cleared out of the room, so he could have my undivided attention. As he approached his face was filled with his usual huge grin. He looked me straight in the eye and said, "Thank you, I did it. I've achieved my own personal Belize!" He handed me a brightly wrapped package and asked me to open it. Inside was a very simple black frame around a sun-faded map of Belize with a photo of five Harley-Davidson motorcycles stuck to it. It looked like a collage from grade school.

Obviously I had a confused look on my face because, after he stopped laughing, he explained. In a workshop years ago, I had explained how powerful it is to have your compelling vision in both words and pictures so you can look at it every day. That night, he raced home and developed a vision so clear and so real that it became his underlying source of energy and enthusiasm for the next three years. During that time, all of his real estate decisions were based on whether the investment got him closer to his vision or farther away. He only acted on the ones that moved him closer; his vision made all of his decisions easy.

So here we were, just over three years later and he was standing there beaming with a grin from ear to ear saying, "I did it!" The funny thing is I still didn't know what he had done. He then handed me a piece of paper with his vision clearly written on it. It was one of the clearest and most focused vision statements I had ever read. Here's what it said (remember he had written this three years previous to handing it to me):

> *I did it! I have now used the ACRE system to fulfill one of my life-long dreams. I am now sitting in my white beachfront house in Belize with the ocean breeze blowing lightly through the window.*

I am here with my wife, Natalie, who has never looked happier in her life. I get up in the morning to walk down the white sand beach to our Harley-Davidson rental business, where I have five brand-new Harleys waiting to be rented to the tourists. Every day I go to the local market to smell the amazing smells of the Caribbean, taste the exotic tastes, hear the rhythm from the local bands and meet my new Belizian friends. I run my business for fun, not just for profit, because my real estate has set me up financially for life. Friends from across Canada visit throughout the year, so we are always surrounded by happy, excited and positive people. I have many ideas for the charities I volunteer for and am making a difference in any way I can using my enthusiasm and knowledge.

After I'd caught my breath from reading this remarkable story, he handed me two other pieces of paper. One, a photocopy of a sales invoice for five Harley-Davidson motorcycles, and the other, a picture of a white house on a beach with a sold sign in front of it. I had never seen anyone so proud. He had achieved exactly what he had set down in his vision statement three years earlier.

Armand's smile was even wider now, which I didn't think was possible. He said, "For the last 10 years, I had tried everything to try and get rich, but it was only when I listened to you and stepped out of my comfort zone and created this vision that things started to really happen for Natalie and me. Before I created this vision, it felt like I was running at full speed, but I didn't know where I was running to. Then, as soon as the picture was done and hung on my wall for me to see every morning, the finish line became clear.

"I could now put my energies to running straight for the destination, my own personal Belize. I eventually moved this picture into our living room so we and everyone we knew could see it, and now the vision has come true. Both Natalie and I would like to thank you from the bottom of our hearts for giving us this gift of focus, and we want you to keep this picture and use it to help others achieve what we already have."

My response was, "Wow, what a wonderful gesture! But really it was all you. All I gave you was a tool to use. If you hadn't put it into action, it would have been useless. Remember, I've shown this tool to thousands of people and only those who use it know the power of it. You and Nat should be proud of what you've done. Thank you for the amazing gift!"

Armand's story is a lesson in how you must change your actions to change your results. As many have before him, he had been running at full speed, chasing the almighty dollar, only to find that even with his best efforts, he wasn't a whole lot closer to the finish line. He decided that he'd had enough of this race, and so he changed his tactics. He clearly defined his finish line by developing a vision so vivid that he could hear the surf, smell the market, see the colours. That's what makes a vision real. You'll also note that not once did he mention a sum of money.

Once Armand's vision was clear, his direction was set. It was simple for him to stay focused and use the ACRE system to create a roadmap that would take him directly there. By using the same energy as before, he could focus on getting to a specific destination: his personal Belize. Without such a foundation, most investors run from one new and exciting thing to the next—until they get bored—always desperately trying to make money. Without focus, people will try anything; with focus, they create results.

• • • •

DEVELOPING YOUR OWN PERSONAL BELIZE— YOUR FOUNDATION FOR LONG-TERM WEALTH

"Richard, note that Armand's vision was written in the present tense; this is a very important point. Writing goals and visions as if they have already been achieved, programs your brain to make it happen. Every day you read the goal, you're reading it as if it were an established fact and this positive self-talk will produce results if you let it.

"Pretend it's five years from today; create a written picture of what you've achieved over those five years. Make it as real as you possibly can. Then, on a piece of cardboard create a collage by pasting pictures cut from magazines or the Internet that help to create a visual picture of your written vision. Have fun with this exercise, but more importantly, look clearly within yourself to see what you really want out of life!

"This exercise will answer your question, 'What will real estate give me?' Real estate will give you whatever you ask it to, if you clearly articulate your goal. To help you develop your vision, here are some questions to ask yourself. Answer them as if it were five years in the future, and everything has come together for you:

1. Where exactly do you live? Describe the house, the town, the colours, the flora and fauna. Describe the smells you experience and the sounds you hear.
2. With whom do you spend most of your time? What is their state of mind? How much "you" time do you get every day?
3. What hobby or business are you spending most of your time on? How is this making you happy?
4. Do you travel? If so where do you go? Describe as in #1 above.
5. How is your health? What is your weight? How often do you exercise?
6. What type of music fills your life? What types of art and books are you enjoying?
7. What experiences are you having?
8. Who are you helping and how are you helping them?
9. How much cash flow is coming in every month from passive investments?
10. How much net worth have you attained?

"Use these as guideline questions to develop a vision that is so strong that every time you read it or look at the picture you will be motivated. If you just put in half an effort on this exercise, it will be obvious not only to me, but in the results themselves. Everything will continue to feel like a struggle. By spending some serious time on this exercise the rest of the ACRE system will feel easy. Does this answer your question about what real estate will give you?"

"It sure does," Rich said.

"Great! Bring your results to me on Monday afternoon at five. Then, after a quick review of your vision, I'll share with you the key questions you need to ask to determine if a town will Boom or Bust. See you Monday."

On this note, I walked Rich to the door where we shook hands enthusiastically and said our goodbyes.

And now it's your turn. I bet you haven't created a collage in years and this one has the potential of turning your dreams and ideas into realities, so I urge you not to skip this next exercise:

Your vision is critical to turning your dream into reality. If you're tired of only dreaming about success, now's the time to start to make it come true.

Use the above questions to create a vision so compelling that you can't help but be excited about the prospect. Whether it involves three pieces of real estate or 300, it doesn't matter. Create a personalized picture of what you want real estate to do for you and write it in the present tense as if it has already occurred. Your vision will be a constant work in progress. As you grow, so will your vision. Make it compelling today and then keep going back and refining it throughout the years.

E-mail your vision to vision@reincanada.com.

Today's date: _____

My vision: _____

_____

_____

_____

_____

_____

_____

_____

_____

_____

_____

_____

_____

_____

_____

_____

_____

_____

_____

_____

Richard's Personal Belize

On Monday a little before 5 p.m., Richard showed up at my office with a huge smile on his face. His eyes twinkled with a childlike enthusiasm and there was a definite spring in his step. I was almost afraid to ask him how his weekend went! As he bounded into my office, I noticed a large black artist's portfolio that he was hugging to his chest. I had a feeling his enthusiasm had taken over during his Personal Belize exercise.

"Hey, Richard," I said. "You look a lot different from when I first saw you squished into that airplane seat! How are you doing?"

"Amazingly well, considering that someone else still controls every aspect of my financial life," he chuckled. "Wait until I show you my Personal Belize creation! My kids thought I was a bit nuts, sitting there with their glue and a pack of magazines, and I'm sure Emma thought I had finally gone off my rocker. But the outcome was worth the little critical comments they made. The two exercises you've given me, the one on the plane and the one last Friday, have completely changed my outlook on life—and we haven't even started talking real estate yet. I can't wait to get going!"

"Well, don't you worry," I said. "We're going to dive straight into real estate today. But first, tell me about your Personal Belize. What did you discover about yourself?"

"Don, when I left you last Friday I was feeling a little disappointed. You had just given me another exercise that wasn't real estate related. I began to think that none of the stuff you were talking about was important. I just wanted to know about real estate, not all this other stuff. Honestly, I thought you were a bit 'off,' if you know what I mean. So, all day Saturday I refused to work on my Personal Belize and instead made excuses about being too busy.

"Then, I was reviewing some of the notes I took during our discussions and noticed one key phrase: 'To change your results, you must change your actions.' And that's when it hit me—I was going back to my old pattern of not completely following through. So despite my frustration and my lack of belief, I decided to complete this exercise. Why? Because at similar times in the past, I wouldn't have. If that makes any sense...."

At this point I interjected, "Richard, it makes perfect sense. This isn't the first time I've heard this story. The key thing is you actually did complete the exercise and didn't allow your past patterns to get in the way. So you are to be congratulated!"

"Congratulations?" Richard said. "Forget that—let's save the celebrating until this becomes real!" And with that he reached for his portfolio and started to open it.

"Wait!" I said. "You've just brought up a very important point that we need to address, even before we see your masterpiece. You mentioned that you wanted to save the celebrations until you've fully achieved your vision. That is a huge mistake. Let's remember that real estate investing, like life, is a journey not a destination, and we need to enjoy every step of the way. That's why I stress that you celebrate each accomplishment, large or small.

"For instance, every time you buy a new property, go out and celebrate by doing something you and your family love to do. Reward yourself with small rewards along the journey; not only will it make real estate investing more enjoyable, it will also program your brain to keep taking positive steps just so you'll have an excuse to give yourself a small reward. Make it fun to become successful, rather than a struggle."

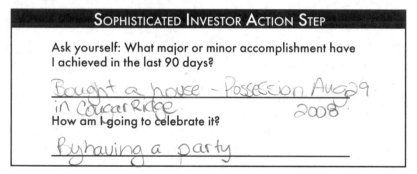

SOPHISTICATED INVESTOR ACTION STEP

Ask yourself: What major or minor accomplishment have I achieved in the last 90 days?

Bought a house - Possession Aug 29
in Cougar Ridge. _2008_

How am I going to celebrate it?

By having a party

"That's a fantastic idea. I can see how even small rewards will keep me motivated."

Richard grabbed his artist's briefcase and opened the massive zipper. As he carefully pulled out his Personal Belize collage, his face beamed with pride. On the top left corner of this large piece of cardboard he had stuck a written version of his vision. In it he described in detail exactly the lifestyle that he wanted to achieve in the next 10 years. And what a description it was: a house on a lake—you could hear the loons, smell the pine trees, hear the kids' laughter, see the white and blue sailboat at the dock and see how happy and healthy Richard and his family were. This was one of the best vision statements I had ever read.

Then, to make it even more compelling, he had filled the rest of the cardboard sheet with photos and magazine cutouts that captured the inspiration of his vision. It was obvious that he knew exactly what boat he wanted and what lake he wanted to live on; they were clearly pictured. He had many pictures of smiling and laughing people. The photo of the house must have been from a Cedar Homes catalogue; it was gorgeous. It really didn't matter if I read his vision or just looked at the collage; it was clear what Richard wanted; the detail was exact. I noticed in the bottom right corner a black and white photo of a young child at a lake with a toy boat, so I just *had* to ask, "Who's the kid in the picture?"

He looked up and said, "That's me, one of my favourite memories of my whole life. Every summer we went to the lake and spent time with friends and family, having fun and generally goofing off. As I got older and entered into my teens and twenties, I continued to go up to our cabin, and every time I drove up the driveway I would think how lucky I was to have this paradise in my life. I want to capture that enthusiasm for life again; I want working to be an option, not a requirement. You know why? Because for most of the time we were up at the lake, my dad had to stay back home and go to work every day. He could only get one week's holiday in the summer so he missed out on these amazing times. As I bring up my family, I want to ensure that I've got more time to spend with them. In fact, in my vision, I want to be living in this paradise, not visiting it periodically."

I congratulated him on the clarity and emotion in his vision and encouraged him to hang it in his house so he, Emma, Sam and Alison could see it each and every day. A vision this thoughtful and clear is the key foundational step to successful investing. It will ensure that you stay patient and follow the system. Richard propped up his collage on the chair beside him as we began to dive into the next phase of the ACRE system.

 **KEY INSIGHT**

Remember: *To Change Your Results You Must Change Your Actions*

The Four MOST IMPORTANT Words in Real Estate Investing: "What's Behind the Curtain?"

4

A man may fail many times, but he isn't a failure until he begins to blame someone else.

—J. Paul Getty

The next two weeks passed by in what felt like record time. During that period I closed on another 20 buy-and-hold rental properties, all of which had been negotiated in the previous months. You'll find that there will be some months when you purchase no property and others when you are overwhelmed with solid deals.

Because I have built such strong relationships with the professionals that I need on my real estate team, including a lawyer, bankers, accountant, realtors and property managers, closing on these properties was almost *boring*. Yes, that's right, boring. While there is always a bit of excitement whenever you take possession of a new property, the process itself has become boringly precise. And this is as it should be.

 **KEY INSIGHT**

> Make your investing so automatic that it becomes boring. It will then allow you the freedom to find excitement elsewhere in your life!

That's the key: your job as an investor is to make the process so automatic, so systemized, that it becomes boring, and then don't mess with it. The mistake many investors make is getting the system working well and then altering it to put some excitement back into it. They look for adventure when they should be looking for results! There are many places in life where one can find excitement—go skydiving or ski racing—but *don't* create unneeded excitement in your real estate investments.

Investors who start to mess with their proven system catch what I call the "invincibility" or "professor" virus. This virus gives investors a feeling of infallibility. They begin to believe that they, not their system, are creating these amazing results. With this virus coursing through their veins, they begin to write complex and confusing offers to vendors (so they can prove their expertise), or they start to buy property types or in geographic areas that don't fit their system. Why? Because they feel invincible. When investors catch this invincibility virus, the eventual crash is inevitable. Ego can get in the way of success—if you let it.

Not only do investors catch this virus—they can also spread it! And that's when it becomes very dangerous. Because these "gurus" feel above their system, they begin to share their "wisdom" with rookie investors. They start to teach their newfangled system (an old system with their new, unproven changes) even though it has never been tested through a complete real estate cycle. They enthusiastically spread this virus to others more vulnerable than themselves.

The sad part is, I've seen people who have only ever bought 15 properties in their lives start calling themselves real estate experts or mentors. They train other people in a system that has never been tested in both up and down markets. Let's be realistic: *anyone* can look like a genius or feel invincible in an up market, and that's why we see so many "experts" out there in the field today.

Sadly, the real trouble doesn't show itself until the inevitable minor correction or major negative market turn occurs and these self-proclaimed experts are thrown out of their element, scrambling to give people advice without having any experience,which leads directly to disaster.

We've all heard of unscrupulous stock market salesmen who load up on a certain stock at a low price. Then they start telling their clients how good this stock is going to be and recommending that they buy some. These stock market salesmen show stats; they show graphs; they even show projected values. They justify the sale in any way they can. These actions create a demand for the stock, which inevitably drives the price upwards. As the price nears a peak, the salesmen and their friends sell their stock, leaving the poor client with an overpriced stock.

As an Investor, You're an Obvious Target!

In the real estate world, you'll see a similar scenario play out. Someone will create a dazzling presentation that outlines why the value of real estate in a certain city or town is ready to skyrocket. They'll show you their graphs, they'll have a nice PowerPoint presentation for you, they'll feed you a nice meal and they'll seem like nice and trustworthy people. Why? Because that's their business: providing you with a very strong argument for buying the properties.

In this scenario, they have their role that they play, and you have a role that you play. The difference is, when armed with the ACRE system, the role you play changes. It shifts the power into your hands as you play the role of the Sophisticated Investor. Your one job in this role is to cut through all the hype and complete your own investigations as the ACRE system will teach you—*before* buying the property.

Notice that I am not advising you simply to ignore these types of presentations. However, before you do commit, you *must* remove emotion from the decision and complete your own "What's behind the curtain?" investigation. Ensure that the property fits your vision, that your numbers match the presenters', and that you're investing based on fundamentals—not emotion.

When you've completed that process, and everything still looks good, that's when you act—not before. Never allow yourself to become a lazy investor. You can tell if you are when you start to use the excuse that you don't have the time for due diligence and simply dive in, rationalizing that it will save you time. If the deal turns out poorly, and you haven't done your homework, it's not just the sales company's fault. The investor who has blindly followed along is just as much to blame.

KEY INSIGHT

Make sure you are doing your absolute best to ensure that every deal you transact has been investigated to the fullest of your ability.

Then decide if the investment gets you closer to your Personal Belize.

Keep real estate investment in perspective; you're buying a property worth tens (if not hundreds) of thousands of dollars. It is worth spending more time investigating the property than you do trying to decide what movie to rent at the local video store.

Choose Your Investment "Guru" Wisely

These days, there are many people out there calling themselves real estate experts, many of whom do a great job. However, even a below-average investor can look like a genius in an up market, and if they are good speakers it makes them even more attractive to investors. Always go back to fundamentals. To help you choose your "gurus," look for people who have at least the following credentials:

1. **They are currently investing in real estate, using the strategies they're teaching.**
2. **They have a bare minimum of 20 real estate transactions to their name, so they have the experience of dealing with different buying and selling situations.**
3. **They have been investing for at least five years (absolute minimum), so they have experience in different market conditions. It is even better if they've been through a full up and down real estate cycle (often a decade or more).**

There are many pretenders out there—some who are excellent in selling the "I'm helping you" story. In reality, with a little "What's behind the curtain?" you can ascertain their real intentions. You will discover if the pitch is based on emotion or fear of losing a deal (act now or miss out!), or if the pitch is based on making others look bad. Don't be taken in. In other words, integrity and unwavering commitment to disclosure are critical in considering investment advice—of any kind.

KEY INSIGHT

You don't go to a dentist to get your foot fixed, so don't go to a real estate pretender to learn seasoned real estate strategies.

THE THREE ESSENTIAL COMPONENTS TO REAL ESTATE INVESTING

There are three key components to becoming a successful real estate investor. Surprisingly, they are not money, luck or talent, despite what many believe. Veteran investors, who have a long-term, successful track record, focus on these three things:

1. **Systems**
2. **Relationships**
3. **Follow-through**

Here's how the system works:

1. **SYSTEMS:** The foundation on which you'll build your wealth. Follow a proven system and stick to it. It must be a system that has been proven to work in your geographic area and focuses on the type of property in which you want to invest. For instance, the ACRE system you will learn about is Canadian-specific, and investors have used it to purchase close to a billion dollars of residential real estate across the country. That's the type of track record you're looking for. Once you have a system that works, don't mess with it; let it work for you.

2. **RELATIONSHIPS:** Surround yourself with the best of the best experts and utilize their talents as much as possible. Relationships will fuel your business and make it easier for you to become more successful than you ever thought possible. Conversely, if you focus on money instead of relationships, you will find yourself continually running after the next deal, you'll feel exhausted and anxious, and you'll be constantly wondering where the next deal will come from. That's why, throughout this book, you will learn how to find these ultimate relationships. Some of the key relationships you'll need to develop and nurture are:

   a. *A realtor for your system* who understands your type of properties and your target geographic area. You may need to go through many until you find the right match.
   b. *A banker or mortgage broker* whose expertise lies in the investment residential real estate arena, someone who has expertise in getting financing on difficult deals. Often this will not be the banker you are currently using. Later in this book you will discover the exact steps in choosing and working with a quality banker.
   c. *A real estate-specific lawyer.* There are lots of lawyers, but the one you want is someone with 10 years or more of investment real estate expertise. Do not choose your lawyer based on price: that is the ultimate in false economy and could end up costing you thousands and thousands of dollars more in the long run when something goes awry.
   d. *A network of like-minded, success-oriented individuals.* Even

if you only see them once a month or so, this network will become a lifeline as you progress along your real estate investment path. Your network will provide you with the positive outlook and impetus to keep moving towards your Personal Belize, even as others question you or try to steal your dream. Make sure your network is real estate specific, and make sure your peers are action takers not talkers, players not pretenders. And most important, pick a group that will continually challenge you to get better. You should always feel a little behind whenever you get together with them. This will ensure that the word "average" never enters your real estate vocabulary.

3. **FOLLOW-THROUGH:** This is the component that most don't want to talk about. Even with the best system in your hand and the most powerful relationships in your life, nothing positive can or will occur without you taking action. Following through on the steps needed to achieve your personal vision is critical. Dreams are for dreamers; results are for action takers! Even if you're not fully confident in what you're doing, at least take the first few steps of a proven system. Even the longest journeys begin with the smallest steps!

You'll discover in the following chapters the rest of the steps proven by the ACRE system, including how and where to find properties, how to analyze them, how to buy them and how to manage them. You'll also discover how to build the quality relationships that propel any ultra-successful investor.

 **KEY INSIGHT**

- Choose bankers, lawyers, accountants and other professionals who own or who have owned investment real estate. This will ensure that their advice is based in real life, not just theory.

- Make sure that each of the professionals on your team has investment residential real estate specific expertise and extensive experience in working with investors

Focus on fundamentals...not emotions.
—Don R. Campbell

Still energized by the completion of his Personal Belize statement, Richard was primed and ready to start talking real estate. During our last meeting, I had promised Richard that we would be looking at the first major analysis tool of the ACRE system—picking the right town and neighbourhood to invest in.

Just like the stock market, not all towns see real estate values increase in a booming market and many underperform even in an average market. Our job as investors is to pick the areas that will provide us the best returns for the lowest risk. There is a simple and easy strategy for doing this, as you and Richard are about to find out.

How to Identify Where to Invest

"Richard, it's time to start discovering how to find properties that are going to help you create your vision. Are you ready?"

"Absolutely!"

"I want to remind you," I said, "that this system is designed to remove the emotions from the real estate equation. Here's how it works.

"By removing emotions, you are left with making decisions based solely on economic fundamentals, which will give you a huge edge in the marketplace. If you focus on fundamentals, you will keep a level head during the market's inevitable gyrations. While others are buying and selling their properties based on an emotional reaction to a news event, you'll be able to stick with your system, buying properties at a price that agrees with your assessment and selling properties only when the fundamentals say you should.

"For instance, in Alberta, recall the fear-based selling frenzy that occurred when the Kyoto Protocol was first announced. The government announcements were filled with stories analyzing the potential negative economic impact this accord would have on the oil industries of the province. Doom and gloom were thick, and fear took over the whole province.

Fear led people to stop buying and, in fact, many people bought into the negative hype and sold their properties under market value.

"At the same time, those of us who study the economic fundamentals knew that the demand for real estate in certain cities would actually increase because of all of the other indicators in the oil patch. So we bought whatever we could during this dip in the marketplace. Since then, of course, these property values have skyrocketed.

"The same thing occurred in 2004 in Ontario when the government announced their changes to the rent control laws; many pointed to this as the end of the real estate market in Ontario, when in reality it will prove not to be. Sure, it has put a damper on the market, just like the Kyoto scare did in Alberta; however, economic fundamentals always win out over the long term. The moral is that fear and confusion provide sophisticated investors with fantastic opportunities, if they are focusing on fundamentals.

Where Are the Towns with a Future— Not a Past?

"The first fundamental step is to identify a city, town or neighbourhood that has a future, not a past. I've found that many investors like to invest based on past performance. They'll jump into a town because over the last three years, property values have increased, even if the investor doesn't know why. That's like buying a stock because it's increased in value three years in a row. Both instances are called *speculation*—not investing.

"Sure, the values in some towns will continue to go up; however, others will falter and may even decrease. And that's why identifying the future potential of a town is so critical. First we investigate the macro, then we'll drill down to the micro and identify specific properties.

"In order to make the macro investigations simple, I developed a Property Goldmine Scorecard that allows you to rate a town's potential by asking the right questions. Investors have told me that using the scorecard is like having a crystal ball that allows them to look into the future. Would you like to know more about it?" I asked.

"Sure would!" exclaimed Richard.

"Good, but first let's discuss the fundamentals behind what drives real estate values both upwards and downwards. That way you'll clearly understand how to use it."

• • • •

The 12 Keys that Unlock the Vault

There are 12 major events that affect real estate values in a town, some of which sound obvious, but others are a little more surprising. Each of these events affects real estate prices both up and down, and each one is an important component in finding which way real estate values will be going.

You will use media and government announcements to start looking behind the curtain, and you'll soon be watching the news with a whole new set of eyes—eyes trained on finding real estate opportunity.

Sophisticated Investor Action Step

For this exercise, it is important to picture in your mind a property or region where the event is occurring. This will help implant the habit of watching for opportunities everywhere you go. During this exercise, if you're not sure of a region that fits the rule, take a wild guess and write it down. It may or may not be correct, but you can check it later. What you'll have by the end of this exercise is a list of areas that have investment potential. Then you'll take your list and narrow the regions down to the areas with the best potential.

The Passive Factors

Let's start by analyzing factors over which you don't have any control. I call them the passive factors. They are the micro and macro economic forces that drive market values. The ultimate investment property will feature as many of these factors as possible, making it a true Goldmine opportunity.

After each of the factors is presented, you will find either questions or action steps to illustrate their application. Take the time to analyze each one separately.

1. Mortgage Interest Rates

Mortgage rates are discussed in the media just about every day. Yet, even though they have become a national obsession, many people don't understand how interest rates work. The most obvious assumption is that low mortgage rates drive values upward, while high interest rates keep values down. Using this theory, you would think that a low interest-rate environment is good for the real estate investor. However, this assumption is false. Sure, a low mortgage interest rate keeps the investor's expenses down, but it also allows more renters to become home owners, thus increasing vacancy rates. So actually, low interest rates are more of a neutral issue for investors. Values increase but vacancies also increase.

Bottom Line: Lower mortgage rates will help drive values up and keep an investor's expenses down, but this positive effect is offset by the increase in the vacancy rates that low rates bring. If you're buying and flipping properties, low interest rates are good for your business; if you're buying and renting, then a little increase in interest rates can prove to be a very good thing over the long term of your investment.

SOPHISTICATED INVESTOR ACTION STEP
Which way are interest rates going today? Up ☐ Down ☐ Flat ☐
How do today's rates compare to historical numbers?
Low ☐ Average ☐ High ☐

 **KEY INSIGHT**

When analyzing each of these 12 economic components, you must put them in context by comparing them to local averages. For example, compare a town's population growth percentage to the provincial population growth percentage. You are looking for a town with a higher percentage growth than the province.

2. INCREASE IN AVERAGE INCOMES

This factor is often overlooked, or discounted, by investors. But it's one of the most important numbers to track as an indicator of future value. If a town's average income is increasing faster than the provincial average, real estate prices will do the same. Demographer and futurist David Baxter, the president of the Urban Futures Institute, has studied population trends and their effect on Canadian real estate markets since 1994. One of his major discoveries has been the direct correlation of income to property values. Simply put, as average incomes increase, real estate values also move upward.

SOPHISTICATED INVESTOR ACTION STEP

When you see articles in the newspaper or on the web discussing increases in average income, save them as part of your research. When you see an increase in median income or average income in an area, it's huge news, and a direct indicator that you should investigate what else is going on in that town. Remember to compare the numbers to the provincial and national averages.

For instance, if your target town's income is currently low, yet increasing at 5 percent per year, while the provincial average is only 3 percent, this is a sign that real estate values also have a strong potential to move upward. Remember, what we are looking for is a town that will outperform the rest of the marketplace. Even if the values across the whole province are increasing, a town with a higher gross income increase will often do even better.

Be wary of towns where demand is driving values upward, while the average income is remaining flat or decreasing. This is often true of towns that are attracting a lot of retirees. The town may be a good short-term investment, but without an increase in the average income, increases in real estate values will not be sustainable over the long term.

BOTTOM LINE: As people earn and spend more money, values of real estate in that town will increase. Focus on towns where income and retail sales are increasing at a higher rate than the provincial average.

QUESTION

What areas do you know of where incomes are increasing quickly? List them below.

Areas Where Incomes Are on the Increase

1. _____
2. _____
3. _____

3. INCREASED *IN-MIGRATION* AND DEMAND

A major increase in demand, without a corresponding increase in supply, will always drive prices upwards. But, in the real estate market it is important to know the reasons behind the increase in demand, so you can be assured that the increases are driven by fundamentals, not speculation.

When analyzing this component, you're looking for cities, towns and neighbourhoods in high demand because of an increase in jobs or easier access to jobs. You want to find areas where the population is growing faster than the provincial average and that are gaining a reputation as a great place to live.

Analyze both components of *in-migration*.

1. **Immigration—people from other countries moving into the area.**
2. **Intra-migration—people moving from other parts of Canada into the area.**

BOTTOM LINE: Look for areas to which people are moving at a rate faster than the provincial average. Watch for major announcements of new jobs or major new businesses moving to an area. This is always a good sign of future increase in demand.

QUESTION

What neighbourhoods or small towns do you know of where there seems to be a large influx of people moving there? List them below.
Neighbourhoods and Small Towns with Large Influxes of People

1. _____
2. _____
3. _____

4. THE RIPPLE EFFECT

To picture the "ripple effect," imagine you're standing at the side of a pond holding a large stone. Now throw this stone out as far as you can into the pond. There is an initial splash where the stone hits the water. Then, in a perfect circle around this initial splash, a large ripple flows outwards. Subsequently, outside of that ripple another ripple forms, this time a little smaller. This phenomenon continues outwards until the ripples vanish.

This phenomenon occurs exactly the same way in the real estate market. When a specific area has a boom in prices, the real estate in the surrounding areas follows, but often not at the same rate as the initial splash area. You can use this factor to identify areas that are poised for a strong increase in values.

On the macro scale, for example, when Calgary, Alberta had a late 1990s boom, property values in areas surrounding it were pushed up along with it. The value of the real estate in towns closest to the city increased at a rate slightly less than Calgary's, and this boom lagged the city's value increases by about six months. Then the areas outside of these closest towns began to feel the effects of the boom. Even today you can witness the effects of the real estate ripple occurring around Calgary.

This also works on a micro scale. When a neighbourhood is redeveloped or goes through a gentrification (which we'll talk more about later), the older untouched neighbourhoods near it also increase in value. A specific investment strategy is to look for these redeveloping areas and then purchase in areas surrounding them where it is still possible to find good properties at great prices, before the positive boom ripple affects the area.

BOTTOM LINE: Look for cities, towns and neighbourhoods where values are already increasing dramatically or redevelopment is occurring. Then look outwards from there until you find an area that has not yet felt a major impact of these changes.

QUESTION

What older neighbourhoods do you know of that are located very close to new development? List them below.
Older Neighbourhoods Located Near New Development
1. North Haven
2. Beddington
3. _____

QUESTION

What towns do you know of that have not vastly increased in value, yet are located close to major centres that have already begun a rapid increase in values? List them below.
Towns Close to Boom Towns with Real Estate on the Rise
1. _____
2. _____
3. _____

5. LOCAL, REGIONAL AND PROVINCIAL POLITICAL CLIMATE

This factor could easily be called the "leadership effect." As a real estate investor, you must keep your eyes and ears open to the shifts in political winds. What you're looking for is a business-friendly environment with minimal taxation (both income and property) and with a fair landlord and tenant law structure.

In the perfect world, you are looking for an area with strong growth in both new industries and new jobs so that there are more potential renters. As a real estate investor, it is important to understand that you are in business (even if you only own one property), and anything that enhances your business's ability for success should be applauded and supported.

For instance, whether you like Ralph Klein, the premier of Alberta, or not, he has taken a province that was vastly in debt, with high taxes and a generally unfriendly business atmosphere, and turned it around so that it now officially has zero debt and some of the lowest taxes in the country. Alberta has been called the "Cayman Islands of Canada" and has become a magnet for high tech, manufacturing, resource and distribution businesses—and that means more jobs and more renters.

On the other hand, you may notice that other leaders are making their provinces less attractive for investment by implementing restrictive landlord and tenant laws that negatively affect both landlord and tenant. Some leaders also make their province less attractive to new industries and job growth by increasing taxes at all levels of government.

Once again, this leadership effect works on a micro scale as well. For example, you can have two geographically well-positioned towns in your province. They can be the same size and the same distance from a major city, yet one always attracts the new jobs and investments, while the other continues to be the poor cousin. The major reason is the leadership in the towns. Each town has its own leadership and its own bylaws, and the progressive town attracts investment while the other loses it. In business, it is important to choose the environment where you have the best chance of succeeding.

I witness this every year when we are completing our annual "Top 10 Canadian Towns to Invest In" reports. We speak with the political and bureaucratic leaders of over 100 towns, and the differences are staggering. Some completely understand the benefits of their town and they work hard to sell it, while others are completely uncooperative and often fearful of saying anything at all. Obviously, it is the towns that promote themselves that end up growing and bringing in new jobs and renters.

A special commendation should go to the small cities and towns that are actively promoting themselves to the world. These include towns such as Barrie, Orillia and the Tri-Cities areas of Ontario; Sylvan Lake, Grand Prairie, Red Deer and Devon in Alberta; and Abbotsford, Kimberley and Ft. St. John in British Columbia. Although these may or may not be great places to invest, these towns have decided that their future is in their hands and they are promoting the influx of investment to their towns.

BOTTOM LINE: We have a very mobile workforce in this country, and if the jobs disappear in one area, these workers just pick up their families and move to another area. Watch for areas that are attractive to businesses because you'll find those areas have the strong long-term potential you're looking for.

These next two factors are my all-time favourites to watch for because they are true indicators of potential real estate goldmines.

6. TRANSPORTATION EXPANSION

This is another instance where reading major and local newspapers every day can pay off. You'll see opportunities everywhere!

When you read an announcement of a major transportation improvement occurring, get off your couch and go check it out. Transportation equals accessibility; accessibility means population inflow; population inflow means higher demand; higher demand equals increased property values and lower vacancies. That's how simple the formula is.

KEY INSIGHT

In addition to using these analysis tools on cities and towns, you can also use them to identify key neighbourhoods in larger cities. If you are investing in a large city, you will find areas that are great investments as well as those that aren't. Analyze the neighbourhood as if it were a town on its own.

In Canadian society today, distance is no longer measured in kilometres, but in minutes. Commuting and access times are critical to a town's fortunes. Anything that shortens the time and makes it easier to get into and around the town will eventually drive prices skyward. In fact, many surveys of the real estate market have shown that easy access to rail or rapid transit can drive rents an additional 5 percent above the prevailing market. This factor alone will increase your income and the value of your property.

For example, when the recent expansion to the Toronto area GO train announcement was made, sophisticated real estate investors saw a huge opportunity to see where the next major increase in long-term demand for real estate would be. These investors are already investigating where the new stations will be built and buying within a short commute of them—and then sitting back and waiting for the trains to start running. The majority of Canadians have historically waited until the transportation improvement is complete and only then have they started thinking about moving to an area. The sophisticated investor waits until the project is actually begun (announcements can be reversed) and then takes action.

Back in the 1980s when the Coquihalla Highway was built in British Columbia, sophisticated investors started buying properties as soon as the shovels started digging the highway. Once again, history has proven their actions to be on the money with dramatic increases in property values in Kelowna and the surrounding areas.

Transportation improvement also includes expansion of regular scheduled airline service. When WestJet Airlines begins to regularly service an area, it is a strong indication of future real estate growth. It is uncanny how this happens. This airline has assisted many towns in growing more quickly. Look at the impact this company has had on Grande Prairie, Alberta, or Abbotsford and Comox, British Columbia; the growth in these areas has been spectacular. Some consider airline expansion an indicator of potential growth, while other investors use it as a sign that a town or region has begun to come of age. I urge you to watch newer airlines across the country as they expand, and pay special attention to the smaller regional airports they are targeting.

Bottom Line: Look for major transportation announcements by watching the media and reading the newspapers that cover your target area. One warning: don't buy on the announcement; only buy after the work begins so you know it's actually going to happen.

What areas have recently begun major transportation improvements? List them below.

Areas with New Highway or Rail Service

1. _____

2. _____

3. _____

7. AREAS IN TRANSITION

Areas in transition are my favourite places in which to invest because they have consistently proven to provide the biggest bang for my investment dollars. Transition areas are best defined as neighbourhoods that are moving up from one economic class to the next. These tend to be older areas that are rediscovered and redeveloped. Often these areas will be described as "tough yet funky," meaning that the neighbourhood has character, and with a little cleaning up will prove to be an amazing place to bring up a family.

You can identify these neighbourhoods quite easily by getting in your car and driving up and down the streets in an area. In transition areas you'll see a mixture of old run-down homes that have a lot of character, and houses that have recently been fixed up, along with new homes being built where older ones were torn down. Pride of ownership will be starting to shine through; telling signs are window and patio boxes with flowers, new siding or paint on the houses, attractive fences and well-maintained gardens. What you'll also discover in many of these areas is that the lots are larger than they are in new subdivisions and the landscaping is much more mature. People love the mature feel of the neighbourhoods, which provides an added ambience.

Another indication of transition is the conversion of old rundown warehouses into funky or luxury lofts or apartments, or old industrial buildings being torn down to be replaced by new households. Look for in-fills being built, which means developers have knocked down old buildings and are constructing narrow, zero-lot-line houses (or townhouses).

Be aware as you drive through the area and take a look at the cars on the street and in the driveways. If you've caught the area at the right time, you'll see a mix of older cars and new vehicles. As the number of newer and upscale models increases, the more the transition has progressed.

The important thing is never to be the first into an area you believe or hope will go through a transition. The truth is that sometimes neighbourhoods that seem to have transition potential never sustain a long-term transition. Make sure the transition has already begun before you jump in.

This process is sometimes called *gentrification* and you'll see it in the human-interest stories on the news. Often residents in transition areas say that they intend to kick out the prostitutes and drug dealers and make their neighbourhood one to be proud of again. In other words, they are taking back their neighbourhood.

Every city and most towns have areas like this; however, it is often the locals who are the last to discover them. Why? It's really rather simple. The locals have perceived beliefs and emotions regarding these areas. The local perception is the most difficult to change and often remains negative long after the transition has been completed. The local investors make the fatal investment mistake of letting their emotions rule their decisions. The good news is this provides an intelligent investor an amazing opportunity. The investor with no preconceived biases about the area can look at a property's transitional investment potential and base his or her investment decision on reality.

Areas like Forest Lawn in Calgary, the Junction in Toronto and Queen Mary Park in Edmonton are all in differing levels of transition, providing investors some major opportunities. Look at Yaletown in Vancouver; it was once a rat-infested warehouse area, and now it's one of *the* places to be in the city.

BOTTOM LINE: Never be the first into an area you believe is going to be in transition. Transition areas have lots of long-term profit potential. Just remember that when you are buying you will often be buying in an area where there is a tougher tenant profile and lower-than-average rents, but the tenant situation will improve and the values will increase as the transition progresses.

That concludes the first group of factors. I call them the passive factors
because all seven are out of the investor's control—unless of course you're
the Minister of Transportation and can get a new highway built! All you
need to do is be aware of and take advantage of them as they occur.

ACTIVE FACTORS—THE ONES YOU CAN CONTROL

This next group comprises factors you can directly influence. Each one of
them will affect the overall value of a property by either increasing the income you get from it, or increasing its attractiveness to a potential buyer.

8. CREATING HIGHEST AND BEST USE

Highest and best use is a term you will see in many professional property
appraisals. This means that the property is being used to its potential.
Your opportunities lie in finding properties that are not being maxi-
mized and then changing their use.

To go to an extreme to make a point, consider a plot of raw land on
the edge of a growing city. Obviously, having cows wandering on it is
not maximizing its potential use as a piece of investment real estate.
Depending on the zoning, building a subdivision or industrial park
would obviously drive the value skyward. You'd have to sell a lot of milk
from those cows to make what you would from redevelopment.

On a smaller and more common scale, you'll be looking for properties that can be changed to increase the income they produce. For
example, developing warehouses into loft-style apartments is a change
of use that will dramatically increase the value of the property. A
popular trend right now is converting old office buildings into condominiums. Imagine that scenario for a second. You could end up
buying and living in the exact same space your Dilbert work cubicle
used to occupy; now *that* would be depressing.

On an even smaller scale, you can make simple changes to a house in a university district so that it can be rented out by the room, instead of renting out the whole house. Often you can get close to double the income from a property by doing this, if the zoning allows.

BOTTOM LINE: You will run across many different types of real estate opportunities as you're out in the marketplace. A small number of them will allow you the opportunity to change the use. Make sure that you have the expertise and the funds to complete the change you are contemplating. If you don't have the knowledge and experience, you can always partner with someone who does, especially for large projects.

SOPHISTICATED INVESTOR INSIGHT:
Easy Change of Use Can Drive Up Your Income

Thinking outside the box can really assist you in the real estate investment game. One of the more creative, yet simple, ways in which to drive up the income on single-family homes is by renting out the unattached garage separately.

The assumption is that garages always go to the person renting the main floor of the house. Well, that's not a rule. Remember, as the business owner, your job is to provide quality housing to quality tenants, while at the same time maximizing the total income you generate from the property.

Renting out your garages separately, under a separate agreement, is just one additional way to maximize your returns. Sophisticated investors rent unattached garages for anywhere from $50 to $300 and up per month, depending on the area and the demand. Sometimes they are rented to the tenants renting the house, but in many cases they are rented to someone else. In most cases, garage renters use them for storage or for parking.

The additional income vastly increases your profitability. The good news is that, in most provinces, garage rental is not covered by the landlord and tenant laws (make sure you have a separate lease for it, not a residential lease). This provides you much more freedom to set garage rents.

---

9. BUY WHOLESALE; SELL RETAIL

Sounds like your local store at the mall, doesn't it? You can buy property wholesale any day of the week, in any town across the country; you just have to know what to look for.

There are companies whose sole business is buying properties at wholesale and selling them to investors or homeowners at retail. This area of real estate investing can be very profitable if you know what you're doing.

Here's how it works: you purchase a larger multi-family property, an entire apartment building, for example. You then convert the property so that each suite has an individual title. This is known as *condominiumization* or *stratification*. Now you can sell the individual units one at a time for substantially more than you paid for them. Sometimes these individual units can be sold almost immediately, while at other times you must hold them in your portfolio for years before you can sell them at a worthwhile profit. Development of raw land is also covered under this scenario. You purchase raw land and convert it to individual lots to be sold at retail.

BOTTOM LINE: If you don't yet have the expertise or the deep pockets for this type of investment, you can still watch for areas where it is already occurring. Then you may be able to take advantage of the ripple effect as these projects drive values up in neighbouring areas and properties.

PROCEED WITH CAUTION!

This process of stratification takes a unique talent and some deep pockets to get started. All of your costs are up front and your return is derived only from the sale of the property.

10. QUALITY MARKETING

Marketing is a critical tool for investors. You need to become proficient at it if you wish to get higher-than-market rents and values for your properties. By using proven marketing strategies, you can attract the type of buyer, seller or renter you want, while at the same time reducing the effort it takes for you to run your business. Quality marketing is a real estate investor's best-kept secret. It allows you to maximize your income, minimize your purchase price and maximize your selling price.

For instance, if there are two similar houses in the same neighbourhood, the one that is properly marketed can easily sell for 5 percent to 10 percent more than the other. And when you're talking real estate, 5 to 10 percent is a lot of money. The same is true for rental properties; simple marketing strategies can allow you to get a higher rent (if your local landlord and tenant laws allow) than you would for the exact same property that is poorly marketed.

That's how valuable quality marketing is. The good news is, you don't have to be overly creative to be a good marketer. Marketing is not an art; it is a science with proven formulas that you can follow to be successful.

11. Renovations and Sweat Equity

Doing renovations on a property can dramatically affect its value. Many investors start this way because they don't have a lot of working capital, but they do have time and expertise. It also helps if you don't mind your house being a construction zone for a few months. If it is your primary residence, make sure you have a very understanding spouse!

Areas of transition are a great source of properties that need improvements. Look for well-built, but somewhat neglected, properties in areas that are showing an increase in pride of ownership. The first step is to buy a property in a location that is poised to boom. Make sure the property is structurally sound and just needs simple things like lumber, new flooring, drywall, paint, cabinets and so on. You buy it, improve it to increase the value and the curb appeal, and then either sell it or rent it, making it a part of your investment portfolio.

Your labour and expertise play a major role in the value increase. The key is, if the property is going to be a rental or you're just going to sell it, keep the work simple. Remember, you are ultimately trying to appeal to the renter or purchaser, not yourself. For example, you may love a dark purple feature wall because it goes with your furniture; however, that colour may put people off.

Make sure you understand which upgrades give you payback and which are a waste of money. There is a whole system for calculating this, including knowing what colours to use in which rooms, which areas never to renovate and which areas you must. The renovations that provide you the best bang for your dollar are often not what conventional wisdom might tell you to be true.

Bottom Line: Look for properties that need touch-up renovations—non-structural improvements that have an immediate impact on the appeal of the property. Improvements can include those mentioned above as well as landscaping and exterior work. The key to this strategy is to ensure that you put a value on your time and make sure the effort is really worth it.

KEY INSIGHT

Many investors complete the renovations on the first one or two properties on their own and from then on use trusted contractors to do the improvements. You will start to really make money when you focus on buying properties with great investment potential and let others do the physical work.

QUESTIONS

What properties do you know of where a few cosmetic renovations could drive up their value? What neighbourhoods do you know of with a number of these types of properties? List them below.

Properties with Potential for Good Return on Cosmetic Renovations

1. _____

2. _____

3. _____

Neighbourhoods with Properties with Potential for Good Return on Cosmetic Renovations

1. _____

2. _____

3. _____

12. Speculation: The Secret Tip That Turns Out Not to Be So Secret!

You hear about speculation in the stock market every day of the week. Your neighbour hears of a hot tip about a stock that is about to go crazy. The rumour spreads and as more people buy, the price goes up. Unfortunately, the hot tip proves not to be real and the stock tanks.

This also occurs in the real estate market. For instance, your neighbour, who knows someone whose brother is the neighbour to someone on a planning committee somewhere, tells you and all of his friends about a new development or golf course that's about to be built. He says you should go up there and buy property because he's heard it's a sure thing. In this situation, people start buying based on greed, and this emotional behaviour drives up the values. These speculators forget about economic fundamentals and neglect doing their homework, once again proving that emotions lead to bad decisions and are the downfall of most real estate investors.

However, speculation *can* prove to be a very profitable business, as long as you know what you're doing and you are armed with facts, not rumours. When the Vancouver Olympic bid was approved, speculators jumped into the Sea-to-Sky corridor between Whistler Mountain and Vancouver, driving the values into the stratosphere. Money was made by those who got in and rode the wave. In this case, the speculation paid off as the values went up and stayed strong. Speculative investing can be quite profitable, as long as you know that you are in for just a short time and the real economic fundamentals don't work in this case. It has substantial risk because it isn't based on fundamentals.

Bottom Line: Although there is money to be made in speculation, it is not part of the ACRE system because there are too many variables that are out of your control. You need very deep pockets to speculate well, and the bottom line is that you can make just as much money—with less risk—by investing according to economic fundamentals.

What areas have you heard rumours about? List them below.
Areas Where Real Estate Values Are Rumoured to Take Off

1. _____
2. _____
3. _____

The final exercise is to take a look at all of the areas you've written down in the 12 key components above and see whether any areas are listed more than once. The more references to an area, the better the chance that area will boom. In today's market, you're looking for areas that have at least 7 of the 12 components to make it a potential home run. Write down the areas, in order of the number of times they showed up on your lists, starting with the best.

EXERCISE

Areas Listed in Order of Their Investment Potential

1. _____
2. _____
3. _____
4. _____
5. _____

In the next chapter you will be given a very powerful tool, which is designed to ensure that you pick only the towns that are poised to boom. Use this tool, combined with all of the insights you have gained in Chapter 5, and you will give yourself an amazing head start in the real estate marketplace. It works like a crystal ball, pointing you to the areas in which to invest and the areas to avoid.

If there is no dull and determined effort, there will be no brilliant achievement.
—Hsun-tzu

After Richard had systematically worked his way through the 12 factors that influence real estate values and compiled his list of prospective areas and properties, he was ready to move on to the next step—due diligence in the form of key questions designed to look behind the curtain to clearly identify anw investment opportunity.

"Well, Rich, that's quite a bit to get your head around in just a couple of hours. How are you feeling?"

"To be honest, I'm very excited to finally be talking about real estate!" he said in a slightly tired voice. "The one problem I have is how am I going to keep track of all 12 of these points? I've already forgotten some of them! You see, I've got a great memory; it's just short," he chuckled.

"Don't worry," I replied. "I've got that covered. Here's a very special card titled the 'Property Goldmine Score Card.' It encompasses all 12 of the key factors we just discussed, as well as adding additional questions to prompt you as you progress in your investigations.

"Each and every time you review a property you *must* ask every one of these questions. It forces you to look behind the curtain and not get caught up in hype or your emotions. Successful investors across Canada have been using this for years with amazing results."

With that, I handed him one of the most important pieces of the ACRE system and explained how it works.

• • • •

HOW TO USE THE PROPERTY GOLDMINE SCORE CARD

As a sophisticated investor, you are looking for cities, towns or neighbourhoods that have as many of these factors in place as possible. For instance, if you find an area that has just one or two of these keys, then it's not a sure bet. However, as you reach seven or eight, you're starting to see a town with huge potential. Any score above that mark means you should personally go and check the area out, because that area may hold substantial opportunity. You should keep blank copies of the score card in your car at all times, because you never know when opportunity might strike. Keeping the card close at hand will ensure that you remember all of the critical questions to ask *before* you take action.

To find the answers to the questions on the score card, start with the economic development department of the city or town. Their job is to provide you with reasons to invest in their town, so they'll have most of the stats you need at their fingertips. Check out the town's website, too; many have superb statistics sections. Go to the provincial government's website to get the stats against which you're going to compare the town's numbers. To answer the rest of the questions, start digging. Talk to realtors, developers and other investors. Hang out at the town hall and talk to councillors and the mayor. Don't quit until you have the answers to all the questions; then, and only then, can you be assured that you've got your first level of due diligence complete.

If you want to be a successful investor, you need to do this due diligence for every property. Not doing it leads to mediocrity or worse. Those willing to do that extra 10 percent that others aren't willing to do are the people who become very successful. Those who skip the work or try to take shortcuts invariably create unremarkable results.

No Shortcuts to Belize

The scorecard is a foundational piece of the ACRE system, so let's talk about the importance of systems for a second. Systems are a combination of all of their parts. Systems work when all the parts are in place. For instance, your car is a system. To operate, it needs fuel, air and coolant. And it needs to be properly maintained. If you take shortcuts around maintenance, or go without fuel, you aren't going to get very far, no matter how compelling your destination.

Quality systems only work when all the parts are there; shortcuts around the difficult parts destroy systems. These shortcuts inevitably seem like they are saving you time; however, they always lead to frustration and below-average results. It's basic human nature to look for a shorter and easier way of doing things. But realistically, if the system is the right one, it will always provide the fastest route with the best results. If you're serious about making your Personal Belize come true, it's worth a little effort to get it right.

REAL ESTATE INVESTMENT NETWORK™

#1018, 105 – 150 Crowfoot Cres. NW,
Calgary, Alberta T3G 3T2
phone (403) 208-2722 fax (403) 241-6685
www.reincanada.com

Property Goldmine Score Card

Property Address: _____

Town: _____ Prov: _____

Source: _____ Tel: _____

Property-Specific Questions

❑ Can you <u>change the use</u> of the property?
❑ Can you buy it substantially <u>below retail market value?</u>
❑ Can you substantially <u>increase the current rents?</u>
❑ Can you do small <u>renovations</u> to substantially increase the value?

Area's Economic Influences

❑ Is there an <u>overall increase in demand</u> in the area?
❑ Are there currently <u>sales over list price</u> in the area?
❑ Is there a noted <u>increase in labour and materials cost</u> in the area?
❑ Is there a lot of <u>speculative investment</u> in the area?
❑ Is it <u>an area in transition</u>—moving upwards in quality?
❑ Is there a major <u>transportation improvement</u> occurring nearby?
❑ Is it in an area that is going to benefit from the ripple effect?
❑ Is the property's area in "<u>Real Estate Spring or Summer</u>"?
❑ Has the <u>political leadership</u> created a growth atmosphere?
❑ Is the area's <u>average income increasing</u> faster than provincial average?
❑ Is it an area that is attractive to the baby boomers?
❑ Is the area <u>growing faster</u> than the provincial average?
❑ Are <u>interest rates</u> at historic lows and/or moving downward?

_____ = Total ✔s

Does This Property Fit Your System?   ❑ yes ❑ no
Does It Take You Closer To Your Goal?   ❑ yes ❑ no

"Well, I now have a very clear picture of where real estate is going to take me. That collage gives me something to shoot for and it's the first time I've had that clear of a goal. I also have a very clear idea of how to analyze cities and towns. I didn't know it was that easy. So easy, in fact, that I've already made a list of locations to check out. And I guess the best part is I'm starting to see that I can dig myself out of this situation I find myself in."

"Richard, I've got two questions for you," I said after he had looked over the Property Goldmine Score Card. "First off, what do you feel you've accomplished so far?"

"Well, I now have a very clear picture of where real estate is going to take me. That collage gives me something to shoot for and it's the first time I've had that clear of a goal. I also have a very clear idea of how to analyze cities and towns. I didn't know it was that easy. So easy, in fact, that I've already made a list of locations to check out. And I guess the best part is I'm starting to see that I can dig myself out of this situation I find myself in."

"That's a great start, but really it's just the beginning. The second question is even more important. How are you going to celebrate accomplishing this first step?"

"What are you talking about? Why should I celebrate? I haven't accomplished anything yet."

KEY INSIGHT

Remember to celebrate all your successes along the way, both large and small. This will make the journey much more enjoyable and program you for continual action.

"Are you kidding me, Richard? You've already defined your vision and discovered the first steps to making it real. I'm willing to bet that previously you would have made excuses and not done any of these exercises. So you've already broken one of the major habits that have held you back. That in itself is worth celebrating, not counting what you've already accomplished. Celebrating is the next habit you've got to get into."

"Celebrating sounds like it costs money and takes me away from the time I need to focus on taking action. Isn't it a big waste?"

"It's far from being a waste; it's actually a critical part of any success program. Without the celebrations along the way, it's easy to get weary and to tire of following the system. Imagine this: you're a number of years away from achieving your vision. If you wait all that time to acknowledge your results, you may get frustrated and quit following the system because you don't see any progress. Celebrating keeps you on track, makes the journey more fun and, most importantly, helps you feel great about the progress you're making. It's an amazingly powerful tool that many people don't even know about!"

"I get it. If I make the journey fun, I'll stick with it and so will the family!" Richard's face lit up. "I've got an idea! I have a town that came up in 8 of the 12 categories. It's about an hour's drive from here and it has a beach. I'm going to go check it out, but I'll make it a celebration now that the family is back from their vacation. I'll take all of them with me and make it an outing with fish and chips on the beach. I'm not known for doing something like this, so it may also show Emma my commitment to this new endeavour and help bring her onside. Combining a little work with celebration—how does that sound?"

"What a great start!" I said. "And that also sets up our next meeting perfectly. A week from today, meet me at 6:30 p.m. by the pond across from your house. Let's meet in the parking lot and you can take me to the spot where you sat when you took your personal inventory. I suggest calling the economic development office before you head up there and making an appointment. In growing towns, administrative staff are often very busy and work six days a week, so respect their time. I'm looking forward to seeing what you discover. Bring the results of your family trip, both personal and research."

With that Richard jumped out of his chair, carefully placed his "Personal Belize" back in his artist's case and bounded out of the office throwing a "See ya later" over his shoulder.

SOPHISTICATED INVESTOR ACTION STEP

Review your list of areas and choose one to go visit in the next 30 days. Take a look around the area, speak to the city representatives and ask the questions from your score card. Be observant as you drive around. The goal is not to buy a property on this first trip; it is just to familiarize yourself with the area and prepare you for the next step in the ACRE system.

I wanted to change the world, but I have found that the only thing one can be sure of changing is oneself.

—Aldous Huxley

It was a beautiful day as I pulled into the parking lot near the pond. As I sat there, I reviewed a number of e-mails from successful users of the ACRE system. It is a real pleasure reading about all the success that investors are creating by following the system.

There was a knock on the car window. Richard was standing there with a smile on his face and a sunburned nose. Obviously he had enjoyed his time at the beach with the family.

"Great seeing you, Richard, and nice Rudolph nose. It looks like you followed through on your celebration trip. Congratulations."

"It was awesome; everyone had a good time, even the kids. The fish and chips had that beach combination of sand and ketchup, just like I remember as a kid. And the best news is that Emma got to see me doing the background homework on the town. I spoke with the economic development officer and used the score card to get as many answers as I could. Emma and I even went through the local real estate newspaper together while the kids enjoyed the beach. She's not completely sold yet, but I think she's seeing how I've changed, especially when I kept repeating the mantra—focus on the fundamentals and remove the emotions." He paused and added, "Anyway, why are meeting here?"

"I thought it would be a good place because it's really where this whole journey began for you. I'm sure you remember that day, when you looked at your financial life and scared yourself into action."

Richard nodded. "Oh yeah. Now that I look back, even though it was only a month ago, I can see how important that was. I've brought some of the real estate newspapers so we can review them and pick some properties. I can hardly wait. Let's start walking and I'll show you the spot where it all began."

And with that, we headed off down the pathway. As we walked, he told me he had spent quite a bit of time in his target town, driving around the neighbourhoods, speaking with town representatives, calling a few realtors. Rich really didn't know what he was looking for at this point, but he wanted to get all of his Goldmine Score Card questions answered.

Richard had discovered that some of the information is not easy to get. You have to do a bit of digging and you have to ask the question of more than one person to get the right information. The Internet plays a strong role for investors, but you can never really investigate a town or city without visiting it in person and driving and walking around to get the feel of the streets.

I've seen too many investors get themselves in trouble by blindly buying in an area based only on numbers and hearsay. If you do that, you're giving up the most important part of investing—due diligence. For instance, let's say that all of the numbers look good. The town is growing, the property is below what the average property is selling for and the pictures look great, so you assume it's a winner. You break out your chequebook and buy the property. However, what you don't know is that it's the best property in the worst neighbourhood in town, only a block away from the busy rail yard. A transition is not occurring there and probably never will. You could only know all this by going there, looking around, keeping your eyes open and talking to the locals.

 **KEY INSIGHT**

You must always personally visit the town or neighbourhood you're going to invest in. Only by driving or walking around the area will you see what the real truth is!

SKIPPING STONES

Richard had stopped walking and stood looking out over the pond; it was peaceful, yet we were right in the heart of the city. I walked over to the small rocky beach and called Rich down. I said, "Let's skip a few stones. I just can't resist because the water is like glass. We'll talk down here."

"Sure," he said as we walked down to the water. "A lot of people have skipped rocks from this beach before, so you may have trouble finding a good one."

"Did I tell you that real estate and skipping stones are incredibly similar?" I asked while digging in a pile of rock and sand.

"No, and if you did, I'd have thought you were a bit off your rocker." He chuckled as he hunted for a stone.

"Let me explain. This summer I was walking on a beautiful rocky beach. This was a busy spot where hundreds of people wandered by every day. As I walked along looking for stones to skip, I was contemplating how blessed I was that I had allowed real estate investing to provide me with financial freedom.

"It was the first day of holidays and 'decompression' hadn't quite set in yet. I could still feel the pull of the office. It always takes those first two days to shift gears from office to holidays.

"There were literally thousands of rocks on the beach and lots of people were sifting through them. I began my hunt for the perfect stone. I knew that I could make just about any stone skip with enough energy behind it, but I wanted the perfect one so I could break my record of 14 with 11 true skips. Yes, I even want to do the extra 10 percent on my holidays!"

On Richard's first try the stone hit the water and sank. He looked over at me and said, "Not many good ones left; they're pretty picked over, so I usually just chuck whatever I can find. If I throw them hard enough, I can usually get a couple of skips off them."

"You're right. You can get any stone to skip if you have enough energy behind it. Of course, with some stones you'd need a cannon, but you could still make them skip. But on this day I'm talking about, I wanted the perfect stone. I hunted and hunted, kicking piles of rocks and sand around, digging deeper and deeper. I looked around to see a number of other people doing the same, and that's when I started to feel frustrated. I started to believe that all of the good rocks were gone because others before me had taken them all.

"I began to make excuses about why I couldn't find a decent skipping stone anywhere. Others had taken them all; the tide was too far in; all the good stones were farther out; I was standing in the wrong spot. I started to think of all of the baloney excuses I could think of. So I started to pick stones I knew were not flat enough to skip. I wanted to skip stones and nothing was going to stop me.

"I've skipped rocks all my life, so I decided I could make any one of them skip, even if the shape was wrong. I allowed my excuses, my frustration and my emotions to lower my expectations. It was almost like I had created an artificial deadline—I had to find a stone to skip *now*! When I look back, I can see how silly it was, but at that moment I found it easy to get caught up in the game.

"So with my lowered expectations, I started to skip stones that I knew had very little chance of skipping and used a ton of energy to try and make them hop, skip and jump. The amount of extra energy needed made the whole process a lot less fun and, of course, I came nowhere near my record. So my frustration grew even more. It wasn't fun and I wasn't very successful, so I quit and walked back to the resort, frustrated and suffering from a sore wrist."

Richard looked over and said, "Sounds like a great way to start a vacation."

I ignored the jibe. "The next day vacation mellowness began to set in as I walked along the same beach. I ended up at the exact same spot where I was standing the day before, only this time feeling a little more relaxed. This time I told myself, 'You don't have anything planned today, so only choose a flat stone, even if you end up with only a couple of throws.' There was no time pressure. So I started looking again, but with a different attitude and goal—only pick the best.

"After about 10 minutes the same frustrations started to set in; no flat stones anywhere! But this time I ignored my negative thoughts. Here I was: same beach, same conditions, different thoughts. Another five minutes went by and there it was: the perfect stone. I grabbed it and ran down to the water's edge and with a quick and easy flip of my wrist I launched it. It skipped and skipped effortlessly 10 times. Not a record, but still great—and easy!

"With renewed enthusiasm, I continued looking. My negative emotions tried to work their way in, however, I just kept blocking them, by focusing on that last rock's success. It took another 10 minutes, but I wouldn't allow myself to grab any old stone. I rejected dozens. And once again there it was: another perfect rock.

"Just like the other flat stone, it skipped effortlessly across the quiet, calm lake: 10 skips again. This was a lot more fun, a lot less effort and a lot more satisfying. Although they didn't take me to my goal of 14, I could see how to get there by never compromising on choosing the perfect stone. I sat back on a log to enjoy the sun and that's when it struck me—skipping rocks is exactly like real estate investing."

Richard had stopped looking for stones and was trying to guess where the story was going. "I think I see the connection," he said with a bit of hesitation in his voice.

"It's rather simple. When you're filtering through hundreds of pieces of real estate to find the one that will take you closer to your goal, your emotions need to be kept in check or you'll choose poor properties just for the sake of buying a property. Then, as you try your best to make these underperforming properties work, your frustration will grow even more."

• • • •

KEY INSIGHT

Real estate is not a race; it is more like a transit system. If a property comes along that's not going to take you towards your destination (your Personal Belize), then let it go by and wait for the one that will.

LINING UP THE FUNDAMENTALS

1. Yes, you can make just about any piece of real estate work just as you can make almost any stone skip, but the point is, how much effort does it take to do it? <u>Look for properties that will become effortless over time.</u>
2. No matter how many people before you have looked in your target area, there are always deals to be found—if you're patient. Vendors' circumstances change every week. Don't let the excuse "all the properties are gone" even enter your mind.
3. If you let them, frustrations and excuses can force you to choose properties that don't quite fit your system. Many investors feel that investing is a race, and they need to purchase properties just to purchase properties. This is the absolutely wrong reason to buy a piece of real estate. There are no deadlines. All you need to do as an investor is to focus on your next piece of real estate.
4. Properties that fit your system feel effortless, just like the perfect skipping rocks. Those that don't fit take a huge amount of your time and energy. Make your real estate investing easy and you'll buy more, reach your goal quicker and have much more fun doing it.
5. Location and fundamentals are critical to success. For skipping rocks you need flat water and a flat stone. For real estate you need a "Goldmine Town"—strong economics combined with a quality property that fits the ACRE system. Never compromise on the fundamentals!

KEY INSIGHT

Focus on fundamentals, not emotions.

As an investor, you may begin to feel frustrated when you haven't written any offers in a while. However, that simply says you are following your system and waiting until you find a property that does fit your system. Investors, both veteran and rookie, feel frustrated at one time or another. The successful ones don't let their frustration distract them from their end goal—their Personal Belize.

• • • •

I looked at my watch and called out to Richard, "Let's walk back to the car. My wife Connie is hosting a party to celebrate our purchase of another property and there is no way I want to be late for her amazing cooking. Richard, are you free on Tuesday evening?"

"Yes, my kids don't have any dance rehearsals or hockey this Tuesday—a break in the action, so to speak."

"Great, let's get together after your work. I want to introduce you to the filter system I use to pick only the best properties in the best towns. Interested?"

"Absolutely!"

"Okay, 6:00 p.m. it is." We entered the parking lot and I turned to Richard. "Hey, I'm thinking of bringing along a very successful investor, who has a very interesting way of looking at the cycles of real estate. I don't know how much time he'll have, but we'll give it a shot. I've told him about what you and I are doing, and he sounded excited about the whole process. He's free on Tuesday."

I jumped in my car and headed home. Connie, my wife and business partner of 18 years, is an amazing cook. As I drove home I thought about how our real estate business really started to take off when she started to believe in it. The power of a family working together is unbeatable. We had to make Emma comfortable with Richard's choices based on the ACRE system and the positive impact these decisions have on their family. I already knew how to do this, and Rich was going to find out soon.

Always leave something on the table for someone else.
—Tim Johnson

It was 6:00 p.m. and my staff had all gone home. Sonya was the last to leave as she is in charge of preparing all of our workshop materials, and with a huge event right around the corner, we were all working at breakneck speed.

I appreciate very much the quality of the support team I have around me—Connie, Sue, Ginger, Deb, Russell, Barry and Sonya. Each plays a major role in the success of our company. Rich will soon come to understand that he too will require a small support team to assist him as he grows his portfolio. His lawyer, his accountant, his banker and his realtors will all have a hand in his long-term success. These relationships will develop over time.

I value strongly the relationships I have with a number of very successful investors across the country. One is with one of the most focused investors I've ever met. His name is Tim Johnson, and he took his real estate investing to a whole new level. In fact, starting with very little, he built a portfolio that has provided him with financial freedom—over $61,000 per month of pre-tax cash flow. Tim developed and used the exact same strategies that Richard is learning about.

One of Tim Johnson's key ideas is a unique way of looking at the cycle that real estate goes through and what actions you should take in each phase of the cycle. That's what he was about to share with Richard at our meeting. As Tim and Rich came into the office, I could hear their chatter all the way back in the boardroom.

"Well, it looks like you two have already met," I said.

"We sure have. This Richard is quick with the jokes—let's hope he's as quick with his real estate," Tim responded. "Don, I don't have a whole lot of time today. I'm getting quite a charge out of coaching my girls' soccer team and we've got a game later. This soccer is quite the sport, but we'll save that talk for another day," said Tim.

"Sounds good. Richard, how's Emma?" I asked.

Rich smiled. "She's doing well. A night off from running around with the kids, it's almost like a holiday," he chuckled. "We discussed real estate a little more last night and her interest is definitely piqued.

I told her about your skipping stones analogy and she said it actually sounded like my life, always looking for but never finding the perfect stone. And you know, she's right."

Tim jumped in. "Richard, we all have a bit of that in us. You should have seen all the crazy things I tried before I finally figured out how simple real estate is."

"You and me both, Tim," I agreed.

"One of the more simple things I discovered is that the real estate cycle follows a very predictable pattern. Once I identified the pattern, I knew exactly what action to take, no matter where we were in the cycle. By following this cycle, your friends and family will call you lucky, when in fact all you are doing is paying attention. I'm sure Don has talked with you about paying attention to what's behind the curtain. This cycle is another piece of that system," Tim explained.

Richard popped open his briefcase and grabbed his notebook. "Hey, I'm not the sharpest tool in the shed, so anything simple and predictable fits my personality perfectly. Can you describe the cycle for me?"

"Sure," Tim continued. "I call it the 'Four Seasons of Real Estate.' Just like in nature, there are four distinct and separate seasons in real estate. For simplicity let's call them winter, spring, summer and autumn. Rich, do you know any farmers?"

"Yes, a lot of my family still farms out here. What a tough life that can be! I sure wish that non-farmers appreciated these hard-working folks more. Without them we'd all be pretty hungry."

"I agree," said Tim. "We can look at real estate investing the same way that farmers look at the seasons of the year. What do your relatives on the farm do in the winter?"

Richard responded, "They spend time on the computer, take a vacation, curl with their buddies, spend time with their families—some of them add to their family if you know what I mean."

"That sounds about right; however, you missed one thing. They plan and they get ready for spring, making sure their equipment is ready to go when it's needed, and they research which crops to plant in which fields. But there's one major activity they don't do in winter—planting," said Tim. "So, tell me, what do farmers do in the spring?"

"They hope for an early thaw so they can get out into the fields before the rain comes," Richard replied. "Then as soon as possible they plant like crazy. I don't hear from them for almost a month in the spring, they're so busy planting."

"You nailed it exactly," said Tim. "When spring comes, all of their planning and preparation turn into action. They know very well that there is a deadline for planting their seeds in time for them to have enough time to grow for harvest. Without their winter planning, in the spring they would be disorganized, they'd waste time and the harvest would be terrible. Then summer comes along; what do they do?"

"They watch their crops, they complain about the weather, they play golf and they tend the plants to maximize the harvest," Richard replied.

Tim continued, "They also do a little overseeding in some areas. Planting additional seed in bare spots as well as adding some shorter maturing crops. But you're right; the bottom line is they tend to the seeds they already have in the ground and prepare for harvest.

"Then, as you know, when autumn hits, and the plants have matured, they harvest like crazy. They spend weeks out in the fields working all hours of the day and night to harvest their precious crops. They know they have a very short period of time to get the mature crops in from the fields before the weather once again turns nasty and their profits are ruined."

Richard replied, "You're right, I can never get a hold of my family during harvest. The last thing they want to see is all the fruits of their labour destroyed by an early winter storm or killer frost. But tell me, what does all of this have to do with real estate?"

"That's easy. Real estate markets follow this exact same cycle with one major difference: each real estate season can last for years. So although spring for a farmer is only two months long (April and May), for an investor real estate spring can last for four or five years and this is the same for all of the "real estate seasons." And, like farming, during each real estate season investors have specific actions they should take and others they should avoid. Your Property Goldmine Score Card will help you identify where in the cycle a particular area is and which way it's heading," Tim explained. "The more checkmarks you get, the earlier the area is in real estate spiral."

With this, Tim and I began to explain how the cycle works and what actions to take during each real estate season.

• • • •

The Four Seasons of a Real Estate Cycle

Real Estate Winter

Most of us have been through a real estate winter. It is the time when real estate values drop or stagnate. The economic fundamentals of the market are all out of whack and the future doesn't look very bright. Some parts of the country, where markets remain inactive, are in a continual real estate winter.

Investor's Actions

During real estate winter, which can last decades in some areas, astute investors will study, research and educate themselves about real estate opportunities. They'll analyze other areas in the country looking for signs of real estate spring. They will work on and perfect their Personal Belize. They will prepare financially for the time when real estate spring appears.

Bottom Line

During winter, just like the farmer, investors wait for the signs of spring before they plant their seeds (or in real estate buy any long-term hold properties). They do not buy any buy-and-rent properties hoping for equity appreciation until they see signs of real estate spring.

Real Estate Spring

When the market enters the spring segment of the real estate cycle, this is the sign to start buying. In fact, if you're following the ACRE system, spring is the season when you should buy as much as you can. These are the seeds of profits that you'll harvest during real estate autumn. Real estate spring is the time for action because it only lasts a few years. The ACRE system shows you how to choose the best seeds. Just follow the steps so you can achieve your Personal Belize after harvest.

Investor's Actions

During real estate spring, you buy quality investment properties that fit your system. You add them to your portfolio, making sure they are well looked after (planted in great soil such as a Property Goldmine town), and then you add some more. Never feel pressured to buy, and always make sure you complete your due diligence.

BOTTOM LINE

During spring, don't get caught in analysis paralysis or allow other opportunities to distract you. There will be plenty of time to focus on other investment schemes after the harvest. However, if you allow your focus to be distracted by something other than adding to your real estate portfolio in real estate spring, your harvest will not be anywhere near as sweet. The power of focus is the power of success in spring.

Real Estate Summer

After a number of years of real estate spring, the market begins to change to summer. This phase of the real estate cycle is an exciting time for a real estate investor. You will start to see the seeds (properties) you planted in the spring growing into profit centres. By following the ACRE system, you will have bought the right property in the right town. The values will have begun to increase, and you'll notice that your tenants have paid down your mortgage. In other words, once the summer hits, you'll see a jump in your net worth with all of the equity you have created.

INVESTOR'S ACTIONS

In real estate summer, you have many options. You can sit back and tend your properties, managing them for maximum positive cash flow, cleaning and painting them and getting them ready for the harvest. You can also go through the process of re-financing them—taking some of your cash out now. The equity that you take out today won't have any tax payable on it until you sell the property in the future. And just like the farmer, you can overseed—in other words, buy the odd new property that fits your system by using the money you've taken from the equity in your other properties when you refinanced.

BOTTOM LINE

During the years of real estate summer, don't ignore your properties just because they are all running well. Tend them like the valuable crops that they are. Real estate summer is another time when some investors allow themselves to become distracted from their real estate holdings. Watch that this doesn't happen to you, as the profits you are about to harvest have been hard won; you don't want anything to jeopardize them.

Real Estate Autumn

This is the part of the cycle when real estate investing becomes very enjoyable. During these years, the phase we call real estate autumn, you begin to reap the rewards of all your hard work. You begin to harvest all of the real estate seeds you planted way back in real estate spring. How? By selling off your properties—one by one.

INVESTOR'S ACTIONS

In real estate autumn you use a whole new system to begin selling your properties while maximizing profits and minimizing taxes (we'll be discussing these strategies in a later book). And as you sell, you will witness the real power of the ACRE system. If you have followed it step-by-step, you will be ready to take the profits and make your Personal Belize a reality.

BOTTOM LINE

During autumn it is important to pay attention to the economic fundamentals. I have often seen investors start to believe the hype surrounding a market and they don't sell when they should. They are overly concerned with selling right at the peak. Invariably, when you shoot for the peak, you end up missing. The key is to sell before the peak, cash in your chips and then go live your Personal Belize, because inevitably real estate winter follows real estate autumn. You don't want to be still holding property when that hits.

It is easy to get greedy in real estate, and if you let that emotion enter into your investment decisions it will get you in deep trouble. Never believe your own press clippings. That is why it is critical to commit to the insight: "Always leave something on the table for someone else." This will ensure that you never try to sell for the absolute top dollar. You let the person who buys from you ride the market upward for a while. That way you'll never get stuck with properties after the market peaks.

 **KEY INSIGHT**

Veteran real estate investors will tell you that it will take at least three years of real estate investing before you will start to see the real fruits of your labour. Make sure you are emotionally prepared for this investment timeline.

If you follow these cycles and take the recommended actions in each real estate season, you will create amazing results. The ACRE system will help you identify towns and areas that are experiencing different seasons. One point I forgot to make—just because it is real estate spring in Toronto, does not mean it is real estate spring in Edmonton. Each area has its own cycle.

One final thought: real estate investing is not about money; it is about the freedom that this money will provide you. It is a means to an end. Make sure you have fun along the way, keep your focus on what's important in your life and don't let anyone steal your dreams.

• • • •

Richard said, "I never thought lessons from farming would help me much living in the city, but I see they're going to serve me well. It's been a pleasure to meet you."

Tim shook Richard's hand and said, "You must be willing to do whatever it takes to be successful. Have a laser-beam focus and don't mess with the system. If you do that, you'll be amazed at what you create." He then turned to me and said, "You've got a winner on your hands here, Don. See you at our monthly brainstorm meeting next week!" Then he was off.

"Rich, what did you think?"

"Great insights! I bet your monthly brainstorms are amazing. I drew a picture to remind me of the cycles and the actions I need to take. It's a little rough, but I'll make it nicer on the computer later."

The Four Seasons of Real Estate

Richard continued, "So, in the town that I'm looking at, I would guess by the large number of check marks on my Property Goldmine Score Card that it was in real estate spring. Correct?"

"You're right," I affirmed. "Even though values have increased over the last few years, if you follow the underlying fundamentals, you can see that they have a long way to go. If there were only a few checkmarks on the items that indicate future growth (such as increasing average income, increasing in-migration), then it would indicate you were in real estate summer. Remember, though, like the Goldmine Score Card, these give only a macro view of the marketplace. Just because these overall market indicators tell you it's time to buy doesn't mean that any piece of real estate will do ... that's a mistake that some rookie investors make. The next piece of the ACRE system will help you decide exactly what property to buy and what properties to avoid. Are you ready to start drilling down into the micro?"

"You bet I am," Rich said.

"Good. Then, once I've outlined some more tools at our next meeting, you'll go off on your own to find some properties we can analyze," I replied.

SOPHISTICATED INVESTOR ACTION STEP: IN WHAT SEASON IS YOUR LOCAL MARKET?

Real estate markets are living and breathing entities. They are in constant flux, moving forward and backward as the years progress. It is important for you to keep in touch with the latest research and trends so you can identify what season your real estate market is in.

To do so, make sure you visit www.reincanada.com and sign up for the free *Canadian Real Estate Insider* newsletter. The latest trends and economic shifts are discussed, keeping investors apprised of where the markets will be moving.

I urge you to put this book down now, visit the website and register so you don't miss out on the latest findings.

All it takes to be succesful is doing the extra 10% others aren't willing to do.
—Don R. Campbell

The Property Analysis Pyramid

As Richard and I sat in the boardroom, I brought out the next step of the ACRE system—the Property Analysis Pyramid. On the boardroom table sat a model of an Egyptian pyramid, which I had placed in the middle of the table so that Richard could see it clearly.

"Richard, before I send you out into the cold harsh market, I'm going to arm you with some very important criteria for buying real estate along with a few more checklists to keep you on track. I call this section of the ACRE system the Property Analysis Pyramid. As you can see in this model, a pyramid is built on a strong and wide foundation. Without this foundation, the pyramids in Egypt, for example, would have toppled long ago.

"In our Property Analysis Pyramid, the strong foundation is the Property Goldmine Score Card. On top of this we add layers of due diligence and investigation; each layer is designed to filter out the poor properties and to leave us only with the best."

"Let's get on with it," Richard said, calculator and pen at the ready.

"All right. The rest of tonight's discussion revolves around the elements of time and positive cash flow, the two keys that must be measured and valued in order for you to become an overachieving investor." I began with an explanation of what comprises positive cash flow.

• • • •

The Two Resources of a Real Estate Investor: Positive Cash Flow and Time

A property will give you positive cash flow if, at the end of the month, the rent you take in exceeds the expenses of operating and owning the property. These expenses include any item you, not your tenant, pay for during the month. Such expenses can include utilities, maintenance, management and insurance, and they always include mortgage and tax payments. You deduct these from the rent you've collected and, if you end up with a positive balance, you have a positive cash flow. However, if you come up with a negative balance, this is not good news and you need to fix the situation immediately.

The other important resource is time. Your time is valuable and it would be literally impossible to look at and analyze every single property that comes on the market. You want to focus your time only on properties that have the potential of creating positive cash flow. The Property Analysis Pyramid does just that. It will save you, your realtors and vendors a lot of time. It allows you to have a life outside of real estate, even in real estate spring when you'll be buying like crazy.

The 10 Percent Rule

Because time is so important, the first level to build on our pyramid's foundation is a filter: a way to discard (as you will) the majority of properties quickly and effectively. This filter is a simple yet powerful mathematical formula that has been developed from the results of a much larger and more complex analysis tool.

The complex formula took lots of time to work through, and it had many components such as interest rate, expense ratio, property price, down payment, market demand and other factors. Then one day, while analyzing the results of all of these calculations, a very clear mathematical pattern became obvious. Every time a property worked under this formula, there was a direct correlation between the amount of rent it generated and the purchase price. So rather than completing a complex, detailed analysis up front on every property, you can now use the following formula as your first filter:

The annual gross rent must be at least 10 percent of the purchase price.

If the annual gross rent is 10 percent or more of the purchase price, then the property is worth further investigation and a more detailed analysis. If the rent is below 10 percent of the purchase price, or the property doesn't have the potential to drive the rent to that level, walk away and keep looking for a better property.

You'll notice I said *annual gross rent.* That means the monthly rent multiplied by 12 months, gives you the annual total. Compare this number against the purchase price.

Monthly Rent x 12 = Gross Annual Rent
Purchase Price x 10% must equal Gross Annual Rent or less

For example:

A property rents for $925 per month and you can buy
it for $100,000.
Does this property warrant more of your valuable time?
$925 x 12 = $11,100
$100,000 x 10% = $10,000
The math shows that this property does warrant
more investigation.

SOPHISTICATED INVESTOR ACTION STEP

Try this quick analysis to see how easy this method is.
Purchase Price = $125,000   Monthly Rent = $1,100

_____ x 12 = _____

_____ x 10% = _____

Is this property worth more of your time: Yes or No?

By following this quick math, you can see that the rent far surpasses the 10 percent mark and the property is worth more detailed analysis.

You may miss the occasional property that has potential by applying this formula; however, remember you are focusing your valuable time on the best of the best.

Now for a dose of reality. In some areas of the country, properties that fit the 10 percent rule are difficult to come by, while in other areas, they are abundant. There's more good news. In a low interest-rate environment (with the Central Bank's prime lending rates below 6.5 percent), you can actually use 9 percent as your initial filter due to the lower mortgage interest payments.

A Profit Centre in the Garage

You can see that the total amount of income a property can produce is critical. And now I'm going to let you in on another sophisticated investor secret. You will remember our earlier discussion on the rental of detached garages. Using this 10 percent formula, you can see how important this extra income can be; it can make the difference between a property working financially—or not.

Currently, across the country, there are thousands of detached garages being rented out separately by investors and homeowners. You can see the advertisements in almost every newspaper in every town. These garages are rented out for anywhere from $50 to $300 per month depending on the area, the condition and the prevailing market. That's an extra $600 to $3,600 of income every year!

When you pop these numbers into your 10 percent equation, you may find that a property that didn't quite make sense when analyzed conventionally suddenly looks like a wonderful cash-producing investment.

SOPHISTICATED INVESTOR ACTION STEP

Look in the classified ads of today's newspaper. You are likely to see several listings of garages for rent. The weather in Canada can be harsh, and many renters don't have access to a garage. By offering your detached garage for rent, you can solve their problem.

Additional Strategy: Arrange for your garage leases to end during the wintertime; you will have a much easier time renewing the lease when the weather is colder.

Always ask the question, "What total revenue can I generate from this property?" Then, armed with that number, you can run the 10 percent rule. By asking this question, and truly analyzing a property's potential, you will be able to say yes to properties that some unsophisticated investors will pass up.

The 10 percent rule is only a rule of thumb, a coarse filter designed to save you time. Since the filter is unrefined, you will miss out on a few properties that would have worked, but that's a very cheap price to pay for the vast amounts of time saved. Time is a non-renewable resource: once it's gone, it's gone. However, potential real estate deals will keep coming at you like a raging river, so if you miss the odd one, it's no big deal.

SOPHISTICATED INVESTOR ACTION STEP: THREE KEY QUESTIONS

Use these three simple questions to save yourself time whenever you are speaking with a vendor or realtor. The answers to these questions will help you decide whether to spend any additional time on the property. They will allow you to complete a quick "10 percent solution" analysis on the property.

1. For how much can we purchase the property?
2. What is the current rent the property generates? Or, if it isn't rented, what do you believe the market rent will be?
3. Does this property have a detached garage?

IDENTIFYING MOTIVATED VENDORS

Once the property fits the 10 percent rule, you can feel comfortable spending time analyzing it. The first step is to determine the motivation of the vendor. This includes finding out how motivated they really are, and what the underlying motivations are.

Unmotivated vendors will waste a ton of your time. They don't care if you ever come to an agreement; in fact, you could give them the price they are asking and they still won't accept it. On the flip side, motivated vendors will be proactive in making a deal. They are also much more apt to give you a good price and good terms.

If you ask the basic question, "Is the vendor truly motivated to sell?", in most cases you'll hear in response, "Yes, the vendor is motivated"—whether this is true or not. Your job as a sophisticated investor is to cut through this first line of response and look behind the curtain to discover the truth.

The good news is motivated vendors exist in all markets, hot and cold. The sellers may be transferred to a new town or are about to move into a newly built house. Perhaps they are downsizing or retiring. It doesn't matter why they're motivated, as long as they are truly ready to sell.

It is a much simpler process to determine motivation when you are talking directly to a for-sale-by-owner seller as you can ask questions directly. It's a little more difficult when realtors are involved because they'll have to ask the questions for you. The best way to determine the vendor's motivation is to provide your realtor with a list of questions, or when circumstances permit such as when you're inspecting the property and the vendor is there, you can ask them yourself. Write them down so you'll be sure to get the information you need.

1. **Why are you selling?** (Many vendors have a pre-determined answer. This often requires a follow-up such as "Tell me more … that sounds interesting …")
2. **How long have you owned the property?** (This question is designed to determine if the vendors like to flip properties or, conversely, if they have an emotional attachment to the property.)
3. **When do you have to move?** (You'll discover if the vendors have a deadline; if so, you'll know their main motivation.)
4. **Would you accept a full-price offer if it worked for me/ the purchaser as well?** (This helps to discover if price is the main concern.)
5. **Can I/my client see it tomorrow at 7:00 a.m.?** (If the vendors are extremely motivated, they will jump at the chance to show the property at any time of the day or night. If not, you'll be brushed off.)

As I mentioned above, you can ask these questions yourself or have your realtor ask them for you. This is another reason why you want to build a great relationship with an investment-savvy realtor who's not afraid of doing whatever it takes to get the deal done, including getting the answers you need.

The answers you get will reveal the vendors' motivation level and, as an added bonus, you'll discover whether the most critical motivating factor is time or money. You should also note that a vendor's motivation level often increases when the property has been listed for sale for some time. Watch for properties that have been listed for a while; it may be a sign of increased vendor motivation.

KEY INSIGHT

Motivated vendors will provide you with the opportunity to solve the problem of selling their property. By doing so you'll be rewarded with some or all of the following:
1. Below-market price.
2. Terms and conditions that suit you.
3. Access to the property before closing so you can do minor renovations and conduct showings to potential renters/buyers.
4. Information about additional properties the vendor may wish to sell.

THE POWER OF THE
DUE DILIGENCE CHECKLIST

We started by using the 10 percent rule to narrow down the massive list of for-sale properties to a manageable size. Then, we shrank this list even further by focusing only on motivated vendors, and still none of this has taken very much of our time. We're now left with a solid list of properties that have potential, so let's dive into the details of the property itself.

Here is a checklist of questions that you need to answer for every property you are analyzing. You'll see it is a fairly extensive list. This is your due diligence checklist, so make sure every question is answered. If the vendors hesitate to provide answers to some questions, consider it a signal and dig a little deeper to find out why. Are they hiding anything behind the curtain?

Completing this checklist fully is another piece of that extra 10 percent of effort that many aren't willing to take on. Your job is to collect all of this information in one place and look for any inconsistencies in the answers.

As you use this checklist, you'll discover that it forces you to look at the fundamentals behind the property, further removing your emotions from your decision. You'll also hone your instinct for identifying quality properties by having these conversations with the vendors or realtors. At the beginning it may feel like a lot of extra work; however, the more practice you get, the quicker and more efficient you'll become. And the more efficient you become, the more successful your investments will be.

By asking these questions, you may discover something about the property that makes it unattractive to purchase, such as outstanding city workorders on the property that would be too expensive to fix. This checklist will help protect you just by reminding you of all the critical questions, just as a pilot's checklist helps him or her ensure the plane is ready for flight. Pilots never skip their checklist, no matter how many hours they've flown, and sophisticated investors never skip their due diligence checklist, either.

Every Property Due Diligence Checklist

Due diligence is critical for ANY property you are considering investing in. Whether you are a silent partner or the actual person finding and investigating a property, you must do your own independent due diligence. This checklist will provide you a foundation from which to work, and will assist you in asking the critical questions. Remember, it does all come down to the accuracy of numbers. DO NOT SKIP ANY STEPS!

Location:

❑ How many checkmarks does the area get using the **Property Goldmine Score Card**? *(6 checks or more is best)*

❑ What is the nature of the local economy? ❑ Diverse or ❑ Single Industry

❑ In what area of town is the property located? ___Older ___Newer ___Transitional

❑ What is the type and quality of the surrounding properties?
Type:_____

Quality vs. rest of neighbourhood:

❑ What amenities and services are nearby?
❑ Transit ❑ Shopping ❑ Schools ❑ University/College ❑ Major Employer

Building:

❑ What is the overall curb appeal? (scale 1 to 10) _____

❑ What is the overall interior appeal? (scale 1 to 10) _____

❑ How well has the property been maintained? (scale 1 to 10) _____

❑ Are there any deferred maintenance repairs required in the next 12 months?

If YES, list them: _____

If YES, estimate cost of repairs: $_____

❑ Are there any appliances you need to purchase? YES / NO

❑ Has a complete professional inspection been completed? YES / NO

If NO, when are you scheduling it for? _____

❑ Is a Real Property Report (site survey certificate) available from vendor?
YES / NO

      If YES, is it acceptable to your lawyer for closing? YES / NO

Financials:

❑ Have you completed a **Property Analysis Form**? YES / NO
(You must complete the form for EVERY property before you make your offer.)

❑ Do the results of the **Property Analysis Form** fit your investment system?
YES / NO *(If NO, look for a different property.)*

❑ If currently a rental—are financial statements available for the property?
YES / NO

      What is the expense to income ratio? *(35%–45% is workable)*

      Are the numbers believable? Do they fit market norms? YES / NO

❑ What is the current rent on the property? _____
(If not currently rented, what should it rent for when analyzing the market?)

❑ What are rents for similar properties in the area? $_____

❑ What is the vacancy rate history of the property? _____%

      When vacant, does it seem difficult to re-rent? _____

      What is the vacancy rate history for the area? _____%

      How does that compare with the property's history? _____

Additional Critical Due Diligence:

Check the following items to ensure you're not buying unknown trouble:

❑ Confirm taxes and other charges are current (city hall).

❑ Confirm no outstanding workorders or compliance orders
(city hall—health department).

❑ Open or past complaints registered to the address? Known as a problem
property (police)?

❑ Who will be managing the property? _____

> If YOU—is there a reliable company when you get tired of managing?
> YES / NO
> ☐ What banker/broker has a program to assist you with the financing
> on this property? _____
> ☐ What is the vendor's REAL motivation level?
> (0 = none, 10 = extremely) _____
> ☐ Do you plan on keeping the current tenant—do they fit YOUR tenant profile?
> YES / NO
> ☐ Do you need vacant possession to make it fit your system? YES / NO

We were at the halfway mark of the complete Property Analysis Pyramid. Richard now had the tools to eliminate the majority of properties on the market and spend his time and energy focusing on the best of the best. It was time for him to get out into the market and try out this first part of the system in real life.

Then, after he experienced first-hand how simple the system was, I would introduce him to the heart and soul of the ACRE system—the tool I call the "Decision Maker."

THE DECISION MAKER

"Richard, the next piece of the Real Estate Pyramid is where all of your homework and analysis come together. It's called the Decision Maker. At the decision-maker stage, you will be focusing on the real life numbers of a property and analyzing them in extensive detail. Then, and only then, can you truly make an informed and unemotional decision about purchasing the property."

Richard nodded in agreement, ready for the next piece of the system, even though he still hadn't turned on his calculator. He seemed a little impatient. "Don, I understand the pyramid idea, but we've not done a whole lot of math yet. How come?"

"Simply stated, we don't want to waste our time on properties that don't have even the slightest chance of working. Let's only do the more difficult math on properties that have a very good chance of making it into our portfolio!"

"Makes sense to me," Richard replied. "I'm not a huge fan of math anyway, so I might as well only do it when it's going to make me money. So let's get to it!"

"Not quite yet," I said. "Your job in the next two days is to find at least three properties that you are interested in. You've already identified the area from your Property Goldmine Score Card; now it's time for you to go see if there are any good properties for sale there."

"How will I know whether it's good or not if I don't have the Property Analyzer Form? It seems to me to be a bit of a waste of time." Richard's frustration was showing.

"Believe me, by the time you've completed these first steps of the Property Analysis Pyramid, you'll have narrowed your search down substantially. Just follow the first steps we discussed today, and then meet me at Starbucks down the street from your office on Thursday. I'll be in the area around 5:45 p.m. Does that work for you?" I asked.

"It does. Sam's hockey practice isn't until 8:00 and Emma will be visiting her mom at the hospital. By the way, I sure hope real estate will provide me with the freedom I'm looking for. I'd love to be able to take care of Emma's mom and dad so they don't have any financial concerns. I think that would be a huge load off their minds and a way for me to thank Emma for sticking through all of my past financial adventures."

"In the long run, real estate can and will provide financial freedom, if you have the patience to stick with the system," I said to reassure him. "See you at Starbucks. And bring your due diligence on three properties you think could work. And your calculator. Have fun!"

"I will! I'm glad I finally get to analyze properties. I never thought we'd get through all of the foundational work. Yes, I know, that stuff is important, but I can't wait to get going on these properties!"

As usual I had one last thought before he left. "Hang on, Richard. Before you go, let's talk about the types of properties that best fit your Personal Belize. I often get the question, 'What types of property make the best investment?' The answer is, it all depends on where you are in your life, how much extra time you have and, of course, what your Personal Belize looks like.

"Richard, you've created your vision and you're committed to making it a reality. That's the first step in identifying the types of properties to focus on. The second step is analyzing your financial situation. Once again, it all stems from your vision and the available time you have.

"For example, if you have a lot of spare time, then buying properties that require renovation can be a great strategy. You buy them undervalued and use your spare time and knowledge to increase the value.

Then, when they're fixed, you have the option of selling them for a quicker profit or holding them as rental properties. If you buy right, keeping them is often the best model as these types of properties will provide you with income and an increase in your net worth as the value increases. In other words, you get the best of both worlds.

"In your case, passive income plays a major role in your vision. You mentioned that you want work to be an option not a requirement, when you're living at the lake in your dream home. So obviously buying properties for passive income will drive this portion of your vision. Single condominiums are often much easier to manage. They're usually located in buildings with a manager. You can arrange with the building manager to take care of your property. However, single-family homes and multi-plex properties often create higher cash flow. The downside is they are more difficult to manage and often the fees you'll pay to a property management company will be two or three times higher than what you would pay to manage a condominium.

"Many successful investors have a portfolio that contains a mix of condos, single-family homes and multi-plexes. But most important, they all have positive cash flow and are located in areas identified by the Property Goldmine Score Card as having a positive future."

"Does that mean I should limit the types of properties I'm looking at this week?" Richard asked.

"Yes! You should just look at properties that fit the 10 percent solution (a very small number of properties) and are located in your target area. Leave the rest up to the Property Analyzer Form I'll give you on Thursday.

"And one final tip. When you go to a property, take your digital camera. Shoot as many photos of the property as you can, inside and outside. Make the first picture a shot of the address of the property. As you get busier you'll find this will help you organize your photos. Photograph both the good and bad features of the property, and ensure that you get a minimum of one photo for each room, including the basement. You should also take a photo of all the appliances, the roof and any outbuildings such as garden sheds and garages. Then, when you download your pictures into your computer, rename the files to match the address of the property, for example, 123–45th Avenue, kitchen."

Richard looked up from his notetaking and asked, "Should I bring my photos along when we meet?"

"Sure, why not? I'll be able to show you how I'd look at a property. Now get outta here. I think you have a hockey practice you're chauffeuring for tonight."

"That's right," Richard said as he looked at his watch. "Gotta go." With that he packed up his stuff and dashed out the door into the rain—and off to a new real estate adventure.

**SOPHISTICATED INVESTOR ACTION STEP:
START TO OWN THE PROCESS—IDENTIFY REAL PROPERTIES THIS WEEK**

Now that you've identified an area you think has potential, it's time to identify a few properties—before you do the financial analysis. Look up properties in a newspaper and speak to realtors and vendors. Over the next seven days, compile the answers to the Vendor Motivation questions as well as the Due Diligence Checklist questions.

Of all the properties you review, list the top three addresses below. You will analyze these properties in the next chapter.

1._____

2._____

3._____

The PROPERTY ANALYZER Form: Where the Rubber Hits the Road

10

All great truths are simple in final analysis, and easily understood; if they are not, they are not great truths.

—Napoleon Hill

Jazz was playing as the after-work crowd mingled and talked about the coming weekend over the aroma of roasted coffee. The energy in Starbucks was electric; the perfect setting for doing math, I thought to myself with a chuckle. I'd arrived early and grabbed a corner booth that was both quiet and had a good-sized table so that we could spread out our paperwork.

As I got settled with my latte, I reviewed the latest Property Analyzer Form that I had just completed on a property I wanted to buy. This got me to thinking—in all my years of investing, had I ever bought a property without using this form? After quite a bit of thought, I remembered just two instances. In one case I must have been lucky; I had owned the property for only a year, but so far it had worked out. However, the other property turned out to be a financial mistake, which is often the case when you don't follow every step of a system.

This is a great lesson for both veteran and rookie investors alike: make sure that no matter how many properties you own and how proficient you get at buying, *always* follow your system. Don't skip any of the steps. They are there for a reason—to protect you from yourself and from inevitable market shifts.

 KEY INSIGHT

Never allow yourself to fall back into your old habits, as they lead you to create the regrettable results you experienced before.

Finding the Right Realtor

When Richard bounded through the door, it was obvious he didn't need another cup of coffee.

"Hey, Richard, great to see you! By the look on your face, I'd say you enjoyed your search this week."

"You bet I did, even if I did come across some very grumpy vendors and some very, shall we say, standoffish realtors."

"Don't be too hard on the realtors. I'm sure they've had their time wasted and have probably met some underhanded investors in the past. Once you prove that you're working from a base of integrity, the good ones will warm right up to you. It really is sad how some realtors have been treated."

"Funny you should say that. At least three realtors told me that they don't work with investors and didn't want my business. What's with that? In my job, I'd like to work with someone who is going to buy lots of my product on an ongoing basis, rather than someone who purchases one item every few years or so. Oh well, I guess some get it and some don't. But hey, I found one realtor who loves investors and has been working with them for over 10 years. She completely understands what I'm looking for; we even sat down and met for an hour and a half.

"On the telephone, before we met, I had given her my basic parameters and she came to the meeting with properties that might fit the system. We then narrowed these down to a few key ones. The best part of the meeting occurred right when we sat down together. She didn't start off by talking about a specific piece of real estate; she actually took out a notebook, just like the one you always carry. She then looked me straight in the eye and asked me what my goals were for the next five years. I couldn't believe it! I had never been asked that in my life and now, over the last month, both you and she have pitched that question. I think I might have shocked her because I recited my Personal Belize statement and told her that I'm looking for a team to help me get there."

Richard continued, "The pleased look on her face said she'd found the type of client she was looking for. She told me that most investors she talked with only had a vague idea of what they wanted to achieve, usually something like make a bunch of money, and that she had to start from scratch with them. This realtor completely understands relationships! Thanks for preparing me."

"Congratulations. By having a little patience, you may have found yourself a great team member. But we'll only know by looking at the properties she's brought you."

Richard took out a file and said, "I've narrowed it down to two potential properties in my target area. I know my homework was to find three, but only two fit the system."

I smiled. This guy was really getting it! "Only two, that's great. That tells me you did follow the system and didn't allow the emotions of 'needing three' to get in your way. If the due diligence only says two, then there's only two. Well done!"

Richard was quite proud of his homework, so he dove right in. "One property is a little more expensive than what I was first expecting, but so far the due diligence looks good. The other one is smaller and cheaper. I think I'll buy the smaller one first."

"Wait, wait! Richard, I need to be clear here; you're nowhere near buying a property yet. We haven't even done the math. *All* of your due diligence must be done before you buy—no skipping steps. And this rule applies no matter who's selling you the property. It could be a stranger, a trusted friend, a company you've done business with before or even your mom. There can be no exception to the following rule:

KEY INSIGHT

For every property, you must complete all of your due diligence and number crunching before you buy it. No exceptions!

THE PROPERTY ANALYZER FORM

"Remember, Richard, it's easy to become complacent as an investor, but complacency leads to trouble. Each investment property you look at needs just as much analysis as the previous one, even if it's in the same neighbourhood or the same building as another property you've bought. If you rely on luck you get a 50-50 chance, but if you rely on fundamentals and a proven system, your odds of success increase exponentially.

"In addition, you can never blindly believe the numbers you're given regarding income and operating expenses on a property. In most cases they'll be accurate, but it's imperative that you confirm them by doing your own homework and reviewing the actual bills. Remember, you're 100 percent responsible for the results you produce with this property, so always go that extra 10 percent that others refuse to go. You'll be very pleasantly surprised by your final outcome," I concluded.

Richard nodded in agreement as he sipped his coffee.

"Now, here are the five key steps to take next:

1. Identify a town and a neighbourhood with a future, not a past.
2. Discover a property that has potential in that town.
3. Ensure that the rent is at least 10 percent of the purchase price.
4. Identify if the vendor is truly motivated and why.
5. Work your way through the critical due diligence questions.

"Veteran investors understand that these first five steps are just as, if not more, important than the number crunching. The math becomes easy, now that you know the solid potential of the area and you've asked the critical questions. Veterans know, if the property has passed the test to this point, there's a very good chance they'll be submitting an offer soon.

"You've already saved yourself so much time by not doing extensive math on all of the listed properties. For instance, how many properties did your realtor bring you?" I asked.

"Eleven that she thought might work."

"Now, imagine how much time you would have wasted going over all the details and all the math, if you hadn't had the first parts of the due diligence rules in your hands. You would have had to spend more than 15 to 20 minutes per property. That's more than two hours you just saved yourself! That's time you can spend with your family or looking at properties that do fit your system.

"Let's take a look at how your two properties are really going to perform. This is where the Property Analyzer Form comes in—REIN (Real Estate Investment Network) members and sophisticated investors have been using it for over a decade.

"The form, when completed, will not only play a major role in your decision-making process; it will also help you get the bank to finance the property. I'll show you later how that part works. But first the analysis. Let's walk through the critical parts of the Property Analyzer Form.

NOTE TO THE READER

In Appendix 2 you will find a Property Analyzer Form. Throughout this chapter we have broken it into its components to make it easy for you to follow along with Richard's analysis. As a registered reader of this book, you'll be able to download a full-sized version at www.reincanada.com.

"At the top of the Property Analyzer Form you'll see a section for property data. Most of this information will come from your previous due diligence questions, and possibly a walk through the property. It's important to complete all of the information in this section because you will need to reference it later in the process.

"Write down the address and the date you walked through the property. This is important for a number of reasons. As you become increasingly active in the real estate market, you will be looking at a substantial number of properties and it will become impossible to remember every one you look at. In fact, many of us look at a dozen properties in one day. That's another reason why photos are so important," I explained.

RICHARD'S ANALYSIS

Richard brought out all of the information he had gathered on the first of the two properties he had found.

"Richard, on the very top right-hand corner of the form, write down either the photo numbers from your camera or the location and main file name of the photos on your computer. This will provide you a quick reference later in the process." Richard circled the top right corner of the form as a reminder.

R.E.I.N. ™ Property Analyzer

PROPERTY DATA

Address: _____ City/Area: _____ Date Viewed: _____

Asking Price:$ _____ Size (sq. ft.) _____ Age: _____

Major Repairs: _____ Est. Repair Cost: $_____

Owner: _____ Tel.: _____ Fax: _____

Source: _____ Tel.: _____ Fax: _____

Overall Condition: 1 2 3 4 5

"Next, rate on a scale of 1 to 5 your initial gut feelings for the overall condition of the property. This is very subjective, but it's designed to hone your instinct for properties. I recommend that you make a note of your rating right after walking through the property."

"Do I rate it as if I were moving into it?" Richard asked.

"Great question. Don't rate the property on whether you'd move into it or not. Just rate it based on the condition of the place. If it seems to need a ton of work before you could rent it out, then rate it as a '1'. If it is immaculate and you could put a tenant in immediately, rate it as a '5'."

"That's going to be hard. I'll be looking at all the properties wondering if I would live there with my family or not."

"You know, Richard, you're not unlike most beginning investors. The toughest part is cutting emotions out of the process. What you're looking to do is provide good, clean and safe housing for your tenants. It may not have the fanciest appliances or the most amazing view, and that's okay. Quality suites for quality tenants—that's the key.

"The next section of the Property Analyzer Form is where you capture some of your inspection notes and the main income of the property. You'll note that a number of suites or income centres are designated for each property. This is to remind you to review the rent levels and income opportunities for the entire property."

"You mean like the detached garages we spoke about earlier?" Richard asked while taking notes.

"That's right. Plus you may find the upstairs suite is rented at or above market, while the legal lower suite is substantially under-rented or not rented at all, which would provide you with additional income possibilities.

KEY INSIGHT

Depending on the province you live in, you may be able to raise the rent to market level 90 days after taking possession, or you may be restricted by rent controls that only allow you specific increases. Landlord and tenant laws are continually changing, so make sure you refer to the most recent legislation. The latest rules and regulations can be found on provincial websites.

"Write in the suite number or description, e.g., garage, basement suite, etc., and beside it write down the current rent (if rented) and the projected rent—what you believe you could get for rent for that unit after you purchase it.

"Rich, what's the rent on the property you're looking at?" I asked.

Richard flipped through his notes. "It's currently rented for $825 per month, but the tenant has given notice that he's moving at the end of the lease in four months." Richard continued with a smile, "And it has a detached, single-car garage. I checked some ads in the local paper and they're going for about $125 per month in the area."

"That's a good start; what do you think the real market rent is for that property?" I asked, assuming that he hadn't done this homework yet.

"That's easy! I went to the library and looked at a few weeks of classified ads in the newspaper, trying to determine what a house like this would rent for. After a little digging, I discovered that similar properties are renting for about $850 in the area, on average. I made some calls and found out that at this rate, some included a garage space and some did not. What surprised me is that the ones without a garage weren't really renting for much less than the ones with a garage. Without the garage the property fits the 10 percent solution, and with the garage the numbers are substantially better."

"What you just discovered with these rent differences is that some of the owners know the secrets to good ownership, while others don't.

INCOME & INSPECTION

Suite # or Desc.	# of Bedrooms	Current Rent	Projected Rent	Increase Date	Inspection Comments

Total Monthly Rent $ _____

Total Annual Rent $ _____

"You'll see these anomalies throughout the real estate industry," I explained. "So let's get back to your property. You've written down $825 and $125 in the projected rent columns. Now, total that up on the Total Monthly Rent line and multiply it by 12 to get a total annual rent."

I looked over his shoulder and said, "I see that the asking price is $101,000. So far so good—with total rent of $10,200 per year without the garage, and $11,700 with it, you're fine either way. However, let's look at the expenses. Even if it fits the 10 percent rule of thumb, it doesn't mean the property will always pass the final test.

"As you'll see in this section of the form, it's critical for you to have accurate information. Often at this stage you will only have estimates that the realtor or the vendor gives you. You can confirm these numbers later in the process by getting copies of actual bills, but at this point you must work with the information you have. Did the realtor happen to have any of this information for you?"

"Yes she did—another reason I knew I was dealing with a quality professional. She anticipated my needs as an investor and brought along all that she could. This is my first time; don't they always come prepared like this?"

"Yeah right!" I said sarcastically. "The good ones who work with investors do. They know you're going to need these numbers and that there's no need to waste time waiting until you ask. That's why they sell so many more properties than their competitors; they anticipate their clients' needs and then give them what they want. You really have found a gem in this realtor. Congratulations. Let's enter the numbers on the form.

"As you probably know, the major expenses here are heat, electricity and taxes. And if it's a condo, you have to enter condo fees. You'll notice that there is also a section to capture key notes as you do the analysis. For instance, who pays for the heat? You need to know this. Utilities are one of the main reasons you don't buy based only on the 10 percent rule of thumb. In some cases the landlord pays for the heat; in others, it's the tenant. In most situations you want to find properties where the tenants are responsible for their own consumption of gas, hot water, electricity, etc., but that's not always possible. I see that the heating is a gas furnace in this property, so the tenant will be responsible for the heat and electricity. With a condo, often the property is heated by a central boiler and therefore the heat is paid in the condo fees.

"That's a great start, Richard. Write in the rest of your numbers and circle the appropriate words in the comments section," I instructed.

EXPENSES

	Current Annual	Current Monthly	Projected Monthly	Comments
Heat (gas, oil, elect., hot water)				Paid by tenant/Landlord
Electricity				Paid by tenant/Landlord
Water/Sewer				Paid by tenant/Landlord/Condo
Taxes				Included in mortgage payment?
Condo Fee				Last increase date:
Insurance				
Property Management	%			Current mgmt. rating 1 2 3 4 5
Vacancy Allowance	%			Current vacancy _____%
Rental Pool Mgmt.	%			
Repairs & Maintenance	%			Overall condition 1 2 3 4 5
Resident Manager				Current on-site impression 1 2 3 4 5
Other				

Total Monthly $_____
TOTAL MONTHLY INCOME less TOTAL MONTHLY EXPENSES (before debt service)
Current: $_____ Projected: $ _____
TOTAL PROJECTED INCOME: $ _____

"I don't have any numbers for insurance; what do I do?" Richard already hit his first hurdle.

"That would be easy to calculate if this was a condominium, because in most cases the condo fees cover building insurance as well as sewer and water expenses. However, in this case, you'll be paying these. Do you have the realtor's telephone number? Why not give her a call and ask her to estimate the insurance cost on this property? We'll confirm it with an insurance agent tomorrow, but as she works the area she'll have a good idea."

Richard called and, because the realtor knew her area, she estimated the property insurance at $600 per year. (Richard later called my insurance broker and found out that the cost was $615.)

I continued, "If this was a condominium property, you'd have to pay a monthly condo fee. This fee is designed to provide the building management company with money to maintain the common areas of the building, including but not limited to the parking lot, the entranceway, the roof and the pool. In other words, everything outside of the suite or apartment. Often these fees include heat, hot water and sometimes electricity.

"The condominium board, made up of owners in the building, directs the management company as to how it would like the money to be spent. Many provinces now have strict regulations on condominium reserve funds and how those funds are managed. Make sure that you've reviewed the latest legislation for your province," I advised. "Finally, make sure you confirm what your condo fees include, so you can factor in any additional expenses in your analysis.

"Okay, Richard. You've got the first set of numbers. Now for the bottom half of the expenses. Let's start with taxes. This is where you list the property taxes; make sure you use the upcoming year's property taxes, not the previous year's. The discrepancy between the two can be quite large in some jurisdictions. Break the taxes down into a monthly payment so we can get an accurate picture of the monthly performance of the property.

"Now let's look at property management costs. Here's another very important point: it doesn't matter if you're going to manage the property yourself or hand it off to somebody else—you must always factor in a cost for management."

KEY INSIGHT

Always factor in a property management expense, even if you are managing the property yourself.

Richard had a confused look on his face. "Why should I factor that in, if I'm going to be saving money by managing the property myself? That doesn't make sense; I'll just be paying myself."

"Richard, do you value your time?"

"Of course, that's one of the key things you've taught me," Richard reminded me. "Guard my time like it was Fort Knox."

"Well, if you value your time, you need to get paid for it. That's one of the reasons to factor in a management fee. Another reason is opportunity cost. As an investor you make most of your money buying properties, not managing them. If you insist on managing the properties yourself, you'll soon discover that you can own only a limited number before all of your time is used up in management. Which means you'll have no time to do the thing that makes you money—finding and buying good properties.

"That's when you'll realize that it's time to hand your properties over to a qualified property management company," I continued. "It's false economy if you believe you're saving money by managing your properties yourself. The 4 to 10 percent of your monthly rent you pay to a management company will soon seem cheap by any measure. In this case, even if you have to pay 8 percent of the rent for someone to babysit your property, it's only $68 per month.

"Even if you do decide to manage your first few properties, you'll eventually hand them off to a management company, so we need to factor this cost into the analysis. Be realistic and you won't go wrong; underestimate your costs and you've got a recipe for trouble down the road," I warned.

"This theory is the same when factoring in a vacancy allowance. For your calculations, you should use a percentage that is about double what the going vacancy number is for the area. You can get this figure from Canada Mortgage and Housing's annual reports, or from a provincial report or even from a veteran property manager or realtor. Take this number (in your case 2 percent) and double it to factor in a buffer. Like you'll do for property management, you should always put an expense in this column even if the property hasn't been vacant for years.

"As we work our way down the expense column, the same goes for the repairs and maintenance allowance. Sometimes the vendors can provide you with their past annual repair expenses. For example, they've spent $500 on minor repairs such as new taps, etc. over the last year; that would be about 5 percent of the annual rent. As a rule of thumb, if the property is renovated and in great condition, you can use a number between 3 and 5 percent; however, if the property is not renovated and is in rough condition, you should use at least 8 or 9 percent."

Richard looked up from his notes and said, "This is starting to sound like we're analyzing properties pretty conservatively. It's obvious to me that I won't be paying the vacancy allowance or the repair amounts every month, but I guess factoring them in gives me a more realistic picture. We're continuing to remove the emotions, eh?"

"You're right—removing the emotions and at the same time lowering the risk. By factoring in these contingencies, we're taking decades of investor experience and planning for the inevitable. How are you doing so far?"

Richard grabbed his calculator and added up his monthly expenses. "Great. By following along on the form, it's very easy to see that I'm not going to forget any critical number. Simple, just like Napoleon Hill says. Great truths are simple. I've added up my expenses and have come up with $450. I guess I subtract that from my rental income to come up with my profit."

"I wish you were right! But you've forgotten about one key expense that's covered on the back of this form—the mortgage payment. Take your net income and transfer it to the top corner of the back of the form where it says Total Projected Income.

MORTGAGING/DEBT SERVICE
Total Projected Income:$_____

	Balance	Interest Rate	Expiry Date	Monthly Payment
1st Mortgage		%		PIT
2nd Mortgage		%		PIT
Vendor Take-Back		%		PIT
Other		%		PIT

Total Debt Service $ _____

Net Cash Flow $ _____

"In the boxes below, enter the balance of the mortgage, along with the prevailing interest rate and expiry date. From these figures you can calculate the monthly mortgage payment. There are many on-line mortgage calculators available that do this calculation quickly.* Be sure to note if the payment is PI (principal and interest) or PIT (principal, interest and taxes). If you factored taxes into the equation on the front of the Property Analyzer Form, don't repeat the expense on the back. Some financial institutions insist that you pay the property taxes through them. Just be sure you don't factor the cost twice in your calculations.

"The calculations are much easier from here on in. Subtract the Total Debt Service line from the Total Projected Income line to give you your estimated monthly cash flow, or your profit as you like to call it."

With fingers flying, Richard completed doing the math, which he concluded with a bright smile. "By my figuring, this property will give me at least $105 per month positive cash flow, and that factors in all of those estimates that I won't really have to pay every month."

"Great start. Actually, if you're buying a property in an area that your Goldmine Score Card told you has a great future, you ought to be happy with this number because values will be increasing as you own it. Not bad for your first property! Remember, you're looking for properties that will take care of themselves financially and provide you with some extra income while you ride the wave upwards in the Goldmine Score Card town," I said. "Now, let's go through the same exercise on the second property."

This time, Richard raced through the calculations, then we flipped the form over. We then factored in what his mortgage payments would be and instantly Richard's smile turned to a frown. As I suspected, this property wasn't nearly as profitable and, as a matter of fact, Richard was going to be over $200 per month out of pocket. This was a negative cash flow property. Even though it initially met the 10 percent solution, after all the numbers were calculated, it no longer fit the system. It was a good example of why it's so important to do *all* of the due diligence.

"So Richard, what do you think of this second property?"

"I'm pretty disappointed. I thought because it fit the 10 percent solution it would work out like the other one."

---

* Registered users can access an on-line mortgage calculator at www.reincanada.com.

"That's what a lot of people think," I said. "They believe that if it fits the rule of thumb, everything will take care of itself. That's why we do the real math on these properties. The 10 percent solution is just a tool to quickly evaluate properties and dispense with those that aren't worth your time and interest. Only by doing the detailed analysis can we know if a property will really work out or not."

"I've heard a theory that negative cash flow properties are good to have in your portfolio because they save you tax while at the same time the property values increase. What do you think?" Richard asked.

"Let's get back to reality here," I replied. "Always look at what your desired outcome is. In your case, your Personal Belize is all about freedom—working less and enjoying life more by living on the monthly profits from your properties. With this in mind, does a negative cash flow property get you closer or farther from financial freedom? And the second question is: how many negative cash flow properties can you afford to own before you end up broke?"

PROCEED WITH CAUTION! BEWARE OF ALLIGATORS!

Negative cash flow properties take money from you each and every month and impact your lifestyle. In addition, you can only own a few before your monthly job income gets eaten up by feeding these black holes.

With negative cash flow properties, you'll become emotionally and financially drained long before you'll become wealthy from properties whose values are increasing. Negative cash flow properties can eat you alive—that's why we call them alligators.

I went on, "One additional thing to remember is this: reducing taxes is an emotional, strong pitch for Canadians. That's why many are drawn to these negative cash flow tax savings strategies, when in fact over the long run, many of these strategies will just eat you up financially. Heck, we all like to save taxes, but not at the cost of our dream. If the cost of saving taxes is the loss of my Personal Belize, I'm not willing to pay the price.

"But enough of that talk. Let's get back to analyzing the property that does meet our benchmarks. If you could buy the property for $100,000, a conventional first mortgage would be $75,000, which means you need a $25,000 down payment."

Richard's smile returned. "That means that if I have $25,000 to invest, I could buy this property today and start getting my positive cash flow? Awesome!"

"Whoa, wait a minute. The down payment is only a small portion of what this property is going to cost you. It's time for the Property Analyzer Form to bring you back to reality. As you'll see, the next portion lists the additional cost considerations that you'll often end up paying for when you buy a property. Let's look at a few of them:

1. **Professional Inspection:** In every case you should have a very well-respected professional provide you with a detailed inspection report of the property before you buy it. This will be the best couple of hundred dollars you'll spend. If there is something wrong with the property, you can go back to the vendor and get it fixed *or* get compensated so you can fix it. And if the problem is too big, you can often walk away from the deal. We'll talk later on about how to do that.

2. **Appraisal:** Your bank or mortgage broker will require an appraisal for your property. The banks will only lend against the lower of either the appraised value or the purchase price. In some cases, if you have built a strong relationship, you can ask your bank to pay for all or part of the appraisal.

3. **Property Survey or Real Property Report (or title insurance):** This is called by many different names across the country. It is a document that clearly provides a picture of the land and exactly cites where the building is located on the land. It must be certified by the city or town and provided to the lawyers. This ensures that the property conforms to the local structural by-laws. As title insurance becomes increasingly popular, it will circumvent the need to acquire this document. However, costs will stay about the same.

4. **Mortgage Costs:** In some rare cases, there may be a mortgage broker fee or mortgage setup cost not covered in the legal costs. Ask your bank or mortgage broker if you will be charged this.

5. **Legal Costs:** As part of your closing costs, you'll need to pay a lawyer or legal professional to conduct the closing of the property. This will include working with banks for the mortgage documents

and working with the vendor's lawyer for the transfer of land and money. Along with their fees there will be disbursements, which are fees they must pay on your behalf to the land registry, etc. Speak with a recommended lawyer so you're aware of the total costs. In this case they will be about $1,000.

6. **Staying Power Fund:** Once again, we are treating this investment as a business and we would never strap our business of working capital. So for each and every property you own, you should have at least one month's rent in a bank account as a contingency fund. Inevitably something breaks that needs immediate repair. This staying power fund is designed to allow you to sleep at night without worrying about the next disaster.

7. **Repairs and Renovations:** Factor in any immediate repairs you need to do after you buy the property. Maybe it's a little paint, or maybe it's a full renovation. You'll have already decided this during the inspection.

8. **Land Transfer Tax:** In some provinces, you will pay a tax to the government based on the value of your property. Each province's tax rate is different; rates range from zero percent in Alberta to over 1.5 percent in other provinces. Make sure you have built this into your closing cost; you don't want to be surprised when the lawyer asks you for a cheque to cover it.

"You see, Richard, to become an overachieving investor, it's imperative that you look at reality. By adding all of these purchase costs into your equation, you'll now know what this property is really going to cost you. Add up all of these figures and then add them to the down payment required and you'll have the Total Cash Required to Close. In other words, the amount of money you must have to buy this property."

Richard looked surprised. "Wow, I would have completely forgotten about some of these. In fact, when I was talking with the realtor all we talked about was the down payment and the small renovations that were required. I see from my calculations that I would have been surprised with almost $4,500 in costs I wasn't prepared to meet. And I love the concept of the staying power fund. That will take the pressure off, if a vacancy occurs or a hot water tank quits. It will also allow Emma to sleep at night, knowing that we're not living right on the edge. Great system!"

"Richard, I think that the staying power fund is one of the most effective strategies that sophisticated investors use. If you don't use it, you're just waiting for trouble. If you do, you're treating your investments like a business—by reducing the risks and increasing the results.

"You can see why we spend so much time on the Property Analyzer Form. It truly is the decision-maker for my fellow investors and me. Simple step-by-step decision making. I know this has been a lot to absorb. Any questions?"

"This will take some practice to become efficient working with it," Richard said thoughtfully. "But I can see that over a very short period of time I'll get very quick at this whole thing. Just give me some time and I'll be very comfortable asking the questions and doing the math."

"Great! Make sure you use the form for assessing every property, and don't allow yourself to get sloppy just because it starts to feel easy. I guess our next step is to design an offer to give to your realtor. But first, it's important that you take all of this due diligence back to your house and sit down with Emma and show her all that you've accomplished so far. I know you've told her that you were investigating real estate, and that you were following a system. Now walk her through the analysis process we've gone through. By sharing it with her two things will occur. One, you'll get much more confident in the steps of the system, and two, you'll come up with a few deeper questions to ask. And I'm sure Emma will too.

"Talk it over with her, and come to a decision whether you want to go to the next step: submitting an offer on that property. The numbers look great and the area has strong potential; I know I would put in an offer. But, this is your decision to make. Go home and discuss this with Emma after the kids have gone to bed. Run through the numbers one more time. Then, when you've decided, you need to do two things. Call the realtor and tell her you will have an offer to give her tomorrow, and call me. We'll get together to structure the offer. Sound good?"

"This is getting exciting. But, I'm a little afraid of Emma's reaction. Remember, she's seen me go through an awful lot of 'get rich' ideas before."

"Richard, all I can say is that you have to show her the value of following a non-emotional system. Show her all the homework you've done. What will be, will be, but I think you'll be pleasantly surprised," I said hopefully. "Well, I'm off for home. Good luck tonight. Call me as soon as you two decide on your next step."

As I was collecting my coat, Rich looked up and asked, "Have you got any last words of advice for dealing with Emma tonight?"

"Yes, as a matter of fact I do. Be calm, unemotional and really listen to her. If she has concerns, get to the root of them. Ask meaningful questions, address her questions wherever you can and never be dismissive of her thoughts or concerns. Explain once again your Personal Belize and how real estate will play a major part in getting your family there. Explain how this property is the first step. If she asks any questions you can't answer, write them down and ask me. Or if she wants, she can come to our next meeting."

"All right, I'm looking forward to explaining the 'new me' to Emma. Although you say the Property Analyzer Form is where the rubber hits the road in real estate, I think tonight is even more important. Talk to you tomorrow!" Rich said as he headed for the door.

"Just be clear and confident, and things will go well!" I called after him.

This was the moment of truth for Richard; he had found a property that fit the system and completed his analysis. However, he still hadn't placed an offer. Many investors get stuck in this analysis stage. They look for the perfect property—the ultimate skipping stone and even when they find it, they get stuck in analysis paralysis. The difference between the average investor and the truly successful one is this: the great ones feel the fear and use their system to work through it. You can't outright eliminate fear, but you can use it to propel you forward or backward—the choice rests with you. After you have completed your action steps for this chapter, read on to discover how to turn fear into the rocket fuel that propels you forward.

BELOW AVERAGE OR SUPER SUCCESSFUL: YOU CHOOSE!

11

Remember that fear always lurks behind perfectionism. Confronting your fears and allowing yourself the right to be human can, paradoxically, make you a far happier and more productive person.
—Dr. David M. Burns

Richard was no different from many other beginning investors. Over the last 12 years, I have taught thousands of people the secrets and strategies of successful real estate investing. This experience with such a large group of investors has allowed me to study their habits and compile first-hand data on the psychology of success. I have learned that there are fundamentals upon which successful investors base their actions.

The data has also revealed the important fact that average investors can learn to become super successful if they allow themselves. Often, the biggest deterrent average investors have is themselves. If they would get out of their own way, they would create substantially better results in their life. The problem is too many allow fear to hold them back.

The reality is that fear is an ever-present emotion for investors, from rookie to veteran. It has been hardwired into our brains since childhood. Fear reveals itself in many shapes and sizes, and the symptoms are quite noticeable once you know what to look for.

Fear can be paralyzing or very motivating. The choice is yours. Tapping into the positive side of fear is a strategy that the super successful use to rise above the crowd. They all admit that fear exists; however, they've learned the habits of turning their fear into a positive motivator.

Here are the most common fears that real estate investors encounter and the strategies that super-successful investors use to break through them.

Fear of Taking Action: Analysis Paralysis

The ability to take action is the number-one difference between successful real estate investors and wannabe investors. Getting over the initial fear of moving forward is critical.

This *fear of action* reveals itself in many different ways. In most cases you can identify it by the symptoms, the most obvious one being a web of excuses. I'm sure you've met people who are caught in a web of excuses. Over the years I've heard just about every excuse imaginable for why people won't take that first step to become a real estate investor. You may have heard a few:

- I don't think my spouse will support me if I invest in real estate.
- It's too late; I missed the market boom.
- I just need to make a few quick bucks first so I can afford to invest.
- I don't have the time—my job gets in the way.
- I could never own a property that's not within 30 minutes of my house and none that close is a good investment property.
- I need to know everything about real estate before I get started.
- That property is too large for me; I could never get the deal done.
- My credit rating isn't the best; my banker told me *no* when I asked him.
- The guy who was going to fund my investing backed out at the last minute.
- I heard you can get stuck with bad tenants.
- My uncle/dad/neighbour lost a ton of money in real estate and I asked them what they thought about investing in real estate and they emphatically said *no*!
- My dog ate my homework …

I think you get the point. These excuses are entirely fear-based. The web of excuses doesn't just show itself in real estate; you'll witness it in all walks of life. The next time you're talking with someone, listen for how many excuses they throw around in conversation. Often you will find that the more excuses you hear, the less successful and less happy the person is in his or her life.

Excuses are the easy way out. However, looking for reasons not to act is a habit that can be changed. Let's look at how super-successful investors use fear as a motivator to take action.

WRITE, SCRATCH AND QUESTION

There are a number of different strategies to overcome the web of excuses, and one of the most effective is called the "write, scratch and question" technique. One of our most successful clients is a single mom with three kids and a below-average income. She had plenty of potential excuses at her disposal for not taking action. Instead, she uses the write, scratch and question technique, which has allowed her to purchase 27 properties over the last few years.

This simple technique ensures that, rather than running from her fear, she can use it to deal with the enormous challenges she is up against. Her Personal Belize was so compelling that she was willing to do whatever it took to make it come true—despite the fear she felt, and continues to feel. Here's how the technique works: every time an excuse-based fear pops into your head, take these three steps:

1. **Write.** Stop whatever you're doing and write down on a piece of paper the excuse that has occurred to you.
2. **Scratch.** Cross it out with your pen.
3. **Question.** Create a "positive spin question" that provides you with what you need to make the excuse no longer valid.

For example:
Excuse: "I don't have any (more) money to buy real estate."
Positive Spin Question: "I require more money to keep investing. Although this is out of my comfort zone, which trusted advisor can I talk with who can show me how to access more capital?"
or
Excuse: "My job and children fill my days. I don't have any extra time to invest."
Positive Spin Question: "My job and kids are important parts of my life, so how do I prioritize my weeks so I can find a couple of hours to focus on real estate?"

The super successful know that excuses can stop them in their tracks. Using this positive spin strategy, you literally destroy the excuse—by crossing it out—and then turn it into a positive motivator. This strategy is simple yet brilliant. It uses your brain power and the expertise of those who are supporting you.

You do not need to immediately know the answers to your questions; answers may come much later. The key is in posing the questions so you know what you're looking for.

Questions demand answers, while excuses give your brain a reason to stop looking for answers. By asking the right questions you are, in fact, programming your brain to look for the answers. Often, you'll be amazed; the answers often are not what you expect.

Those who use this strategy commit to doing it no matter where they are or what they're doing—and the changes they see are immediate!

THE FEAR OF MAKING MISTAKES: WHERE WRONG IS RIGHT AND RIGHT IS RIGHT!

The second most prevalent fear for investors lies in their dread of making a mistake. This fear has been drilled into us through years of schooling where mistakes were marked with a big red X—the dreaded Red X Syndrome. Once again, the good news is that this fear can be conquered and turned to your advantage!

Throughout our lives, we are taught that mistakes are bad and wrong, when in reality they're not. Mistakes are proof that you're moving forward. Making zero mistakes in your life is a sign that you are not moving forward and are quite possibly slipping backwards. Average investors are afraid of mistakes, while successful investors turn them into very positive experiences.

Just like fear, mistakes will always be present in the life of an investor. No matter how much knowledge or experience you have, mistakes will occur. First, be realistic and follow these three steps:

1. Acknowledge that mistakes are going to happen, and do not characterize them as a negative.

2. Learn from your mistakes. Ask yourself how you're going to ensure you don't repeat the same mistake in your next deal.

3. Talk with other investors about the mistakes they've made, and how they fixed them. Learning from others' mistakes will allow you to grow more quickly than if you had to make every mistake yourself.

Learning from others is called *leveraging knowledge*. In real estate, not only is it important to leverage your cash by using a minimum amount of your cash and financing the rest through the bank; it's also important to leverage your knowledge and the knowledge of other investors.

KEY INSIGHT

We will never live long enough to make all the mistakes ourselves. That's why it is critical to surround ourselves with like-minded people and learn from one another's experiences.

Mistakes will always occur; your job is to minimize their impact. Here's what our survey found to be the steps the super successful use to reduce or avoid mistakes:

1. **Follow a proven system.** Make sure you find a system that fits your goals and has already been proven to work in your area. Ensure that it's simple and easy to follow, and it takes you closer to your Personal Belize.

2. **Don't skip any steps in the system.** Successful investors find the patience to stick with the system, no matter what. This is critical to avoiding mistakes. As average or below-average investors become more adept at analyzing properties, they become increasingly tempted to skip steps, thinking they are saving time. However, these shortcuts lead to two potential outcomes: either a major

pitfall or poor results. Always follow the system to vastly improve your investment results.

3. **Base your investment decisions on economic fundamentals, not emotions.** Emotions are the largest contributor to making investment mistakes, and if you take them out of the equation you reduce your mistakes substantially. Emotional decisions bring huge investment mistakes; fundamental decisions bring results.

4. **Review your system once a year from start to finish.** This is much like an athlete's annual training camp. Sure, Wayne Gretzky knew how to skate, pass and score, but every single year he reviewed hockey basics during training camp. The same is true of one of the most successful football coaches of all time, Vince Lombardi. At the start of every training camp, he would line up all the players, from superstar quarterbacks and 10-year veterans all the way down to rookie kick returners. When the room went silent, he would begin by holding up a ball and saying, "Gentlemen, this is a football!" He knew that results are always built on a foundation of basics. Similarly, successful investors always review and practise the basics of the system, no matter how good they are as individual investors. This minimizes their mistakes and is the key to their success.

KEY INSIGHT

> Super successful investors never wait until they know it all. They are acutely aware that they'll never know everything and recognize that opportunities will pass them by while they sit on the sidelines and wait.

If you're serious about becoming a successful real estate investor, make sure you study the basics, follow a proven system and review the basics at least once per year. If you do this, your results will astound even you.

The Fear of Making an Offer: When Either *Yes* or *No* Makes You Nervous

The bottom line is that in all my years of investing in real estate, I have never bought a property without first making an offer. A good friend of mine, Alan Jacques, describes making an offer as "the critical success event" in real estate, and I thoroughly agree! No offers equals no results—period!

Although it's a well-known fact that the more offers you make, the more real estate you'll buy, my research shows that average investors make significantly fewer offers than the successful investor. Successful real estate investors are continually making offers, whether formally through realtors or informally on napkins, while sitting at a vendor's kitchen table. Active investors know that most of their offers will not be accepted: that's the nature of the game. However, they also know that for each *no* they hear, they have just moved a step closer to *yes*. It really is a numbers game; the more offers you place, the more of your offers will be accepted.

Why is it that most people don't submit more offers to buy real estate? Not surprisingly, this too is based in fear. But this fear is unique. I call it double-edged fear because it includes both the fear of rejection and the fear of acceptance! Let's look at how it works and how you can avoid it.

Up until the time you actually submit an offer to purchase a property, looking for properties can be a lot of fun and quite exciting. You're completing your due diligence, you're talking with realtors and bankers, you're crunching the numbers based on the ACRE system's formulas—you're feeling like a big-time investor. However, you still don't have anything on the line except your time.

KEY INSIGHT

Writing offers is the difference between successful investors and excuse-laden pretenders.

Then suddenly it's time for you to take the plunge and place an offer. Reality stares you in the face as you are about to write the deposit cheque, attach it to your offer and hand it over to the vendor or realtor. Fear rears its ugly head as two of the most common questions pass through your mind:

"What happens if the offer is accepted?"
and
"What happens if the offer is rejected?"

That's right, beginner investors are often fearful of both outcomes! So, how do successful investors cut through these conflicted reactions? They use a very simple and effective strategy, based solely on analyzing the reality—not the emotions—of the situation.

Super-successful real estate investors acknowledge the fear and excitement surrounding placing an offer. But they ask themselves: "What's the worst thing that can happen by placing this offer?" Then they deal with the answers to this powerful question. The truth is there really are only three potential outcomes from placing an offer, and each and every one of them is a positive result. Here they are, along with the no-risk solutions to each.

1. **The offer is rejected outright.** If the offer is rejected outright, then you know you haven't found the motivated vendor you're looking for; remember, dealing only with motivated vendors is absolutely critical. By receiving an outright rejection, you have just saved yourself substantial time, energy and money because there is no use putting any further effort into this property until the vendor is motivated. You may return in a few months when the vendor's motivation level has increased, but today is not the day for a deal, so move on to the next one.

KEY INSIGHT

> Beginning investors are often embarrassed by an outright rejection of their offer; however, successful investors understand that the vendor is rejecting their offer, not them personally. Remember, this is a business proposition, not a popularity contest.

2. **The offer is accepted.** This is great news. You can celebrate because you've just found the right mix of a property that fits your system and a vendor motivated to sell. Once again, because you've structured the offer using a proven system, you can now complete your due diligence before making the final investment commitment. You still have an opportunity to back out of the deal if your

inspections and appraisals don't turn out to your satisfaction. Of course, there is no downside here either!

3. **The offer is countered.** This means that the vendor likes what he or she sees in the offer. However, they are suggesting some changes. Often the changes centre around the price, because that's what most vendors focus on. They make changes to the offer you have given them and present it back to you. The power is now completely back in your court; you can do whatever you want at this point. As a matter of fact, you've just been handed three very clear options, all of which put you soundly in the power position:

- **Option 1:** You can reject the counter-offer outright and move on to another piece of real estate, thus releasing you of any obligations on this property. You receive your full deposit back and you walk away. No downside to this one!

- **Option 2:** You can make a counter-offer to their counter-offer. At this point, if you are following a proven system such as the ACRE system in this book, you will have completed the majority of your due diligence. You will already know the maximum you want to pay for the property and what terms you need to make it fit your system. If you still want the property, make the appropriate adjustments to the offer and send it back to the vendor and the whole cycle starts over again. No downside here either!

- **Option 3:** You can accept the counter-offer as is. If the vendor has counteroffered at a price and with the terms that fit your system, just accept his or her offer and add this property to your portfolio. All that is left is the remainder of your due diligence (inspection, appraisal, etc.). If these reports don't turn out to your satisfaction, you can still walk away from the deal, because you've followed the system and structured the offer with the right protection clauses. Another no-lose situation!

Never be afraid of making an offer after you have done your initial due diligence. If the property seems to fit your system, place an offer. On your offer, include a sophisticated investor clause (we'll talk about this in chapter 12) just to ensure you have a way out of the contract if surprises arise as you complete your due diligence.

KEY INSIGHT

> You have to make offers to make money! If you aren't making offers, you've stopped before you've started.

You have just discovered that although there is often fear around making an offer to purchase a property, there is zero downside to doing so if it is structured using the ACRE system. Acknowledge that your fear exists. However, realize that it is completely misplaced.

No matter what the vendor says about your offer, you still win. It is especially important to note that in all of the above potential outcomes you are always in the power position, meaning *you* decide whether to move forward or not. As the buyer, you are the person who holds all the cards. The vendor needs or wants to sell that property, and you can help that happen. However, if you don't end up buying it, you'll go and buy a different property. No rush, no panic. The vendor doesn't have that option; the vendor needs a buyer, but you don't need the property.

This one simple change in your mindset can give you a huge advantage in the marketplace. While others fret and worry before placing an offer, you'll have already jumped into first place by placing your offer. You will be shocked at the success that comes to you, seemingly out of the blue, when you place offers. Ask for what you want, and often you will get it.

YOUR ULTIMATE ADVANTAGE

You can give yourself an amazing advantage in the real estate marketplace just by being aware of the above strategies of the super successful and acknowledging that fear will always exist. Remember, below-average investors allow fear to rule their lives.

Now that you are aware that excuses are just a symptom of fear, here is an interesting exercise for you to do.

By using the techniques outlined in this chapter, you can turn fear into a positive motivator and follow in the footsteps of some of the most successful real estate investors in Canada. While others are stuck in fear, you'll be moving forward, making offers, buying properties and making your Personal Belize come true. Mark Twain said it best when he uttered the famous words:

"Courage is resistance to fear, mastery of fear—not absence of fear."

SOPHISTICATED INVESTOR ACTION STEP

Carefully listen and watch others around you, at work and at home. Observe how fear manifests itself through their excuses and lack of action. The more you're aware of fear, the easier it is to remove it from your life, allowing you to vastly improve your own real estate investing results. Don't judge others; just observe.

Below, list the three biggest fears you have about investing in real estate. Then follow the write, scratch and question technique to turn them into positive questions:

Fear 1:_____

_____

_____

Positive Question 1: _____

_____

_____

_____

Fear 2:_____

_____

_____

Positive Question 2: _____

_____

_____

_____

Fear 3:_____

_____

_____

Positive Question 3: _____

_____

_____

_____

PLACING Your Offer and Getting It ACCEPTED   12

If you approach life with a sense of possibility and the expectation of positive results, you're more likely to have a life in which possibilities are realized and results are positive.
                                            —Lisa Funderburg

The call came in Saturday morning at 8:15 a.m. The call display showed R. McTavish; it was the one call Richard would make that would change his life.

"Hey Richard, good morning!"

"As a matter of fact it is," he replied. "I think we're ready to go to the next level. Emma has a few questions and she's not 100 percent sold that this is different from my past ideas, but we've decided to give it a shot."

"That's great! We'd better get together this morning," I suggested.

"There's one new condition. Emma wants to be a part of the rest of this process. I know we haven't really discussed this, but I agree with her."

"It's about time! I've been waiting for the two of you to come to that conclusion for a while. You'll be much more powerful as a team. Bring her along if she can make it this morning."

"We'll drop the kids at my parents and meet you at Starbucks in about an hour. Does that work for you?" Richard asked.

"Sure does. Bring your due diligence, your calculator and your chequebook and we'll get going. See you in an hour."

This was an important step for Richard, since he had always tried the financial schemes on his own, with or without Emma's consent. I guess he felt the money making was his duty alone. And so far his lone-wolf strategy hadn't worked very well for him. At one point he had mentioned that his father had always been the breadwinner and he felt compelled to do the same.

I've noticed over the last 15 years an increasing number of female investors in the marketplace. And I've found that, for the most part, they're more apt to follow all of the steps in a system, show patience and allow enough time to ensure results. Many men, on the other hand, have a tendency to get bored with a system that's working well so they begin tinkering with it or even change it radically.

I've also noticed an increasing number of couples investing together as a team. What a powerful combination that can be! The go-it-alone mentality is fine for a while, but once the whole family starts to get on board, the momentum builds quickly and leads to success. Richard's past actions, where he jumped from one scheme to another, had proven that he has a short attention span. But now, with Emma jumping on board, I could see he had potential to break this pattern and build some long-term wealth.

SOPHISTICATED INVESTOR ACTION STEP

Begin to build a team around you. It might not all happen at once, however. Keep your lines of communication open with the people in your life and tell them what you're doing, but don't push them into playing along with you. Some investors have discovered that it took years for their spouse or friends to be fully 100 percent behind them in real estate, while for others it just took a few months.

In either case, being a member of a larger community of like-minded real estate investors, whether with a partner or not, helps tip the scales in your favour. Make sure the group you choose to hang out with is supportive and not just a room of people looking to sell you something.

What you're looking to find is what Napoleon Hill would call your Real Estate Master-Mind-Group. In a good group you'll find the names of the best real estate oriented contacts such as lawyers, accountants, realtors, inspectors, bankers, mortgage brokers, renovators and much more. These references will save you time and money while building your team.

As I walked into Starbucks, I could see Richard facing the door anxiously. I could see in front of him a tall, dark-haired woman facing away from the door leafing through the real estate classified ads. I had to chuckle, when Richard motioned me over by pointing at his watch.

"Hey, it's only five minutes before our meeting time. For you that's pretty late. I didn't think you'd show," he said. He was obviously feeling a little nervous about this meeting and was trying to mask it with a bit of humour.

"I wouldn't miss this meeting for the world. Hi, you must be Emma. It's a pleasure to finally meet you," I said as I held out my hand. She took it and looked up with a pair of intense blue eyes and a bright smile.

"Hi. Richard has told me an awful lot about you and what he's been learning from you. I thought you'd be much older," Emma said in a confident tone.

"Thanks for the compliment," I said as I shrugged off my coat and sat down next to the soy latte that Richard had ordered for me. "So, are you two ready to design an offer to present to the vendor for this property, or is there anything you'd like to cover first?"

Emma spoke up first. "I'd like to start off with a few comments. I've seen Richard try many different things over the years. His enthusiasm is something I've always loved about him. However, he has a tendency not to follow through long enough to get to the finish line. I'm the opposite; I like to think things through a little too much. It's as if I'm afraid of making the wrong choice, so I don't make any choice at all. As Rich and I were talking last night, it finally dawned on me—the combination of the two of us could be pretty powerful: one who gets things started and one who follows through on the details. I guess that's why I'm here."

I nodded my agreement and said, "I too have noticed a transformation in Richard. Although we've just started to work together I can see where, if given the right tools and the right support, real estate can be his thing. As the two of you become more seasoned investors, the roles each of you play will become more clearly defined. It might be that one of you finds the properties and analyzes them, while the other does all the financing and managing of the properties.

"But today we're here to put together an offer for the property so you can take your first financial steps towards your Personal Belize. By the way Emma, what did you think of Rich's collage?"

She looked sheepishly over at Richard before she started. "I must be honest; at first I thought it was rather silly. Why would a grown-up spend hours writing out a fantasy life and then cut pictures out of magazines to make a kindergarten collage? But when he sat down and read his written description to me, I realized I hadn't heard that amount of conviction and strength in his voice for years. It was truly amazing—a goal, a focus, a direction we could all work towards. And the best thing is, it captured my dreams as well. What Richard doesn't know is I've read it every day since and looked at the collage every morning. I can't wait to be a part of it."

"So let's start making this come true, shall we?" I declared to the whole room.

"Absolutely!" they stated almost in unison.

• • • •

THE OFFER TO PURCHASE

Let's begin with a quick review of where Richard and Emma are right now. Using the ACRE system, they found a town or a neighbourhood that scored extremely well on the Goldmine Score Card; they then visited the area and found a few properties that fit the 10 percent solution. Next, they gathered all of the required numbers and details following the checklists. Finally, they crunched the numbers in the Property Analyzer Form to come up with a property that appears to have great potential. Now they are ready to take the next critical step, which is to go after that property.

An investor, in order to purchase a property, needs a contract between him- or herself and the vendor. In most cases, it will be written up in a Contract of Purchase and Sale, often called the Offer to Purchase. Every jurisdiction has its own name for this contract and seems to change its templates frequently. That means you need to be familiar with the current offer contract in your target area, whether you're working with a realtor or directly with a vendor. Make sure you read it and understand it *before* you make your first offer. Have your real estate lawyer explain any portion of the contract you don't understand. You need to take this contract seriously, because you are bound by all that it contains whether you understand it or not.

Clarity is Key

Your offer must clearly define what you're buying, the terms under which you are buying it and at what price. Take charge of this portion of the process; this is your offer, not the realtor's, so you should determine what it says.

Before you determine what your offer will look like, let me discuss a few key parts of the contract so you get a general understanding. The pre-printed offers that the realtors use have been written by lawyers who were paid by the real estate boards. You should run these offers by your own lawyer to get independent legal advice. This extra step will help protect you as well.

 **KEY INSIGHT**

There are many great realtors who are more than willing to assist and give you guidance in the offer process. These quality realtors will provide you with options and ideas, but not demands. When you find one, use that person a lot. Help him or her to become extremely successful, and he or she, in turn, will do the same for you.

On the other hand, there are a few realtors who will want to write the offer their way because that's the way they've "always done it." Your polite answer to them should be, "No thanks, this is my offer and I need you to write it this way." Be as clear as you can in your offer, thus eliminating any confusion or misunderstandings.

The key components to your offer include:

Names: The contract must clearly state the names of the purchasers and the vendors. Make sure you have all of the names of the vendors on the contract. For you, the buyers, it is prudent to put your name followed by the words "and/or assigns," for example, "Richard McTavish and Emma McTavish and/or assigns." This is done in case:

- You wish to purchase the property under a corporate name.
- Only one of you wishes to be on title.
- You decide not to buy the property; you can assign the contract over to someone who does. Just be aware, if you do assign a contract you are still 100 percent responsible if the party to whom you assigned it doesn't live up to their contractual obligations.

KEY INSIGHT

You can only decide how best to own your investment properties by describing your plan to a qualified real estate accountant and getting his or her advice. Every investor's situation is different; consequently, there can be no hard-and-fast rule about whether to incorporate or to own the properties in your own name. There are pluses and minuses to each of these scenarios. Your accountant can help you decide what is best from the perspective of taxes and liability.

This is a good example of why it's important to surround yourself with a quality team right from the beginning, so you don't get caught making decisions based on rules of thumb or what your neighbours, friends or relatives believe to be true.

Address: This should include both the street address as well as the legal address. For instance: 123 Knottingly Avenue, Lot 17, Block 23, Plan 234 Anytown, Anyprovince.

Deposit: This is the amount of money you will be providing as a show of good faith. This deposit should be made out to your lawyer's trust account whenever possible or, failing that, to *your* realtor's trust account. *Never* give the vendor a deposit directly, no matter what the circumstance. I like to provide the deposit in two steps. I provide an initial deposit with the offer, to show that I'm serious, and then the rest of the deposit upon the removal of any of my conditions in the contract (for example, following an inspection and approval for financing). For example, if I am planning on providing a $12,000 deposit, I will provide an initial $2,000 deposit with the offer and a $10,000 additional deposit when I am satisfied that I'll be purchasing the property and I've removed all of my conditions. The total deposit will be credited towards your down payment at closing.

If you live up to your side of the contract, and you have not removed the conditions on the contract (for instance, you weren't able to arrange financing in the time allotted), you can simply advise the vendor that you will not be closing. In that case the deposit(s) will be returned to you without penalty. However, if you have removed all of your conditions and then you change your mind and decide not to go through with the purchase, your deposit goes to the vendor. That's why it is important to live up to all of your obligations.

Financing: This is where you list what your proposed financing will be—in other words, the difference between your purchase price and your down payment. It's just simple math at this point.

Balance Owing (Cash to Close): Add up the deposits and the financing, and subtract the total from the proposed purchase price. This figure will tell you how much additional money you'll need to complete this contract—the difference between your proposed down payment and your deposits.

Total Purchase Price: This is the price that you are paying for the property. One of the most common errors is not ensuring that the sum of the deposits plus financing plus balance owing equals the purchase price. Double-check the math after the realtor has completed the form.

Possession Date/Closing Date: In most jurisdictions, these dates are one and the same— the date the property becomes yours. Choose a realistic date that provides you with time to get your financing in place and time for your lawyer to complete the transaction. This should be no less than 30 days from the date the vendor accepts your offer, and preferably longer.

Fixtures and Chattels: Indicate what items within and around the property you wish to be included in your purchase. Ask for what you want and need. You'll need the appliances to rent the property, so make sure you list all of them—fridge, stove, dishwasher, washer and dryer, plus anything else (such as light fixtures, window treatments, etc.) you wish to be included in the deal. Remember, you are planning on renting this property, so everything that you don't get with the property, you will have to purchase at retail.

With attached goods, it is true that most deals include everything that is physically attached to the property, such as built-in vacuums, garage door openers, large mirrors and security systems. However, not everyone has the same definition of attached goods. So, no matter what you're told, make sure you list the attached goods you want as part of the deal, including light fixtures. It has occurred more than once that the vendor has taken some of the main light fixtures in properties that investors have bought. With a contract that clearly includes them, it is much simpler to receive compensation for the missing items.

A special note regarding garage door openers: always state in the contract that you want the remote controls as well. In the midst of all the chaos of moving day, vendors can easily drive away with the remotes still attached to their car's sun visor. Be specific: if there are two controls, ask for both.

Often there is not enough room to list everything on the contract, so create a separate schedule. Simply attach a piece of paper to the Offer to Purchase, clearly listing all of the items you require.

There are two important statements to include on this separate schedule or elsewhere in the purchase contract:

1. All attached and unattached goods to be in good working order at closing.
2. All attached and unattached goods as seen and photographed on _____
   (insert the date you inspected the property).

This is another great reason to take digital photos as you walk through the property. It will give you a record of what you saw. This subtle mention of photographs often stops a dishonest vendor from switching appliances on you.

A common method is to write down the serial number of all the appliances, but this isn't necessary. I don't know of many sophisticated investors who do this. They rely on the contract as well as the digital photos. If you really want them, your realtor may be able to get the serial numbers for you; you can always ask.

Irrevocable Date: This date advises the vendor how long you are willing to keep the offer open for consideration. You want this date to be not very far in the future, yet it must give the vendor enough time to consider the offer. A date too far in the future allows the vendor to sit back and "shop your deal," meaning he or she can speak with other purchasers and perhaps use your deal as a negotiating tool. I like to use a time frame no longer than three days.

Possession: You must advise the vendor whether you wish to take over the property with the current tenant or vacant. An important note here: make sure you have met the tenants and confirmed that you wish to keep them. In some provincial jurisdictions it can be difficult to take vacant possession if tenants are already in place. In some provinces this can add months to the process, and many vendors won't be willing to wait this long.

An experienced realtor understands the value of working with a sophisticated investor and will appreciate the clarity you bring. Your preparation as well as your checklists can make his or her job much easier because there are no surprises. If you make the process easy for your realtor, he or she is bound to introduce you to more properties. Conversely, if you become a pain to deal with, you'll probably only see the bottom-of-the-barrel properties.

Conditions: These are clauses within the offer that must be met before the contract becomes unconditionally valid. These conditions can be put in the contract by both the vendor and the purchaser; however, the majority of them are placed by the vendor. Work with your lawyer to create condition statements that work for your situation; however, here are some ideas for your offer.

Financing: If you need to arrange financing in order to buy the property, you will want to include a conditional clause such as "Subject

to buyer obtaining financing satisfactory to the buyer on or before
_____(*insert number*) of days from acceptance of offer."
Here are two important points to note:

1. Be sure to include "satisfactory to the buyer" in this clause to ensure that not just any financing will force you to remove your condition. For instance, if you can get financing but it doesn't fit your system, you will want to have the option of not accepting it.
2. Make sure the date you use is realistic. You will not want to put additional pressure on your banker, especially if you want to be considered a sophisticated investor. On most small properties, such as single-family homes, condos and duplexes, 21 days is sufficient. (In the next chapter, I'll be sharing banking and financing strategies.)

Property Inspection: You should have a professional and well-respected home inspector go through each and every property you buy. This is the cheapest insurance you can buy. A quality inspector will provide you a complete report on everything—the good and the bad—in and around the property. It's better to find this out before you own it! With this in mind, make sure you include a condition such as "Subject to the buyer obtaining a building inspection satisfactory to the buyer within 14 days of acceptance." That way, if the inspector uncovers a major problem with the property, you can walk away from the deal and get your deposit back. You may also choose to re-open negotiations with the vendor and ask him or her to do the necessary repairs or to compensate you for them.

Lawyer's Approval: "Subject to buyer's lawyer's approval within 14 days of acceptance" is another clause that can give you some peace of mind. This clause provides an opportunity to have your lawyer review the purchase contract to ensure that everything is clear and acceptable. Often, if you have a relationship with a real estate lawyer, he or she will want to check out your offers to ensure there are no landmines hidden in the contract. If they do find any issues, this clause allows you to address them before the contract becomes unconditional. Be prepared for some vendors to request less than 14 days; this can work as long as your lawyer is available in that shorter period. Check your lawyer's availability in advance.

Additional Considerations: Make sure you add clauses to cover any additional items to which you agree. These might include:

- Seller to remove the three derelict vehicles on the property on or before closing.
- Seller to provide all existing leases and tenant confirmations within 14 days of acceptance.
- Seller to provide confirmation of new roof within 14 days of acceptance.
- Seller to provide copy of current valid Condo Reserve Fund Study acceptable to the buyer's lending institution.

As you can see, developing a winning offer is a simple process. Let's review it.

- Write an outline of what you wish your offer to say.
- Give your outline to your realtor to transfer to his or her form.
- Review the document to ensure the offer clearly states everything you want.
- Have your realtor submit it to the vendor.

The vendor will accept your offer, reject it or provide you with a counter-offer. If the vendor accepts your offer, or you accept the vendor's counter-offer, the clock starts ticking and you arrange the inspection and advise your banker of the deal. By the way, you can always counter the vendor's counter-offer by making changes on the document, initialling the changes and resubmitting the offer to the vendor.

I've noticed a trend towards using electronic Offers to Purchase. These are electronic documents that are e-mailed back and forth between the realtors, purchasers and vendors.

Although this may seem very efficient, it is also a recipe for trouble. Each time the document passes through a party's hands, it is simple to make small and subtle changes without the other parties noticing.

That means every single time you receive a counter-offer, you must read each word of the document before you sign it, to ensure that other changes haven't been made.

Use hard-copy offers to purchase wherever possible. Although it can get-messy, when counter-offers are passed back and forth, it is *very* easy to see any changes.

When the final offer is ready to be signed, read it all one more time, then use your lawyer clause to ensure the contract clearly details what you believe the deal to be.

Multiple Offer Strategy

Because you have asked the critical "vendor motivation questions," you will already know the vendor's motivation. Now you can work out an offer that will help him or her fill this need. However, sophisticated investors do not rely solely on what they've been told by the vendor. They start the negotiations by using a technique we call the "multiple offer strategy."

You will create two clear and distinct offers, for example: one that focuses on a higher price with a longer closing date, and a second one that focuses on a shorter timeline, yet with a lower price. Another example would be: one offer at a lower price and no vendor take back (VTB) mortgage, and another at a higher price with a VTB. By presenting two offers at the same time, you are offering the vendor an opportunity to choose whichever one best solves his or her problem. Please note: the offers should be presented at the same time, not one followed by the second one after the first is rejected. They are given to the vendor simultaneously.

Once a change is made to the contract, for example, when the vendor counteroffers or you counter-offer in return, the contract is not valid until the other party agrees to all of the changes. Be aware that when you counteroffer you are ending the previous contract. Legally, it is as if you are presenting a brand-new offer.

This strategy is a little out of the ordinary and that is why it is so successful. When you present one offer, often the choice for the vendor is simply *yes* or *no*. Conversely, when you present multiple offers, the vendor will often choose one of them to counteroffer or accept. This is basic human nature—when presented with a choice, people are inclined to choose one of the options.

Good investment realtors completely understand the problem-solving power of this strategy; that's why we focus on developing relationships with quality realtors.

AND FINALLY—THE OFFER'S COVER LETTER

The most effective way to get your offer accepted is to attach a cover letter to every Offer to Purchase you submit. This letter is from you and is addressed directly to the vendor. As a sophisticated investor, every single offer you write *must* have a cover letter attached to it, if you are serious about getting your offer accepted. The job of this letter is to clearly communicate to the vendors why he or she should accept your offer; it points out the highlights of the offer and any additional information that the vendor would find comforting, such as your experience, and maybe even a testimonial or two from previous vendors from whom you have purchased.

With the multiple offer strategy, each offer has its own cover letter. Each explains the merits of the offer. There are two important reasons for this:

1. You don't want to rely on someone else's interpretation or biases to enter into the equation. You've probably played the "broken phone" game as a kid. That's the game where a bunch of people sit in a circle and you whisper a clear statement in the ear of the

kid next to you, then, in turn, he or she repeats it to the following person and so on until it gets back to you. And when it does get back to you, your statement has changed dramatically due to all the parties who have passed it on. This often occurs in real estate transactions. You design your offer, you pass it to your realtor, your realtor passes it to the vendor's realtor who, in turn, shares it with the vendor. By the time the vendor hears it, often the story and the reasons for your offer have been watered down and may even be confusing to the vendor. The cover letter gets around this issue by clearly defining the reasons behind your offer.

2. You are the president of your company, and your job is to sell the vendor on accepting your offer. This letter provides you the opportunity to do that, even if you don't get a chance to meet the vendor face-to-face.

 KEY INSIGHT

Every Offer to Purchase you submit must have a detailed cover letter attached to it.

Keep the letter short and to the point. Sign it in blue ink, so it doesn't look like a photocopy; then make sure it's attached to the offer so the letter and offer must be presented together.

These two strategies will dramatically increase how many of your offers are accepted. As the president of your company, that's the result you're looking for. These strategies work on properties whether they are listed with a realtor or are for-sale-by-owners (FSBOs).

• • • •

RICHARD AND EMMA PUT THE SYSTEM TO THE TEST

We created two distinct and separate offers for Richard and Emma to present to their realtor. Whether the offer gets accepted or not doesn't really matter at this early stage of their investment career. The key is that they get out into the world and start writing offers.

That evening, Emma and Richard met with their realtor. And the report back was very positive. The realtor looked at the two offer outlines and the two cover letters and broke out in a huge laugh. She told them that she didn't expect to see this level of sophistication from a couple of first-timers, but was pleased to see how much thought they had put into it.

She wrote up the offers and took them over to the vendor and his realtor. As any quality realtor will do, she walked the vendor through both of the offers, using the cover letters as a guideline to identify the offers' highlights.

The vendor needed time to think about the deal, so Richard and Emma's realtor left. The next morning, the vendor's realtor called back to say he was shocked with the decision of the vendor. He had previously turned down offers with the exact same price Richard and Emma were offering, but he had decided to accept their offer because he felt comfortable with the clarity and honesty of the offers. All he wanted was a slightly larger initial deposit—$4,000 instead of $2,000.

Like Richard and Emma, you will discover that clear communication combined with addressing a vendor's true motivation can inevitably lead to a positive response where others have failed. There is something I learned a long time ago: "A confused mind always says *no!*" Make sure that any confusion on the vendor's part is lifted early in the process by using the cover letter.

As soon as the offer was accepted, the clock started ticking and the deadlines loomed. When Richard and Emma called with the exciting news (they were both on the line and sounded like kids on Christmas morning), I congratulated them on taking the first step. However, there was still lots of work to be done.

We had to get them prepared to talk to their banker—and quickly. I honestly didn't think they would find a property and have an accepted offer so soon in the process. Although this was great news, it put a lot of time pressure on, as we hadn't talked much about banks and financing yet. So we made an appointment to meet the next day. Richard and Emma had their work cut out for them; their next task was to get the bank to say *yes* to their deal.

GETTING YOUR BANKER TO YES!

13

Conceal a flaw and the world will imagine the worst.
                                              —Martial

Your banker or mortgage broker is one of the top members of your real estate success team. The relationship you create with them must be based on trust and the mutual understanding that you'll meet each other's goals. Your bank makes money by saying *yes* to your deals and your job is to give the mortgage broker very clear reasons as to why you should be provided with financing.

Meeting with their banker was going to be the most critical meeting that Richard, Emma and I were going to have, and to make sure they had everything they needed, I invited another expert along. His name is Alan Jacques.

Alan is a long-time educator, financial trainer and investor. His expertise lies in taking a complex subject and boiling it down to "critical success events." Together, Alan and I have interviewed bank managers, loans officers and vice-presidents. In addition, we've worked side by side with other financial experts, MBAs and successful investors with one goal in mind: to develop a powerful yet simple system that compels the bank to say *yes* to investment real estate deals.

KEY INSIGHT

In this chapter, I'll be using the terms "bank" and "banker." This is for convenience only. I want you to think of these terms in their broadest sense. With the word "bank," I mean any institution or organization that lends money. It could be a trust company, credit union, mortgage company, bank or any name for money lenders that may be used where you live. It could even mean a private individual with money to lend.

With the word "banker," I mean any individual who works for or represents a bank, including loans officers, mortgage representatives, mortgage brokers, branch managers, etc. Over time you will develop relationships with a quality banker and a quality mortgage broker, as each provides his or her own expertise. You want both on your team.

Ten minutes before our meeting was to begin, Richard and Emma walked into the office, both looking a little haggard. Since the vendor had accepted their offer, fear was beginning to kick in. They were still excited, yet the reality of buying their first property was starting to make them a little nervous.

"Hi guys! Great to see you. Congratulations on getting your first offer accepted; this is a huge day for you. I hope you get a chance to celebrate."

"Celebrate? I can hardly breathe I'm so nervous," said Richard. Emma nodded along with him.

"Well, remember what we discussed earlier about how fear can be a positive motivator in real estate investing? Now you're starting to understand it a little more, I bet! What's making you nervous?" I asked.

"We're still wondering if we're doing the right thing, plus we don't know any friends or family who are doing this, which also makes us nervous. I guess it is just a little out of our comfort zone ... okay, maybe *a lot* out of our comfort zone," Rich said.

"I understand. Dealing with banks and lenders is intimidating for a lot of Canadians. But think of the positives: we're going to start learning how to make money using the bank's money—and we're going to make them happy to help us do it." With that, I launched into the importance of the investor-lender relationship.

• • • •

LEVERAGE: A POWERFUL TOOL

One of the advantages you have as a real estate investor is a strategy called leverage. This allows you to profit from the full value of the property, while only putting a small portion of your own money into a deal. Leverage is a very powerful tool if you are buying a property in a market that has strong fundamentals with a great future—in other words, investing in a property that fits the ACRE system.

Investment real estate differs from many other investments due to the tremendous amount of leverage that banks willingly provide you. Let's look at Richard and Emma's property as an example. They'll be purchasing the property for $100,000; however, they only need to come up with 25 percent of this value in order to purchase it. If you were buying such a property for $100,000, you would only need $25,000 of your own money, while using the bank's money for the remainder of the value.

Why is this so important? Simply put, as the equity or value increases in the property, you profit from both your money and the bank's. Here's a comparison of how important this is to you. Let's assume that the market value of the property is increasing at 5 percent per year.

CASE 1

- You purchase an investment property for $100,000 and you pay the full price in cash, thus using up all of your investment dollars.
- The property increases by 5 percent, to a value of $105,000.
- Your return on investment (ROI) is 5 percent.

CASE 2

- You purchase the same property at $100,000, but this time you use the bank's money and use only $25,000 of your own money.
- The property again increases by 5 percent, to a value of $105,000.
- However, you only have $25,000 in the deal and therefore your return on investment (ROI) is 20 percent.

Same property, same increase in value, yet in the second case simply using what we like to call OPM (Other People's Money), your investment returns increase substantially.

So when comparing investment returns from real estate with other investments, make sure you're comparing apples to apples. If you read that the real estate market went up 5 percent and the stock market went up 9 percent, what is an investor's real return? When the real estate market increases 5 percent, you're actually getting a 20 percent return, not the 5 percent you hear about, assuming you only invested 25 percent of the total value of the property. That is one of the reasons why so much wealth is created in real estate. The market is less volatile and you profit from using the bank's money.

KEY INSIGHT

After you've purchased your first couple of properties and figured out how the system works, you can get into some advanced investment strategies where you can purchase investment properties with even less than 25 percent down. This will dramatically increase your percentage returns. Remember, the less of your own money you put down, the better your return on investment. We'll be discussing these advanced strategies at www.reincanada.com.

HOW THE BANKER BECOMES YOUR KEY ALLY

Having the bank on your side is essential. However, many beginning investors are intimidated by banks and financial institutions. They don't have experience in working with financial institutions and this lack of experience breeds fear; what you're about to learn will mitigate this fear. As investors move from rookie status to becoming more seasoned, they discover that their banking relationship changes once again. Once they have added a number of properties to their portfolio and their plan is coming together nicely, they hit the inevitable banker's wall. The banks take a look at these veteran investors' portfolios and start to say *no* to their new deals. This lack of support is understandably frustrating to many investors.

For both the novice and the experienced investor, the ACRE system provides a step-by-step process for making banks a part of your success team, not an obstacle. The foundation of this process is the knowledge that *financial institutions want to lend you money*. That's how they make money—placing their money in the marketplace and collecting interest on it. Our job as investors is to present the banks with a compelling business reason to say *yes*.

• • • •

KEY INSIGHT

Our job as investors is to present the banks with a compelling business reason to say *yes*.

We all looked up as the door opened and Alan Jacques entered the room. You could see by the look in his eyes that Alan was excited about working with Richard and Emma. At the last CFL game Alan and I had attended, I had told him about Richard's Personal Belize. Once he heard about Richard's vision, he agreed to meet with us.

After the introductions Alan sat down, threw open his briefcase and said, "Let's create results!" Obviously, there would be no messing around in this meeting.

Alan started. "Richard and Emma, what you're learning with Don will change your life if you allow it to. But let me be brutally frank with you. You have to want to do some things that you will consider unconventional. Are you willing to do that?"

Emma and Richard nodded. "Yes, we are," they said in unison.

Alan continued, "Today, Don will be teaching you how to get the bank to say *yes*. This will be the most critical piece of your real estate puzzle. With the banks on your side, you'll do amazingly well. There are two key elements:

1. Build relationships with quality bankers and mortgage brokers.
2. Make their job easier than anyone else does.

"The relationship is the key. Many believe that they must look for the absolute lowest interest rate or find the bank that's located nearest to them. Ignore these factors and focus on building a long-term, strong and trusting relationship, because that will be your ticket to success. Let's get into the key points of how you should be working with a banker."

• • • •

ALAN'S ADVICE—STAY OUT OF THE GREY AREA

As an investor, you should *never* cross into the "grey area" of how you operate, as many investors believe you need to do. In fact, I would be surprised if someone doesn't tell you about a "grey area shortcut" early on in your investment career. For example, someone might suggest that you could sign a document that isn't really true, assuring you it's harmless and a necessary strategy. But before you know it, you could be bordering on committing bank fraud.

For example, if you don't plan to move into a property, *do not* sign an affidavit or declaration saying that you are. In fact, you should run away as fast as possible from any banker or broker who asks you to sign such a document, if they have the full knowledge that you are not going to move in. This is deep into the grey area, an area that is close to bank fraud. Yes, there may be legal arguments about whether moving in for a weekend in a sleeping bag is really moving in. But what it boils down to is this: what is your *real* intention for the property?

Playing these games is *not* how long-term wealth is created, and they are definitely not something I recommend. Those types of strategies are taught by people who don't understand the true implications, or they do know and decide to ignore them. Your job is to once again look behind the curtain and ask, "If I can't reveal all of the pieces of the deal to my banker or lawyer, what's wrong with this picture?"

Recently Canadian Mortgage and Housing Corporation (CMHC), GMAC and major financial institutions have stepped up their investigations into homeowner loans. They're looking for people who say they're moving into a property as a primary residence, and who have obtained a loan on that basis, but who in fact have purchased the house as an investment. How are they doing this? Quite simply, they are out in the street investigating. In fact, you can now find them knocking on doors of not only the property you purchased, but also neighbouring properties, asking questions about the new neighbours. They have one purpose in mind: to find out if you have fraudulently obtained a loan. If you have, they will go after you with all of their legal might.

In 2004 in Edmonton, 55 people were caught who were involved in a large scheme like this, and these people are not only losing their properties and their credit rating, they're also getting sued for punitive damages. In other words, they are losing their reputation along with a whole lot of money.

PROCEED WITH CAUTION!

Never commit anything that even smells of bank fraud. It may seem like the easy way out, and others may tell you that it's okay because they know people who are doing it; however, it is never worth the risk. Don't mess with the system.

CHAPTER 13

Remember, the difference between a below-average investor and an overachieving investor is only a 10 percent increase in effort. The same principle comes into play in getting the banks on your side. If you are willing to follow the system and do that extra 10 percent, then you are going to do very well and the banks will love you. If you're not willing to do so, then don't be surprised if you get frustrated and hear *no* a lot more than you should. The extra 10 percent of effort doesn't sound like much, yet it is surprising how many aren't willing to do that extra bit.

Put Yourself in the Banker's Shoes

The first thing to keep in mind when you're dealing with a bank is that you're really dealing with a person, a human being—not a faceless corporation. This is an important distinction, because personalities come into play when you deal with bankers. Each banker has his or her own motivating factors; bankers have good days and bad days just like the rest of us. The banker is just a person doing his or her job to the best of his or her ability. Clearly, the easier you make his or her job, the easier it will make the banker's life. And the easier you make the banker's life, the more pleasant it will be to deal with you, and therefore the banker will be more inclined to work with you on your deals.

The Sophisticated Investor—YOU

As a novice to intermediate investor, your banker primarily evaluates you and your ability to pay the mortgage; the property and its income are secondary. Your job at this point is to provide the banker with the information in such a way that he or she feels comfortable saying yes.

As you move to becoming a senior investor, especially if you start investing in multi-family housing (apartment and townhouse complexes), something very interesting usually happens. The property becomes the primary focus and you become the secondary focus. The key here is to provide extensive due diligence as outlined in the following chapter. Your banker will provide you with *their* specific checklist, but you'll impress your banker by doing more.

It's important to put yourself in the banker's shoes. Just as you learned the vendor's motivation for selling in order to accommodate his or her needs in your offer, you need to discover what the banker is looking for in a deal and how you can fulfill that need. Your job is to find the most suitable banker for you and your situation, and then build a strong relationship. Once you've done that, just stick with these three rules:

Rule 1: Understand the motivation of the person across the desk from you. When you know what motivates someone, you then have the knowledge to work with their motivation so you do what works and avoid what doesn't work.

So, what motivates a banker, you ask? Two things. First, in the short term, a banker wants your business. It's worth a few brownie points and often a bonus if the banker brings business to the bank. And, if he or she is a mortgage broker, no mortgage means no commission.

The second motivating factor is the banker's desire to move up the corporate ladder. This means he or she is looking for real estate deals that are clean and easy to support. In the short term, your file has to look good and meet the bank's parameters because often a file is reviewed by at least one other person in the bank (other than your contact). The cleaner the deal, the more confident your banker will be in representing your file.

In the long term, your mortgage must perform as promised. If a mortgage that the banker wrote goes sideways with missed payments, or even worse, it goes into foreclosure, guess what happens? The file is pulled and reviewed with one question in mind: "Was there anything in the file that the banker missed that could have made this mortgage default predictable?" The bottom line? Make it easy for the banker to create a clean file on you.

Rule 2: When you give people what they want, the odds of you getting what you want in return are much greater. By sitting down and discussing your banker's goals and objectives, you will be one of the very few clients who know what makes this person tick and what is needed from you to make a deal work. You'll also discover how you can help the banker achieve his or her goals.

Rule 3: Ask for what you want. If you ask for what you want, people will appreciate your candour and can clearly tell you whether they can provide it. If you don't ask for what you want, your odds of getting it are very slim. You want the mortgage approved, of course, but perhaps you also want a certain interest rate, fast approval or more flexible terms. As the relationship progresses, your banker will start offering you the items that you want without you asking; however, in the beginning, you must ask for everything you need.

These three rules apply to all your business relationships, not just your banker. Clarity in communication is the underlying theme to all of them.

• • • •

Alan stood up, looked at his watch, and said, "I'll leave you with one last thing: the strategies Don will be sharing with you (both the investment and banker strategies) will work most of the time. However, there will be exceptions. Sometimes it means you're dealing with the wrong banker or realtor, or even the wrong property. Don't let these roadblocks get you down; they are just a part of the process. Learn from the hurdles as well as the successes, and keep asking questions."

Looking a bit awestruck, Emma said, "Thanks for your great advice and for taking the time to meet with us."

Richard stood up and smiled his agreement. "Wow, that really makes sense. Thanks a million!"

Alan reached out and shook both their hands and said, "I'm off to my daughters' dance recital tonight. I hear that your daughter dances as well, so you know how important these nights are. I hope to see you again soon, and I'm sure Don will keep me informed of your progress."

"You bet, Alan. Thanks!"

"Good luck!" Alan called over his shoulder as he left with the same energy with which he had arrived.

Emma spoke up. "Don, this is great to hear in person. One of the reasons I jumped on board with Rich this time is because of the underlying integrity your system has. I noticed how he wasn't talking about taking advantage of anyone, how he spoke of long-term wealth and assisting others. This was sounding so different from many of the other ideas he's brought home."

"Thanks Emma," I said. "Once you adopt a long-term outlook on your investments, you soon take the pressure off yourself to go for the home run, get-rich-quick idea. You start to focus more on the journey and the fundamentals of investing.

"Okay, enough of this!" I joked. "Let's get down to helping the bank say *yes*! It's time to move on to the initial steps in developing a quality relationship with your banker."

With this I began walking through the key strategies that Alan Jacques had intially developed and I refined as the banking market changed. Richard and Emma soon had their eyes opened to just how simple banks can be to deal with.

 **KEY INSIGHT**

Always ask yourself, "What is the single most important thing I can learn from this situation and how can I profit from this knowledge in the future?"

Nothing will ever be attempted if all possible objections must be overcome.
　　　　　　　　　　　　　　　　　　—Samuel Johnson

Richard and Emma, like many Canadians, experience fear around dealing with banks and financial institutions. This fear, while largely unfounded and not based on any real experience, is rooted largely in a lack of knowledge—a lack of knowledge about how to work with banks, how banks really work and what a bank is really looking for in its deals.

You will quickly discover that bankers and mortgage brokers are your best friends in the real estate investment business. They want to lend you money; all you have to do is provide them with the key answers so they can confidently say *yes*.

The relationship you build with your banker must be a win for both parties, providing you with what you need while at the same time you are providing the lender with what they need. Once you implement the following seven strategies, you will be well on your way to building this key relationship. These strategies have been developed through the experience of working with investors and bankers for over a decade. You will note that many don't offer conventional wisdom, and a couple even fly in the face of what you may believe to be true. That's okay: conventional wisdom is for the average investors. For you to become an overachiever, you sometimes have to go against the flow.

Strategy 1: Learn All You Can about Banks and Banking

Become a student of banking. By following the ACRE system, you're well on your way, but there's more you can do. Read every article or book you can find about how banks operate—especially the insider stories. Talk to other real estate investors about their banking experiences. Talk to bankers other than your own whenever you get the opportunity. Take your own banker out for lunch, ask lots of questions and listen carefully.

Learn about the advantages and disadvantages of the various types of mortgages and financing options available, including amortization periods, length of terms, payment options, personal lines of credit, the fine print in mortgage documents and tax implications. Learn all you can from every source you can think of. It'll pay off for you, especially as your real estate portfolio grows. The key point is to understand the *facts*, the *hows*, the *whys* and the *why nots*.

STRATEGY 2: CHOOSE YOUR BANKER OR BROKER CAREFULLY

One of the most important relationships you'll ever have as a real estate investor is with your banker(s) or mortgage broker(s). Notice I said banker, not bank! Even though lending policies are dictated by head offices, it's the individual banker with whom you will build a relationship. Many investors have had the experience of being turned down by a banker at one branch, only to get a mortgage at another branch of the same bank.

Why? Because people are people, and the relationship you create with a person counts for a lot more than most of us realize. Individual bankers have a certain amount of discretion. They use their gut feelings or instincts along with the deal's numbers to decide whether to present your deal to their superiors. One banker may not have a good feeling about you, whereas another banker may think you're the perfect client.

Not all bankers are created equally; many great business bankers have very limited experience with, or do not wish to work with, investment real estate. You may already have a relationship with a banker through your business or personal dealings. However, often this will not be the banker you will end up using for your real estate investments. This is because you need a real estate investment specialist, someone who has seen creative real estate transactions and is not afraid of making a deal work.

Choose a banker who's very experienced in residential real estate investing. These bankers are more apt to understand your deal and how to get it approved. A banker whose focus is writing residential mortgages for a typical home buyer may not be experienced with investment financing. Here are five steps to selecting a banker or mortgage broker:

1. Obtain the names of at least three good bankers from other real estate investors. You will usually get your best referrals from experienced investors.
2. Approach the bankers when you do not need a mortgage! This is essential to putting you in control of the relationship.
3. Interview each banker in person, not over the phone. Look for a good personality fit as well as experience working with creative real estate investors. Ask some general questions about their likes and dislikes. Get to know them. Then ask questions about their banks' approval process. Wear business attire and act with confidence. At this point, you don't have to bring any documents with you.
4. After going through this process, begin to trust your own instincts. Select the banker or broker with whom you want to work.
5. Visit the selected banker(s) and tell them you've chosen to work with their bank on building your real estate portfolio. Ask for three copies of the bank's mortgage application form. Put these in your filing cabinet; I'll tell you what to do with them later.

Banking is a service business. If you're not receiving the type of service you want, don't be afraid to take your business to another banker or bank. Your goal is to develop a long-term relationship with your banker, which means you must always feel comfortable with that person and never intimidated. That's what the five-step selection process is all about.

If the relationship does not work out as you would have liked (we've all experienced one or two wrong relationships in our careers), then you may wish to begin your hunt for a new banking relationship. As the CEO of your business, you need to ensure that you are setting the standard. Handle the transition professionally; don't burn any bridges. You never know what the future holds.

Never play one banker against another. That's what junior investors do. Work with the banker, learn their systems, and become a master at dealing with banks. Always have a "Plan B" in case your first option doesn't work out.

KEY INSIGHT

You may have cash to buy only one or two properties with 25 percent down in the beginning. There are a few options that are available to you. Some options reduce the amount of money you need to put into the deal, while others access additional sources of investment capital. A professional mortgage broker can help you to find these types of deals. Here are a few to look at:

1. CMHC-Insured Mortgages
There are a few lending institutions that will allow you to put down less money. For example, Canada Mortgage and Housing Corporation will insure your loan (for a fee) that will allow the banks to make it possible for you to only put down 15 percent instead of 25 percent. There is a cost to this—CMHC insurance fees run as high as $4\frac{1}{2}$ percent of the loan value and, in addition, you have to pay a substantial application fee. The good news is you can ask for the insurance fees to be added to the principal of the mortgage. The other upside is you can usually get lower mortgage interest rates with a CMHC-insured mortgage.

2. Alternative Lenders
There are lending companies in Canada that offer mortgages for up to 90 percent of the value of the property. Often the loans can't exceed $500,000 and you will pay a premium on the mortgage interest rate along with an application fee. By lowering your down payment to 10 percent of the value, you open up opportunities to purchase more properties with your existing funds. The additional good news is that some of these mortgage companies don't have a flexible TDS analysis and even work with recently discharged bankruptcies. Other major banks offer options that allow 15 percent on rental properties without CMHC insurance. Just remember that you won't always get discounted interest rates with these mortgages.

3. Joint-Venture Relationships
As you become better at picking exceptional real estate deals, you can get into financial relationships with others who don't have the time or knowledge to find such good real estate deals for themselves. You can work together with them as an investment partner, pooling your money and expertise in order to purchase more properties. I have seen investors go from zero to 20 properties all by working in joint-venture relationships. It is an amazing strategy you can use after you understand the whole ACRE system.

Strategy 3: Negotiate the Interest Rate—Sort Of

Remember to ask for what you want. When it comes to mortgage interest rates, nothing could be truer. Virtually every time I've asked for a rate reduction, I've got one. Almost any bank will give you ¼ percent to ¾ percent just for asking. You can even get more in some circumstances. With personal lines of credit, it's not unheard of to receive a reduction of up to 2 percent! All you have to do is ask!

However, it's important not to behave like a typical investor. Never threaten to take your business to another bank because they're willing to offer you ¼ percent less—that's what short-term investors do. You're building a relationship with your banker and the ¼ percent is not worth ruining a relationship over.

KEY INSIGHT

The more you grind the banker, the thinner your welcome will become.

Overall, the interest rate is not as important (assuming it's reasonable) as getting the deal approved. Believe me, a good, solid relationship with a helpful banker is worth much more than a small percentage savings on your mortgage. And if ½ percent on your mortgage makes the deal look bad, then the deal was bad to begin with!

Strategy 4: Have a Pre-Approval Discussion with Your Banker

In the beginning, you may not know the amount of mortgage you will need on a property. That should not stop you from having a pre-approval discussion with your chosen banker.

Very few investors do this, but I've found this to be an important step in the building of the relationship. It takes a bit of the pressure off you as well as your banker. You can avoid a lot of the last-minute scrambling and stress that seem to occur with every real estate deal.

During this pre-approval period, a quality banker or broker will even discuss creative ways for getting a deal done, such as working with joint venture partners. Remember, the banks want to lend you money just as much as you want to borrow it. Yes, it is true that you won't know the exact amount of the mortgage you'll need until you find the property, but this pre-approval step will give you a ballpark figure to work with. This is powerful knowledge. The bank still has to approve the property in terms of value (through an appraisal), location, type and condition, but these are usually secondary considerations; approving *you* is more important.

STRATEGY 5: USE PERSONAL LINES OF CREDIT WHEN APPROPRIATE

A personal line of credit (PLC) can be a very powerful financing tool for real estate investors. A PLC is like a bank loan except that it operates like a reverse bank account. You get approved to borrow a certain amount of money (the PLC limit) against which you can write cheques for any purpose you wish. You only pay interest on the outstanding balance each month.

PLCs are very flexible. You can pay them off any time you wish without penalty. On a secured line of credit, the minimum monthly payment is often just the monthly interest due for that month. The interest rate floats, which is a bonus if interest rates are stable or declining, but they're not so great if rates dramatically increase. Interest rates are usually adjusted monthly.

There are basically two kinds of PLCs—secured and unsecured. A secured PLC is backed up by some type of secure collateral, such as the equity in your home, cash on deposit at the bank, or government bonds. With that type of security, you can usually get an interest rate equal to the bank's prime lending rate or up to 1 percent above. If you use your home as security, the bank will effectively register a second mortgage against your home. In that case, you will have to pay the appropriate legal fees that are usually around $500 to $600, or in some cases the bank will pay them. Remember, there is no harm in asking for what you want.

An unsecured PLC has no specific collateral to back up the loan. As with any loan or mortgage, you still have to meet the bank's income and credit-rating criteria. The tradeoff is that the bank charges a higher interest rate, typically prime plus 1 to 4 percent. These PLCs are much more difficult to get.

Personal lines of credit can be very powerful tools to an investor; however, before arranging one, make sure you understand these three cautions.

First, not all banks have the same PLC rules. There are a few banks out there that offer PLCs you may choose to avoid. Here's what to watch out for:

1. The bank requires a minimum monthly payment on a secured PLC, made up of a combination of the interest and some principal. A common amount for these payments is 3 percent of the outstanding balance (as opposed to interest only, which is usually less than 1 percent per month). This can be very expensive. If this is your only concern about a PLC, then it still may be acceptable to you. The following points are of much more concern.

2. The PLC has an annual or monthly fee. Some banks play a game, which is even worse. You can only get the PLC if you sign up for the bank's gold or deluxe monthly package service for a fee, which includes the right to have a PLC.

3. The bank makes you re-apply for the PLC or package service each year. This is almost as much hassle as applying for the PLC in the first place!

4. The bank bases the PLC interest rate on their "personal loan base rate" (or some other fancy name) which is ½ percent or more above prime. You may think you're getting a prime plus 2 percent rate, when in fact you're being charged prime plus 2½ percent, or even more. Always ask how the rates work!

The second caution is, if interest rates take off, because PLC rates are usually floating, you could have a cash flow problem. One way to beat this is to convert the PLC to a fixed-rate loan if you believe interest rates are about to rise substantially. Keep in mind you may (but you may not) have to pay a higher interest rate for the fixed-rate loan.

The third caution, though it rarely occurs, relates to what could be serious financial woes. With most PLCs, the bank retains the right to "call in" the loan on very short notice. And of course this would probably happen at the worst possible time—the economy is in the dumpster, your PLC is maxed, you have no other cash, or you have just lost your job.

When you sign the documents for any type of bank financing, make sure you understand what you are signing! Read, review, re-read and ask questions. Don't assume the lender has drafted the documents for your benefit, when or if things go sideways.

STRATEGY 6: GIVE THE BANK REFERRALS AND SOME OF YOUR OTHER BANKING BUSINESS

Banks are businesses, and their job is to attract more business. If you find an amazing banker, why not honour this person by bringing additional banking into the branch? It may be your own business needs or it may come from people you have referred. Although the banker is not allowed to say, "I'll give you this mortgage if you bring in all of your other banking," it is still an unstated request. If it helps your banker achieve his or her goals, and it does not hurt your position, then it's a great way to build the relationship.

STRATEGY 7: PRESENT YOUR DEAL BETTER THAN ANYONE ELSE

This point is so important that I've created a checklist outlining exactly how you to do this. Making a powerful written presentation is the most important single thing you can do when working with a banker or lender. You only get one chance to make a good first impression. I cannot emphasize the incredible difference the presentation of your documentation can make.

The manner in which your documentation is presented is a key factor in getting your mortgages approved. The quality of the presentation WILL make or break your deal.

KEY INSIGHT

Making a powerful written presentation is the most important single action to take when working with a banker or lender.

As I said, making the right presentation is the key to getting your banker to say *yes*. By following these next few steps, you will create a presentation that will be one of the best your banker will ever see. It's really just a simple collection of documents, but they are documents few others have ever compiled in a single presentation to a banker. It defines you as a sophisticated investor and will assist the banker in making intuitive decisions and allow him or her to get excited about your deal!

To assess the risk of loaning you a mortgage, your banker needs specific information. It is the same information every time. However, compiling and preparing it properly is part of that extra 10 percent that sophisticated investors do. The benefit this extra effort will bring you is dramatic, both in the short and long term.

There are seven essential components to the system. In hundreds of transactions with bankers over the years, I've heard the same reasons over and over again as to why people get turned down for financing. And in most cases these reasons could have been overcome if the applicant knew how to package their information to be attractive to a banker.

SOPHISTICATED INVESTOR ACTION STEP

The most important step is to *answer the questions before they are asked*. This pre-emptive approach is very powerful.

Put yourself in the shoes of the banker. He or she sees dozens of people a week, all looking for loans and mortgages. The majority do not come to the meeting prepared, with many people so woefully unprepared they can't even answer the most basic questions. Contrast that to you, walking in with all of your paperwork in order, all of the information they need at your fingertips. How will you look compared to the others?

The fundamental question that underlies all of the lending rules is the same everywhere: *Will you be able to pay back the loan on time over the length of the mortgage?*

To satisfy themselves, bankers must be convinced you have the financial ability to pay them back as well as the sophistication to run a rental property. Here's what you need for each and every mortgage application to help them say *yes*.

THE SOPHISTICATED INVESTOR BINDER

The first thing you'll need is a one-inch white binder with a clear overlay that allows you to slide in a simple sheet as a title page. This will become your presentation binder. In it you will compile all of the information listed below, and present it in a simple and organized fashion. This step alone will grab your banker's attention and make the statement that you are a sophisticated investor.

KEY INSIGHT

> Make three binders at once, so when you give one to your banker, you'll have two backups in case another deal comes your way quickly. Save one binder as your master; keep it updated at all times and ready for action.

In this binder insert a set of nine section dividers. These will make it easy for your banker to find your critical information. At the end of this chapter you will see how to separate all nine components.

1. Cover Letter

The cover letter must be addressed directly to the person to whom you'll be presenting your Sophisticated Investor Binder. It should have a date and be structured like a business letter. It must clearly state, in no more than four paragraphs, the following items:

- The reader will find all of the information needed to provide a positive response to the application.
- You look forward to working with them to achieve a positive response on this and future deals.
- The date that you expect to hear back from them. This must not be a panicked "three days or less" date. Sophisticated investors plan ahead and don't set unrealistic deadlines. Short deadlines give bankers another reason to say *no*.
- If the person has any questions, ask him or her to call you immediately.

Attach this cover letter to the front of your binder with a paper clip.

2. Proof of Income

This is perhaps the most basic information a banker will require. In order to establish whether you can repay a mortgage, the banker has to be convinced you have the ability to handle the payments. He or she will require written proof that you make a certain amount of income.

If you are an employee and work for a company (other than your own), a letter of employment will usually be all that's required. It's just a simple letter that states that you work for a certain employer and make so much money per month or per year (see a sample below). Sometimes you can get your boss to include information about what a fine person you are, how long you've been with the company, that you have a great future and so on. This also assists the banker in knowing more about your future ability to pay.

Make sure the letter is on your company's letterhead and that it's signed by someone to whom the bank can speak when they are confirming the information. This letter should not be any more than 90 days old when you present it to the bank, but the more recent, the better.

Sample Job Letter

ABC Company Inc.
1234 Business Way
Opportunityville, ON

July 17, 20xx

To Whom It May Concern:

Joe Investor has worked for our firm for three years and earns $54,000 per year, not including bonuses. His bonuses have averaged $3,000 per year for the past three years.

He is a valued employee with a very promising future with our company.

If you require further information, please call me at the above telephone number.

Sincerely,

Joan Owner

Joan C. Owner
President
ABC Company Inc.

If you are self-employed, you'll still have to provide documentation for your income. However, a letter from yourself, or anyone else at your company, is usually not sufficient. Generally you'll have to give your banker copies of your Notices of Assessment for the last two or three years. These are the notices that Canada Revenue Agency sends you after you have filed your taxes.

The problem for many self-employed people is that they use legal strategies to reduce their taxable personal income so they can reduce their income taxes. However, this strategy negatively affects their ability to borrow money. For bankers, the higher your taxable income, the better. Is there a way around this?

Yes, there are two. First, some bankers will accept financial statements of your business as well as copies of your Notices of Assessment. These statements are often more flattering to your income level. These financial statements will provide insights into the real income you have generated over the year. You already have these prepared for your businesses. Make copies of them so they can play a key part in your Sophisticated Investor Binder.

The second item you can provide is a letter from your chartered accountant that is addressed to your banker and clearly defines your business's actual income. This will obviously include your salary, but it will also include money you received in the form of shareholder loan repayments, expenses such as rent from a home-based business, dividends, retained earnings, depreciation and other items that may not appear, or are difficult to find, on an income tax return.

Sometimes it's best to draft the letter yourself and have your accountant modify it and sign it. Remember, your job is to help the banker say *yes* by presenting the truth in the best possible light. The clearer the letter, the better; however, make sure your accountant states in the letter that he or she can be contacted for further information.

Once again, the more information you provide, the better your chance of building a trusting relationship and getting your deals approved. I provide my trusted banker with both the financials as well as my accountant's letter.

3. Completed and Signed Application

Walking into a bank with a completed and signed mortgage or loan application form may sound like an obvious and trivial step in the process, but it has significant implications. Most investors, in fact most people, wait until they wander into the bank and then wait for the banker to start asking for what should be quite obvious information (social insurance number, postal code, employer's address, etc.). You know in advance that the banker is going to require this information, so present it all on one simple-to-follow sheet. Your job is to raise yourself above the masses, and having this information already completed will do wonders for you and your long-term relationship with the bank.

Picture a busy banker's desk. On the right side, he or she has a pile of "pending files" all awaiting follow-up information from other applicants. Then you walk in with your completed binder providing all of the information he or she requires. You have just made his or her life easier. First impressions are critical, and you have just made a very positive one.

You can use any template (they all ask for the same information) as your blank mortgage application, but the more sophisticated approach is to use the bank's application form, which you'll already have if you have followed all of the seven strategies for choosing a banker discussed at the beginning of this chapter. Be forewarned: if you bring in an application that is not specific to the bank, the banker will likely copy the information onto his or her in-house form.

When filling out the application, don't become lazy and start writing "see attached information" as a reference to the other information you're providing in your Sophisticated Investor Binder. Bankers have their checklists to follow for each file. The application is a key step in their system, so you might as well do it properly. Remember, your job is to make life easy for the banker. Your application will summarize all the rest of the documentation in your Sophisticated Investor Binder.

PROCEED WITH CAUTION!

If the banker does transfer your information to his or her bank's form, make sure you read any fine print before you sign it. You must understand the implication of signing an application. Often you are authorizing the bank to do a credit bureau check on you. In very rare instances, there are other clauses hidden in the fine print. If you are not sure about a certain clause, ask!

4. Personal Cash Flow Summary

The bank needs a summary of your personal cash flow to decide if they think you can afford the monthly payments of the mortgage. Make sure you list all of your sources of income on the summary. If you happen to be receiving positive cash flow from other properties you own, summarize it as net real estate income. You will give them the full details on how you calculated this in a revenue real estate asset statement, which I'll discuss shortly.

Make sure your income listed in your cash flow summary is the same as the income on your job letter or other proof of income documents. One way bankers seek the truth is by looking for consistency. If the numbers don't add up, a banker may think you are fudging numbers and this starts to raise red flags! Remember, tell the truth at all times.

When listing credit card payments, put the minimum payment you have to pay on a monthly basis. This only applies if you are carrying a balance from month to month. Here's a sample personal cash flow statement:

Joe and Mary Investor
September 1, 20XX

Monthly Net Income

Joe (see enclosed Notices of Assessment)		$4,500
Mary (see enclosed Notices of Assessment)		5,100
Total		$9,600

Monthly Expenses and Payments

Living expenses	$3,300	
Residence mortgage (joint)	1,756	Bank of Nova Scotia
Visa—Joe	231	Bank of Nova Scotia
Visa—Mary	122	Bank of Nova Scotia
PLC—joint	156	CIBC
Car loan—Joe	337	Bank of Montreal
Total	$5,902	

Total debt service payments $2,602

GDS* =
TDS* =

Signed: _____ Dated: _____

*One way in which your banker decides whether you can afford the mortgage payments is by calculating two ratios: your gross debt service (GDS) and your total debt service (TDS). Let's look at each one of these.

The GDS Formula

The GDS formula is mainly used when purchasing or refinancing a personal residence. So why am I mentioning it here? Because some bankers will use it for investment properties, and because you need to know about it to talk intelligently about mortgages to a banker. The formula for calculating your GDS is:

$$GDS = \frac{\text{monthly mortgage principal + interest + property taxes}}{\text{your monthly income}}$$

For the purchase of your own home, most banks will let you have a mortgage where the monthly mortgage payment (PIT = principal, interest and taxes) is 32 percent or less than your gross monthly income. (Note: The bank does not account for the deduction of income taxes in this calculation.)

The TDS Formula

The TDS ratio is used all the time by bankers to calculate whether you qualify for a mortgage on an investment property. Here's the formula:

$$TDS = \frac{\text{total debt service monthly payments}}{\text{your monthly income}}$$

The TDS formula includes all of your debt payments, including personal residence mortgage payments and taxes (or monthly rent if you're a tenant), credit card payments, bank loan payments, personal credit line payments, etc. Calculate your own TDS and provide this to your banker; it shows that you are aware of the key numbers they are looking for.

Most bankers will not lend you money if your TDS is above 40 to 42 percent.

Here's a trap to watch out for. Let's say you use your credit card every month and pay off the balance every month when you get your statement. In that situation, you would not need to list any debt on your net worth statement or indicate any payment on your cash flow summary, right? The credit card payment is just part of your monthly living expenses. So far, so good.

However, when the bank gets their credit bureau report on you, they notice an outstanding balance of $3,700 listed against your credit card.

Almost automatically, they become suspicious of your information. I've had some clients who've even been accused of lying!

What happened? Financial institutions usually report to the credit bureau on a monthly or bi-monthly cycle. It's all done automatically by computer. So, guess what happens? If, on the day they report to the bureau, your credit card has an outstanding balance of $3,700, this amount will show up on the bureau report, even if you paid it off the very next day. The bank will then want proof you've paid off the balance.

Is there a way around this? Of course; you're going to include a photocopy of at least three months of credit card statements showing that you've paid them off consistently.

Another problem is some bankers include your credit potential in their TDS calculations. This means that you have a credit card or PLC with a significant unused balance, a banker may calculate what the payment would be if you maxed the credit card or PLC, thus reducing your ability to obtain a mortgage. If your banker insists on doing this, go somewhere else because other lenders may not be required to underwrite that way. Make sure you calculate your own TDS and GDS before going to the bank.

As you invest in more properties, part of the wall you may hit is this TDS obstacle. Your total debt service starts to get out of whack with your personal income. The good news is there is a formula that many financial institutions use when dealing with veteran investors. It is called the 110 percent rule. By sticking with properties that fit the 110 percent rule, you will help the bank remove the wall from your path.

This is a very important rule to understand if you are planning to own three or more rental properties in your portfolio.

In most cases, investors with modest incomes hit a financial wall set by the banks. This wall is designed to minimize the bank's risk. The bank looks at your income and compares it to the debt you have against your name and they yell *stop* when your debt service payments hit 40 percent of your income.

Well, if this was the only option, you'd hear *stop* very quickly as soon as you start to add investment mortgages to your debt load. However, with the right banker or mortgage broker, you can avoid this wall once you get three or more properties in your portfolio. That's when the 110 percent rule kicks in.

Here's how it works.

Once you have three properties, certain banks will consider your properties as a portfolio, and will analyze them as a group. They are looking for one key number—the number 110. They want to see rents that total 110 percent of debt expenses (mortgage payments + property taxes + condo fees). If they do see 110 or more, they no longer include these mortgages into your personal debt service calculation. And suddenly your debts-service ratio drops dramatically, leaving you with the option to purchase many more properties.

As an example, if you own three properties with a total rent of $3,300, as long as your mortgage payments + taxes + condo fees don't add up to more than $3,000, you have a winner in your banker's eyes. This means you have just avoided the dreaded wall.

After you reach this level, look for properties that fit the 110 percent rule and you will be able to add as many properties as you wish. You will need to work with a knowledgeable broker or banker to implement this formula, but it will be well worth the effort.

5. Credit Bureau Report

Every time you sign a mortgage application—or for that matter any credit application— you authorize the bank to check your credit bureau file. Their right to do this is written in the fine print just above where you sign your name. Unless the bank has very recently checked your file, they will print off a report from the bureau and review it carefully.

Now for the scary news. Your bureau file can often contain incorrect information!

All it takes is one slip of a data entry clerk's finger when typing in a social insurance number and someone else's information is in your file. The good news is the credit bureaus provide a system to get the bad information removed quickly. However, if you never look at your own credit bureau report, you will never know if it is accurate or not.

All Canadians should review their credit bureau report at least once a year, especially if they are applying for a loan or mortgage. You can do it on-line for a fee, or you can request the report via fax or mail. There is no charge for this service in most jurisdictions.

You might be very surprised at what's listed on your report—errors or a listing of a credit card that you long ago forgot. You need to clean these up right away. On one occasion a few years ago, information from someone with the same name as mine was on my file, and this person had a very bad credit history. The banks would have just assumed that I was this person, if I hadn't cleaned it up in advance.

Check *all* the information on your report, such as correct spelling of your name, address, employer, your credit cards and their numbers, loans, mortgages, etc. Make sure it's all accurate. If you find something wrong with your personal details, the bureau can usually correct your file for you. If the problem is with a bank, credit card or other company, you'll usually have to contact them directly to get the issue cleared up. The credit bureau employee can tell you how to go about it.

Most bankers seem to look for two specific things on your credit report more than anything else. First, they want to see how many inquiries are on your file. Every time a bank or company looks at your file electronically or manually, an inquiry is recorded on your file. The inquiry states which bank or company inquired and the date. These inquiries usually stay on your file for three years and also affect your BEACON® score. Your beacon score is a calculation based on many factors involved in your credit, from the number of applications you have made in the past, to how much current credit you can access, as well as your credit history. This calculation is becoming increasingly prevalent with banks across the country and is usually the first thing they check.

HOW DOES YOUR BEACON SCORE WORK?

Virtually everyone in Canada who has received credit in his or her lifetime has a credit score. This is most commonly referred to as the "Beacon Score." The higher the score, the better your credit rating. Now, the scoring system is not perfect and not all lenders apply it in the same way, but it is safe to say that maintaining a high Beacon Score will increase your financing options in the market and your appeal as a low risk to a lender.

A Beacon Score is a snapshot in time of your credit history and is derived through a complex formula that takes a variety of items into consideration. Its purpose is to provide a lender with a prediction as to the credit risk you represent over the next 12 to 24 months. So what can you do to improve the score? Well, the first step is to understand how the number is derived in the first place.

Beacon and Empirica scores are used by the two major credit bureaus in the country—Equifax and TransUnion. The scores are computed from data from five different categories to track patterns and predict future actions based on past behaviour. The score is based on this data, along with the percentage weighting applied to each category. To help you increase (improve) your score, focus on those aspects you can control:

Past Payment Performance—35%
- The fewer late payments you make, and the fewer judgements, liens or collections you have, the better.
- Late payments are time sensitive. The lender will give more weight to recent occurrences as opposed to those two years or older.

Credit Utilization—30%
- Low balances on several cards are better than high balances on a few cards.
- It is ideal to keep the balance on credit cards at or below 30% of the available credit and your score will be adversely affected once you exceed 80% of the available credit on those cards.

- Access to too many cards can be deemed detrimental. (Be extra cautious about applying for lots of credit cards, no matter what anyone tells you! Because the weighting of this section is so high, 30 percent, applying for many credit cards will negatively affect your score.)

Credit History—15%
- The longer the credit accounts have been open and in good standing, the better.
- A "red-flag" for lenders is opening new accounts to pay out old accounts—or "credit surfing." This will negatively impact a credit score.

Types of Credit in Use—10%
- Finance company accounts score lower than traditional banking or retail accounts.
- Deferred payment options funded by finance companies impact the score accordingly. Having too many of these "buy now, pay later" accounts will be interpreted as a potential for future risk.

Inquiries—10%
- Looking for new credit often can result in having too many inquiries on your bureau over a short period of time. This will be perceived as "shopping for credit" and can be indicative of higher risk.
- As a special note: Promotional or administrative inquiries (i.e., credit grantor updates or your own inquiry to see your credit rating) may show on the report but do not affect the credit score.

(* Source: Peter Kinch, Canada Mortgage Team)

When bankers see a lot of inquiries on your file, they regard you as a credit seeker. And even worse, if there are no recent loans, mortgages or credit cards to match each inquiry, they'll assume you were declined for financing at another institution, and therefore you must be a bad credit risk. (Please note: Your own inquiries about your file at the credit bureau's office are not recorded on your file in most jurisdictions.)

Second, bankers want to make sure you make your loan, credit card and bill payments on time. If you've been really good, there will be an R1 beside each of the credit vehicle descriptions. That means you've made each payment on or before the due date for a particular credit vehicle. If you're one month late, it will be rated R2; two months late, R3, all the way up to R9, which means "bad debt, placed for collections."

Bankers love to see all R1s. They'll usually accept the odd R2, but not much more.

After the bureau employee finishes explaining the report to you, either in person or over the telephone, you should immediately take a copy of the report and write an explanation beside every item (use black pen as it photocopies well). For example, if you paid off or closed a particular credit card or mortgage, write "paid off and closed May 23, 20XX." This makes it easy for your banker to see what your real position is. If your file is long, attach a cover letter explaining each line item that requires clarity. Write this letter in point form and keep it simple.

Why go to all this trouble? Simple. The bank now has accurate information on your credit activities and the banker will be impressed with your knowledge and the amount of homework you've completed. Also, and this is the biggie, sometimes they'll approve a mortgage for you, if the report copy is recent, without pulling a credit bureau file! And this means there won't be an additional inquiry on your file. Once you've cleaned up your credit history to the best of your ability, request a new copy of your report for inclusion in your Sophisticated Investor Binder.

The Big Spotlight

You may have some past credit issues that are accurate but not very pretty. This is where you use a senior level strategy I call the big spotlight. This technique is the opposite of what many people do, but it's part of being a sophisticated investor.

Here's how it works. Review your credit bureau report, or any other area of your application and look for a weakness. It may be that you have an R9 (poor) credit rating from a few years ago that has a legitimate explanation. It may be that you missed two payments on a previous loan; it could be anything at all that might be considered a weakness in your application.

Now this is where I once again differ from conventional wisdom. Take a brightly coloured highlighter and clearly mark this weakness, point it out, shine a big spotlight on it for all to see. Then write a simple (three paragraphs, maximum) note to the banker about this issue.

For example, one of my clients bought furniture on sale at one of those well-advertised "Don't Pay for One Year" events. He had every intention of paying for it the week before it came due, the moment the notice came in the mail. However, during that one-year period he moved to a different city and promptly forgot all about it. The notice went to his previous address, and he didn't receive it. Almost 19 months later, he was pulling his credit bureau report and found that he had been reported as an R9 because he had not made his furniture payment.

Although it upset him, it was a legitimate R9. He made good on the payment immediately, but the R9 stayed on his report. He used the big spotlight strategy to point this out to his banker and explained the situation. His banker laughed and said, "The exact thing happened to my brother. Thanks for pointing it out; your honesty goes a long way. I look forward to giving you approval in a few days."

You see, bankers are human beings; they understand real life happens to us all. They'd much rather deal with someone who's not afraid of pointing out his or her flaws. It shows an additional level of honesty and integrity on your part and assists them in getting behind your deal.

Use the big spotlight strategy in all aspects of your life, and you'll be very pleasantly surprised at the results. You'll attract those who appreciate honesty and repel those who don't, a great way to build yourself a team of professionals based on integrity.

 **KEY INSIGHT**

Shine a big spotlight on your flaws and gain respect and results!

6. Net Worth Statement

This is the easiest document to describe, though it may take you a while to prepare if you haven't done one recently. A net worth statement is simply a list of all your assets and liabilities (see sample below). Hopefully, when you calculate your net worth by subtracting the liabilities from the assets, you will get a positive number! Think of it as a financial scorecard.

I recommend you keep your net worth statement on your computer. Use a basic Excel spreadsheet or a financial management program such as Quicken. The key is to make it easy for you to update as your life and investments change. The more accurate and up to date it is when you submit it to your banker, the better.

Even if you don't consider your net worth very large, include a detailed breakdown of your assets and liabilities. It will make life easier for your banker, and more importantly, it keeps you aware of where you are.

I have included two versions: one shows the net worth of a non-real estate investor (someone just starting out with the ACRE system) and the second is of an investor who has begun to create his or her real estate portfolio.

An important note for your net worth statement: make sure that you can back up every claim you make on the statement. Include this back-up documentation in your Sophisticated Investor Binder wherever possible.

SOPHISTICATED INVESTOR ACTION STEP: YOUR NET WORTH STATEMENT

Hot Tip 1: Make sure the money you're using as a down payment to purchase a property is listed on the net worth statement! Remember, bankers look for consistency in your various documents.

Hot Tip 2: Sign and date your net worth statement. This senior level step is required when purchasing major properties, but it also provides that extra level of comfort to your banker when working on smaller properties.

Hot Tip 3: If someone is giving you money as a gift for the purchase of the property, make sure that you have a letter, signed and dated by the gift giver and stating the amount, the date that you received the gift, and that it is completely non-repayable. Include this amount in your net worth statement and include the letter in your Sophisticated Investor Binder.

Net Worth Statement—Non-Real Estate Investor

Joe and Mary Investor
September 1, 20XX

ASSETS

Liquid Assets

Cash and equivalent	$ 27,256
RRSPs	47,376
Other investment: mutual funds	8,550
Total liquid assets	**$ 83,182**

Non-Liquid Assets

Personal residence	$ 175,000
Rare coins	5,300
Children's mutual funds	17,847
Total non-liquid assets	**$ 198,147**

Personal-Use Assets

Personal property	$ 67,000
Automobile	16,000
Total personal-use assets	**$ 83,000**

LIABILITIES

Personal residence mortgage	$ (97,418)
PLC ($40,000 available)	(0)
Auto loan	(5,346)
Visa—Joe	(2,321)
Visa—Mary	(2,119)
Total liabilities	**$ (107,204)**

TOTAL NET WORTH $ 257,125

Signed: _____ Dated: _____

Net Worth Statement—First-Year Real Estate Investor

Joe and Mary Investor
September 1, 20XX

ASSETS

Liquid Assets

Cash and equivalent	$ 10,256
RRSPs	47,376
Other investment: mutual funds	8,550
Total liquid assets	**$ 66,182**

Non-Liquid Assets

Personal residence	$ 175,000
Investment property (see revenue property statement)	269,000
Children's mutual funds	17,847
Total non-liquid assets	**$ 461,847**

Personal-Use Assets

Personal property	$ 67,000
Automobile	16,000
Total personal-use assets	**$ 83,000**

LIABILITIES

Personal residence mortgage	$ (97,418)
Investment mortgages	(172,160)
PLC ($40,000 available)	(20,000)
Auto loan	(5,346)
Visa—Joe	(2,321)
Visa—Mary	(2,119)
Total liabilities	**$ (299,364)**

TOTAL NET WORTH $ 311,665

Signed: _____ Dated: _____

7. Revenue Real Estate Asset Statement

As you start to add properties to your portfolio, you will need to declare all of the details to your bank. To do this, create a simple spreadsheet on your computer (a sample follows). Once again, this is designed to provide the bankers with the answers to their questions long in advance of them asking.

Be forewarned: if you are dealing with a banker who does not have experience with investment real estate, you will immediately hit a road-block with your debt ratios. However, with a quality banker or broker whose focus is investment real estate and who works with a bank who understands the 110 percent rule discussed earlier, you will find that this document provides them with the opportunity to achieve their goals.

By providing all the details of the property and underlying mortgages, bankers will see that you are monitoring your properties, and just as important, they will see if any mortgages are being held by another financial institution. And, if so, these properties provide them with an opportunity to get more of your business when the mortgages become due. This form becomes increasingly important as you become a more seasoned investor.

You may ask, why use this exact format of the revenue real estate asset statement? Because it's what the bankers want to see, and it has proven to be effective over and over again! Why does it work? Well, there are three reasons:

- The statement makes you look good. You own a portfolio of real estate even if you have just one property.
- The statement shows that you're organized and implies you manage your assets well. You're a sophisticated investor.
- The statement presents your cash flow situation in the best possible light.

This last point is very important. The bank wants to know the details of your cash flow. You provide this for the same reason you complete a credit application before meeting the banker. You already know what questions the banker is going to ask, so the job of the so-phisticated investor is to provide answers in advance.

Typical questions include: "What are the mortgage payments?" "Is there any secondary financing on these properties?" "What are the taxes?" "What are the condo fees?" And so on.

If you wait until the banker asks the questions, the unprepared investor may not look very good to the bank. Remember, they'll do their own calculations from the numbers you give them. However, if you provide the information in a clear and concise manner, guess what usually happens? The bankers don't need to ask any further questions. Your statement clearly shows your properties are paying their mortgage and taxes, and the banker will generally accept it as is. Also, it allows the banker to check on the hidden 110 percent rule. Your revenue real estate asset statement will do all of that for you.

Here are three important points to note:

- Make sure the totals from the revenue real estate asset statement match up with your net worth statement.
- Create a version of this statement (in the same format) on your computer for easy updating.
- Put the maturity dates of each mortgage on the statement. Your current banker likes to know this information. It could be a source of extra business for him or her as these mortgages from other institutions come due. Any banker wants more of your business, especially if it's a simple renewal of existing mortgages.

See the Current Real Estate Owned chart on page 176.

Current Real Estate Owned

CREDIT APPLICATION PART 2

Applicant's Name: _____

Date: _____

Property Address	TITLE IN NAME OF	RENTAL INCOME	TAXES/ MTH	PRESENT VALUE	UNPAID	RATE %	MTHLY PMT	HELD BY & MATURITY DATE
XXXXXXX	**XXX TOTALS**				**XXX TOTAL**			**XXXXXX**

Applicant's Signature: _____

Page _____ of _____

8. Proof of Down Payment

When you apply for a mortgage, your banker will need to know you have the money to make up the difference between the mortgage amount and the purchase price. Although this might seem like pretty basic stuff, many investors have blown the mortgage approval process by not being able to prove they had the down payment! If your income is sufficiently high, your banker may allow you to borrow the down payment using a PLC. However, this doesn't apply in all situations; each financial institution has a different set of rules on this subject.

Many real estate investors use creative ways to come up with part or all of the down payment. While most of these techniques are perfectly legal and ethical, most bankers either aren't impressed by them or they'd rather not know you're using them. The bottom line for bankers is they need to know that if your creative ways don't pan out, you still have the cash to close when the time comes. They need to protect the bank's position.

You would be shocked at the number of times that below-average investors wait right up to closing day to tell their banker that they no longer have the cash to close. As you can imagine, in that situation, the trusting relationship goes out the window.

Now here's the trick. All you need to do is provide your banker with proof that you have access to the amount of money you'll need to put down on the property. Provide your banker with a stock statement, a bank account statement or even your RRSP statement. You can use any liquid asset statement you have to prove you have the down payment to close on the property. You do not actually need to use those specific funds at closing. Keep in mind that this proof of down payment must be in a liquid form such as cash, e.g., in a bank account, mutual fund, government bond or gift letter. It won't work if the money is locked in, as are some corporate retirement funds.

Never fake the information you provide the bank. I've heard of people faking their proof of down payment by doing things like photocopying someone else's bank book or borrowing money from a friend, putting it in their own bank account for a few days and then returning it, or pulling a huge cash advance out of their credit card a couple of weeks before closing so it doesn't show up on their credit bureau report.

Much of this could be interpreted as bank fraud and is absolutely wrong. How do you know if you're flirting with fraud? Simply ask yourself:

What was my intention in this action?
Was my intention to be up-front with full disclosure or was it designed to fool someone?
What would the bank say if they knew I was doing this? If they'd still say *yes*, then you should be okay. If they would say *no* because of the action, then you've stepped over the line.

Be careful of listening to lazy investors who may advise you of these tricks they've developed to get around the system. Such tricks will eventually come back and bite you.

9. Property Information

This is pretty basic, but many investors seem to forget about providing this critical information. Your bank needs to know all the details on the property you're buying before they'll lend you any money!

You need to create a brief one-page outline of the property, providing the bank with the critical information they're going to ask for:

- Property address (both civic and legal addresses)
- Brief written description of size, bedrooms, lot size and distinctive highlights
- Renovations that have upgraded the property in the last five years
- Purchase price and appraised value (if you have it)
- Rent (current and potential)
- Amount of money you wish to borrow
- Financing subject-to-approval date
- Closing date
- Name of registration for the property (and mortgage).

In addition to the property letter, you need to include copies of the following:

- Copy of the accepted Offer to Purchase
- At least one colour photograph of the property
- Copy of your Property Analysis Form from your due diligence.
- Copy of a current appraisal (if you can get one) completed by an appraiser acceptable to the bank. Most banks have a list of acceptable appraisers that you will, of course, already have in your file cabinet because you asked for it when you took the banker to lunch.

SOPHISTICATED INVESTOR ACTION STEP

Many deals have collapsed when the bank had an appraisal done and it came in lower than the selling price; therefore, the mortgage amount wasn't sufficient. I purposely don't tell the appraiser what the asking price is or what price I'm paying. That way I can use the appraisal as a part of my checks-and-balances system, making sure that the value I am paying is market value or below.

Why does this make a difference? There is no exact amount of money a property is worth. An appraisal is just an opinion of value. Even a sale, or comparable sale, doesn't establish an exact value. If it did, the appraisal amount would always be the same as the selling price. In the real world, a property is worth somewhere between two prices—in other words, a price range. Different appraisers will value a property at different amounts within this range.

When appraisers do appraisals for a bank, they tend to value properties towards the low end of the range to protect their trusted position with the bank. When they do appraisals for vendors, they tend towards the higher end of the range. Remember, appraisers are people too, and they tend to give their clients what they want or expect (within their professional guidelines, of course). Our trusted appraisers are critical members of our success team.

To summarize, here is a checklist of the nine things you should include in your Sophisticated Investor Binder. These are put in their own section of the binder making it easy for your banker to find.

1. Cover letter
2. Proof of income
3. Completed and signed application
4. Personal cash flow summary
5. Credit bureau report
6. Net worth statement
7. Revenue real estate asset statement
8. Proof of down payment
9. Property information.

By going to this effort, you have professionally answered the banker's immediate questions, but now you are going to put the icing on the cake and truly make your presentation stand out from that huge pile of file folders already stacked on the banker's desk.

KEY INSIGHT

Creating the Sophisticated Investor Binder is just as important at all levels of investing, from rookie to veteran. As a rookie, it gives you an edge as you present your first deals to the banker.

Then, as you add many more properties to your portfolio, the binder will assist your banker in getting a clear picture of all your assets and make them feel more comfortable with future deals. Clarity in communications always wins out.

THE EXTRA 10 PERCENT MAKES ALL THE DIFFERENCE!

You'll see your banker's whole face light up with excitement if you add the following items to your binder. In fact, they may even call in another banker in the branch so they can show off your binder. Bankers are so often taken for granted that anything that makes life easier for them is important. You will be amazed at the reaction of your banker, especially if this is the first time he or she has seen one of these binders. Here are the extras that will put your presentation over the top. Include the following every time:

1. In the first section of your binder, a 5" x 7" colour photo of you and your family. Any copy shop can do this for you. Make sure it's high quality and captures the essence of your family. I use one of my family outside playing with our dog. This photo ensures the bank knows they are making a loan to a person, not a faceless investor.
2. A one-page bio of you (and your family) explaining who you are, what your interests are, what your background is and where you're heading with real estate.
3. In the property information section, a copy of your Property Analysis Form and Due Diligence checklist. This will show the banker that you've done your homework on the property and you are not just buying blindly. Including these will take you to the next level of sophisticated investing. If you haven't completed these critical forms, then you shouldn't be buying the property yet. Without completing the due diligence, you really don't know what you are investing in. *Always* complete your own due diligence before you buy, no matter who you're buying from.

These three additions make all the difference in the world. You've already provided your banker the required information; now you're making the deal more personable.

For each application and each property submit a complete binder, even if the bank already has a copy from your last deal. Don't be lazy! By assuming your banker already knows everything, you're setting yourself up for failure. When you have a proven system, never skip a step because often it is the smallest detail that can make or break a deal. Present each application as if you were doing it the first time. Even if you're uncomfortable, do it! I've seen too many investors get sloppy and lazy, which leads to the banker's gut feelings about you changing, and then suddenly you're not getting the service or approvals you used to get. Stick to the system!

SOPHISTICATED INVESTOR ACTION STEP: THE EXTRA 10 PERCENT

It's homework time. Whether you have chosen a property or not, you need to get approved for your first investment mortgage. Here's your action plan, which you should get done in the next seven days:

1. Create your Sophisticated Investor Binder. Make sure you compile all of the information outlined in this chapter.
2. Find the names of two recommended bankers or mortgage brokers in your area. Call them and make appointments with each of them.
3. Interview each banker individually and in person. Look for a good personality fit as well as their history of working with creative real estate investors. Be in charge; remember you are looking for someone you can add to your support team.
4. Once you select the banker with whom you want to work, take him or her out for lunch. Do this before you approach him or her for a mortgage. At lunch, don't talk business; focus on the banker's goals and aspirations.
5. Back in the office, present the banker with the property you want to buy (if you have one), along with your Sophisticated Investor Binder and cover letter. Walk the banker through all of your details and the property information. (If you haven't chosen a property yet, have the meeting anyway and outline your goals.) Give the banker a date by which you would like approval.

Follow these steps and you will build an amazing relationship with one of the key people on your investment team—your banker or mortgage broker.

A wise man will make *more opportunities then he finds.*
—Francis Bacon

On Monday afternoon, Richard and I met at Starbucks, ready to go over the next steps. He could barely contain his excitement and nervousness as he shared his banker story from that morning.

Richard and Emma had chosen a banker and presented her with their complete binder along with the accepted offer to purchase. During the first part of the meeting, the banker sat silently, shaking her head as she leafed through their binder. Richard and Emma wondered if they had done something wrong and were about to have their application rejected.

Finally, after about five minutes, the banker looked up at them with the largest grin she could muster. "In all my years of banking, I have never seen such a complete package from an investor. This will definitely make it quick and easy for me to get you an answer on your mortgage. I can't see it taking longer than four or five days. After looking through your information, I don't see any immediate issues. Can I call you on Thursday?"

Richard told me that he and Emma could hardly contain their excitement. Trying not to let the excitement show too much, Richard had told the banker, "Absolutely, Thursday would be just fine."

Richard and Emma had witnessed first-hand the power of doing that extra 10 percent. These brand new investors had already got a property under contract and arranged for a major banker to be on their side. It had been a very productive couple of weeks.

I decided that now was the time to start discussing the next steps to becoming a real estate investor. Investing in real estate is a very different life from the corporate world, and I wanted to give Richard the tools that would make his transition smooth.

"Richard, you come from a corporate background, with a job in a corporate structure that clearly lays out your responsibilities, often in a detailed job description. This rigid structure is a must in large companies; it keeps them ticking and ensures that all facets of the business are looked after. However, this mindset can prove to be a major stumbling block for investors who move from the structured corporate world to that of a real estate investor. Those who make the mental transition become very successful; however, those who bring their corporate baggage and expectations with them quickly run into roadblocks."

"Why's that?" Richard asked.

"The reason is quite simple; as you begin investing in property, you immediately jump from employee to business owner. As an owner, your responsibilities cover all aspects of your business, not just your department. In the real estate world, you start right at the top! How long do you think it would take for you to get to the top of the company you're in now?" I quizzed, already knowing the answer.

"How about *never!*" Richard blurted. "About 500 people would have to quit and I'd have to go back to school to get my MBA before I would even be in line for the top job. But I thought investing meant I was just buying property and getting tenants."

"I'm not surprised you think that—that's what many beginning investors believe. Investing in real estate is not like investing in stocks or mutual funds. Investing in stocks is a passive investment; you put your money into stocks betting that the respective companies will be productive and profitable, so that your stocks increase in value. You don't have a lot of control over the situation, and that's why so many people end up frustrated with the returns on their stocks or mutual funds.

"Real estate investing is more interactive than most investing. Your actions have direct influence on the ultimate financial results they produce. You make the decisions on which property to buy, how it's managed, which mortgage option to use, which tenants you rent to and how you treat them. Even if you use a property management company, you are ultimately responsible and should be a part of the key decisions.

"As the owner, you can no longer say 'that's not my job' and pass on the responsibility to someone else; it all falls directly in your lap. That's the bad news. However, the good news is you and you alone are the recipient of all the profits you create. You are the leader and you will get compensated like one."

Richard was taking notes and looked up to say, "So I'm the president and CEO of my investment company, even if I only ever buy one property?"

"That's right; you're it. As your real estate investments grow, which they will if you follow what you're learning, you'll create relationships and contacts with others who will help you grow the business—but the bottom line is the buck stops with you."

I pulled a shiny new nameplate out of my briefcase and set it up so Richard could see the engraving: Richard McTavish, President and

CEO. "Every day this will remind you that this is *your* business and *you* are responsible for its results."

• • • •

Over the last five years, I've witnessed a mass exodus of people from the corporate world, some full time and others, like Richard, became part-time investors. These people are taking control of their financial future rather than relying on someone else to do it for them. It's true that many investors keep their jobs while investing in real estate; banks love people with great jobs due to the stable income. I have developed a job description for those coming to real estate from a corporate structure. It's designed to assist you in the mental transition from employee to successful real estate investor. It outlines the general duties of your new job as a real estate investor, whether full time or part time. As with all job descriptions, your new one details not only your actions, but also your responsibilities.

In the corporate world, your job description changes as you move up the ladder. In the real estate investing world, things are different; you start at the top of the company and stay at the top. You have only one position throughout your career.

At the outset many investors think of themselves as rebels and invent their responsibilities as they go along. Sadly, this is why so many fail early on. They don't treat real estate investment as a business; they treat it as a hobby.

The following is the job description I handed Richard. It describes not only the responsibilities, but also the personality traits that the most successful investors have adopted. I urge you to pay special attention to this description and to adopt all of the traits and responsibilities. There is no need to reinvent the wheel; just find one that's working and ride the momentum. By following this job description you will create momentum more quickly than you may have thought possible.

KEY INSIGHT

As you grow as an investor, you can find tasks you wish to delegate to a trusted professional, but no matter how much you delegate, you are ultimately responsible for the results.

Job Description of an Overachieving Real Estate Investor—Part I

Key Traits

In your new position of Real Estate Investment CEO, there are five traits you must avoid and four traits you must adopt immediately in order to become successful. No matter how smart, wealthy or experienced you are, these behaviours will either make or break you as a real estate investor.

Let's get the negative traits out of the way first so you can avoid each and every one of them. Some of them are ingrained habits that you must break, while others are emotions that need to be kept under control. The bottom line is this: if you keep these traits in your life, you will be an average or below-average investor and you will never be a superstar investor.

Traits to Avoid or Control

1. Negativity
2. Analysis Paralysis (fear)
3. Scarcity Mentality
4. Win–Lose Relationships
5. Lack of Follow-through or "Stick-to-it-ness"

1. **Negativity:** The world is filled with negativity. People can always find a reason for *not* doing something. We are bombarded every day with negative messages, negative news and negative comments from others. Most people allow this negative outlook to control their life. Your job as a real estate investor is to rise above this noise and focus on the key question: What do I need to do to achieve my Personal Belize? I don't mean that you should become a Pollyanna—realism is important. Just don't constantly look for the downside of everything. Continually ask "What's behind the curtain?" to discern whether you are being manipulated with negative messages.

2. **Analysis Paralysis (Fear):** Fear is such an overpowering and paralyzing emotion that this book provides you with a whole chapter on how to use it to your advantage. If fear begins to take you over in this new job, you will freeze and be afraid of taking a critical step. Many below-average investors feel very productive while analyzing properties, crunching the numbers, working through scenarios—that's the

no-risk component of real estate investing. Because analysis is no-risk, it can become comfortable. Many investors get fearful of the next step—making an offer. We call this analysis paralysis. Investors enjoy the analysis aspect of due diligence, but freeze when it comes to taking the leap to placing an offer to purchase. In this job, only by taking action and purchasing properties will you be successful. Imagine this: in 1949, your grandfather watched as a real estate boom hit your home-town. He didn't buy that property for $7,000 located on the corner because he thought it was too late and he feared the real estate boom was over. Today, that property is worth close to $750,000. Did fear cost him and his family wealth? Absolutely! As CEO of your business, you can't afford to allow fear to prevent you from taking action. If you ever feel fear holding you back, re-read Chapter 11 so you can break through it and get on with becoming successful. If you are prone to making excuses, understand that this is a symptom of fear!

3. **Scarcity Mentality:** Let's get this straight right off the top—no matter what anyone may tell you, there are enough worthwhile real estate deals in the marketplace for everyone. They will not run out. Society has programmed the majority of us into thinking that there is a limit to everything: a limited amount of money, a limited amount of deals, a limited amount of success. We've been programmed to turn every-thing into a race—we must beat the other guy because there is only one winner. I have seen this race mentality destroy hundreds (if not thousands) of average real estate investors across the country. Thinking of wealth creation as a race against someone or something will add a level of frustration and desperation that doesn't exist in the real world; it only exists in your mind. You'll soon discover that there is a deal of a lifetime around every corner. I look at real estate like a good transit system: if you miss one train, another one will quickly come along and if you miss one deal, another great one will come to you.

4. **Win–Lose Relationships:** Avoiding win–lose deals in real estate in-vesting is an important key to success. As CEO, you must focus on ensuring that all of the relationships you create are win–win. The gen-eral public believes that in order to become successful, you must make someone unsuccessful. True overachievers understand that in order to be successful over the long run you must help others to do the same. How do you do this? It's quite simple: help your bankers, lawyers and

realtors achieve their goals and the relationships you create with them will bring success to you more quickly than you ever expected. Ask them what *their* Personal Belize is, and do what you can to help it become real.

As others become winners around you and they enjoy working with you, you will find that more real estate deals will arrive at your door; more investors will want to work with you; your deals will close more quickly at the bank; and your lawyer will pay that extra attention to making sure your deal goes smoothly. It's like you've opened up a whole new, easy way of doing business. Look back at your life: who have you gone the extra mile for in the past? Those who have been enjoyable to be around or those who have taken advantage of every situation? That should tell you why it's important to help others win.

5. **Lack of Follow-through or "Stick-to-it-ness":** I believe this is the most damaging trait of all for the real estate CEO. The only way you can become successful is by sticking with the plan through the good times and the bad, through the ups and the downs, knowing that you're following a plan that has proven itself many times over. That is why your Personal Belize is so important—it will give you perspective and keep you on track, when the easy way out would be to quit. Now that you're following a proven Canadian real estate system, quitting only hurts you and your family. Yes, it's easy to quit when things aren't going exactly how you want them to. However, quitting is what the masses do; they wander back to their comfort zone and give up on taking control of their life. But based on the experience of thousands of overachieving investors, sticking to it will take you to your Personal Belize and beyond. And that is a financial place worth the extra effort.

The graph below outlines the difference between real life and how many people think life should be. The star represents achieving your Personal Belize. The straight line is how most people believe that life should be: set your goal and go straight to your dream, with no ups and downs. Real life is not like that. It's represented by the curved line. There are always ups and downs along the way; however, if you stay focused on your final outcome, your Personal Belize, you will be able to overcome the emotional swings along the way.

Keep this real life journey in perspective. Never allow the little setbacks to force you to quit or to kick you off your track. Wealth takes time to create—enjoy the process.

Success Is Not A Straight Line

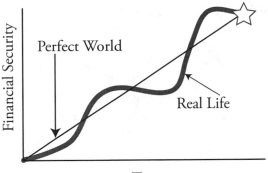

If you allow any one of these five negative behaviours to enter into your new life as CEO, you will create below-average results; you'll feel frustrated and then you'll start to make excuses why you are not doing better. If you're creating results (not excuses), you're still the CEO. If you are making excuses, then there are only two options:

1. Change your thinking to create better results.

   or

2. Fire yourself because you have allowed emotions to take over your decision-making process, and you have started to allow excuses or blaming others to creep into your life. At this point, it's over for you as an investor.

Traits to Adopt and Embrace

Now let's get to the good stuff. Below are the behaviours you *must* bring to the table if you are committed to being an above-average investor. Negative traits are the easy way out for people and have always been the easier behaviours to adopt. You'll find that some of these positive behaviours are initially more difficult to adopt on a consistent basis. However, if you are going to be successful, you have to take a path not often taken by the majority. Success comes from not following conventional wisdom.

While the following traits do break from conventional real estate investing wisdom, they'll help you stay the course and realize your Personal Belize more quickly:

1. **Energy, Enthusiasm, Commitment!**
2. **Ability to See Deals Where Others Fear to Tread**
3. **Willingness to Step Out of the Comfort Zone of the Majority**
4. **Insatiable Appetite for Knowledge**

1. **Energy, Enthusiasm, Commitment!:** This is absolutely paramount to your success. If you go into real estate investing as something you'll try for a little while to find out if you like it or not, you will fail. Wealth creation through real estate investing takes time. That means you must bring lots of energy and enthusiasm and commitment when you become the CEO of your real estate investments. This is true whether you invest in one property or hundreds.

2. **Ability to See Deals Where Others Fear to Tread:** The key here is to become an expert in the geographic area in which you're investing. Know the rents, know the prices, know of transportation changes—know the area better than anyone else. Use the analysis secrets you're learning in the ACRE system. By acquiring this knowledge and removing your emotions from the analysis, you will find deals where others cannot. While other investors analyze the properties based on the current conditions of the area or property, you will be analyzing them based on future potential, thus allowing you to see profits where others see only roadblocks.

3. **Willingness to Step Out of the Comfort Zone of the Masses:** As the CEO and leader of your company, you will continually need to think outside the box, creating solutions to problems, stretching the goals of your company and, most important, looking at situations from many different angles. The majority of Canadians live in what is called their comfort zone. This zone, if analyzed, is not very comfortable for most, characterized by low incomes, unstimulating jobs and underperforming investments (if they have any at all). It is called the comfort zone because people don't take on any additional challenges: they have hit a plateau; even though they know they could do better, they'd rather sit there. They don't get challenged by anything that might put extra pressure on them, so even though they may feel some frustration at how they are living, they believe that staying put is safer than moving off the plateau—a very sad and destructive place to be. Your new job will demand that you step off

this comfort plateau and challenge yourself constantly to do better. Complacency should never enter your mind as a leader and CEO.

4. **Insatiable Appetite for Knowledge:** You will never know everything you need to know—that's a given. As the CEO, you will continually be pushing yourself to learn more, looking for one new idea that will improve how you're doing what you're doing. Overachievers know that a $2,000 investment in a learning opportunity can provide them one simple idea that could make them $20,000 to $50,000 or even more. Cost is not considered—only results. Stretch yourself continually, but don't allow yourself to become distracted. Stay on the path to your Personal Belize and look for ways in which to improve your system.

Your Belief System—It's Up to You

Successful real estate investing is quite simple once you have the mindset and habits for success. As you progress and meet other successful investors, you will find a real similarity between them. You'll notice a calm confidence, a willingness to help others and unending energy. And as you adopt these same traits, you will attract more of these quality people into your life. Like attracts like in the real estate world.

A scarcity mentality is one of the toughest habits to break. The rest of the world believes there are only a limited number of real estate deals and a limited amount of investment capital, and you must fight to grab on to all that you can. Overachievers know there are unlimited deals and unlimited success. The only thing holding a person back is his or her belief system.

For instance, if you still believe there is only a limited amount of money out there to help fund your deals, all you need to do is to think about what you would do if someone came to you and helped put you in a real estate deal where you were making more money than you ever thought possible. You would probably proudly tell your close friends and family members all about the deal. You would be quite proud of the results.

The same holds true for other people you help become successful; they'll tell their friends and family how you helped. The better your real estate deals, the more people will want to invest with you. The more who invest, the more opportunities will come along. The key is working with solid deals and making sure that you surpass what you promise. What you'll find is that the more you associate with successful people, the more success will come your way.

Currently, you may or may not have access to successful people in your life. That's not a roadblock. The best place to start is by spending time with a network of like-minded, success-oriented real estate investors like those found in the real estate investment network. Look to groups where you can network with fellow investors and not be sold a load of books, tapes and seminars. Look for an environment of learning where you don't have to be constantly wondering what's behind the curtain.

The truly successful will have time for you because they too once were rookies and know how to help you. That's what successful people do. If you show initiative and drive, they will have all the time in the world for you. However, if you start to show any of the negative traits we mentioned earlier, they'll drop you like a hot potato. Sounds harsh, but it's true.

As the president and CEO of your new real estate company, you create the atmosphere and the work environment that you want. The reality is that your new life is up to you. Keep your job as you build wealth but remember: as the boss you are now in control of your financial future.

Here is the rest of your new job description, for the time when you've left your regular job behind. There are six key responsibilities in your new job. Each one of these responsibilities is as important as the other. Use the positive traits listed above and apply them to these six areas; you won't believe how simple success can be. However, if you ignore any of these areas of responsibility, you will be just another below-average investor.

JOB DESCRIPTION OF AN OVERACHIEVING REAL ESTATE INVESTOR—PART II

Duties and Responsibilities

As the CEO of your real estate company, you must focus on the following duties and responsibilities at all times.

1. **Build Key Relationships**
2. **Empower Your Team**
3. **Carry Out Due Diligence**
4. **Personally Sign Documents and Cheques**
5. **Be Accountable**
6. **Live the Dream**

1. **Build Key Relationships:** Relationships are the fuel of your real estate success. Many investors believe they need to be a lone wolf, hiding their work from others so they don't give away their secrets. That is a huge mistake. As discussed earlier, key relationships will make real estate investing easier and more profitable. As the CEO, you need to surround yourself with strong and supportive people.

2. **Empower Your Team:** Once you have developed your team and the relationships are starting to strengthen, you *must* get out of the way. Let these key members of your team do what they do best, under your direction and within your parameters. You set the tone, you set the goals, you set the rules and then you empower your team to maximize their talents. Remember, you are the "parent" of the company, while your team members are the babysitters of their respective areas, working under your direction. The clearer your directives are, the better the results will be. Your team consists of:

   - Property sources/realtors
   - Mortgage brokers and bankers
   - Property managers
   - Inspectors, appraisers, lawyers and an accountant
   - Other investors
   - Life partners and joint-venture partners

3. **Carry Out Due Diligence:** You and you alone are ultimately responsible for the bottom-line results of your real estate business. Your job is to be the visionary and the leader. The one thing that you never delegate is the due diligence on a property or area. As the CEO, you must wear the investigative hat—you personally make the final decision on which properties to purchase. That means you must stay up to date on the economics of towns and neighbourhoods where your Goldmine Score Card suggests you invest, continually look for opportunities others don't see, and watch for economic shifts, both positive and negative. Your instincts will get honed to a sharp edge as you pay more attention to what's behind the curtain, when hearing or reading media announcements. Stay true to the ACRE due diligence system and as the leader never skip a step. This will bring consistently good results for your company.

4. Personally Sign Documents and Cheques: As you purchase an increasing number of properties, you will discover that one of your key action steps will be signing your signature. You'll be signing lots of cheques and mountains of paperwork. Understand that each time you sign, you are in the process of creating wealth and freedom. Your job as the CEO is to understand everything that you are signing—never sign blindly just because someone tells you to. If you don't understand a document, have your lawyer explain it to you until you get it. There will be lots of repetition; the closing documents on a property will look like duplicates of the documents on properties you've bought previously, but that is not an excuse to pay less attention to what you're signing. Each signature represents a commitment. Make sure you're making commitments you can fulfill. Find a favourite pen, and make sure your signature is legible. Enjoy the process and remember every signature gets you closer to your goal. Remember, the more you sign, the more properties you buy.

PROCEED WITH CAUTION!

Never sign a document that outlines an action you do not have the intention of fulfilling. For instance, some lazy mortgage brokers will tell you that you must sign a document saying that you're going to move into a property you're about to purchase, even though you have no intention of doing so.

You'll hear that you have to (or others have to) in order to get a good interest rate or good terms. This is wrong and is bordering on bank fraud. If they find you have committed fraud, the bank will go after *you*—not the broker. There are wonderful brokers out there who will work hard and find you the right deal without putting you in harm's way.

Only make commitments you have every intention of fulfilling and that do not put you in a fraudulent position!

5. **Be Accountable:** You are in complete control, so you must be accountable for the results. That means when you make a mistake, you take full responsibility for it; that way you can take full responsibility for the good things. That's right: if you blame others for your mistakes, you must give them full credit for any good things that occur as well.

6. **Live the Dream:** The final duty you have as CEO is to live the dream. Real estate investing is a journey, not a destination, so enjoy the whole ride. There will be ups and downs along the way, so celebrate the highs and don't allow the lows to get too deep. The fun comes from solving the inevitable challenges, being creative in your thinking and, most important of all, in celebrating all of your accomplishments, both large and small. Find some way to reward yourself whenever you take action, for instance, when you place an offer, reward yourself with something small; when you close on a property, reward yourself with something really special. The key is to keep reinforcing that good things occur to you whenever you take action.

Here's the secret I've been saving until now. Real estate success is only 25 percent real estate-based. The remaining 75 percent is about life skills—skills you can transfer to any business. Don't get me wrong; that 25 percent that is real estate-focused is absolutely critical. Every step must be followed and every piece of information must be analyzed. However, if you follow only the real estate steps, you will be a less-than-average investor without all of the other strategies.

• • • •

Richard reviewed the job description and gave a knowing nod. "You know what? It's like you're reading my mind. I was just thinking that in all the meetings we've had only a few have been specific to real estate, which is unlike any real estate course I've ever taken."

"I warned you at the beginning of this process that we would be changing your life, making it more fun while at the same time helping you become wealthy."

Richard looked at his watch and said, "Oh no! It's already 6:25. Alison has a dance recital downtown at 7:00. I really have to get going. Sometimes this success thing gets in the way of real life, eh?"

"If you let it. Make sure the journey is fun for everyone around you. Include your family and friends whenever you can and their support will grow. Obsessing and spending every waking moment thinking about real estate will wear you out and definitely won't help your important relationships. Your family and friends are very important; don't let your pursuit of success get in the way of those relationships. Get going; I'll e-mail you the next exercise tonight."

• • • •

Now that you have grasped the underlying principles of your new career, you will have to take yourself to a whole new level of business knowledge. As the CEO of the business that you are building, you will have to develop an essential skill. This skill is not something you learn overnight; it is a talent that you develop over time and through experience. This critical skill is how to negotiate.

The good news is there are proven formulas and techniques that anyone can use to immediately improve their negotiation skills, and these secrets are what Richard and I are about to cover in detail. Get your highlighter ready as you'll want to make a lot of notations in the next chapter.

SOPHISTICATED INVESTOR ACTION STEP

It's time to get serious about achieving your Personal Belize. Only by clearly stating what you want and how you are going to achieve it can you make it come true. (Plus, you have to have some fun along the way.) You do not have to own any property yet to take these steps.

Go to your local stationery store and order the following:

1. A nameplate for your desk. Have it engraved with your name followed by the title CEO.
2. Business cards with your name and contact information, along with your title, Real Estate Investor. Use these to introduce yourself. You will be pleasantly surprised at the interest they will generate from realtors, bankers and others you meet.

Without a game plan, you'll always end up losing.
—Don R. Campbell

When Richard and I met again, two days had passed since our last meeting and he had received some good news. The bank's appraiser had assessed the property at a value that was slightly above what Richard was paying for the property. He had also spoken with the house inspector, and although the report wasn't finished, the inspector didn't find any serious problems with the property—only some minor cosmetic work would be needed. So far, so good! He was just waiting for the banker to say *yes*.

Now was the time to talk to Richard about the importance of negotiation strategies. Negotiation is an art form in and of itself and can take years to master. However, I have 18 very straightforward strategies and negotiation secrets that investors can start using immediately. And I decided to share these with Richard in this meeting.

"Richard, I'm sure you've noticed that, as a real estate investor, you will be negotiating on just about everything that you do from now on. Often even talking about negotiations can cause fear and uncertainty in a novice investor because, quite frankly, not a lot of people are taught the art of negotiating. Have you had much negotiations training in your life?"

Richard thought back to his training and said, "I remember watching my supervisors and boss negotiating with supplier and courier companies. It sounded more like demanding and yelling rather than negotiating. That's about the extent of my training. Of course, I thought I negotiated a good deal on my last car, but I wasn't very comfortable doing it. And as I was doing it, I was thinking there must be some tricks I don't know."

"Rich, there are a few companies that offer tremendous negotiation workshops to the public, and I highly recommend you attend one in the future. However, to save us all time and effort, I've developed 18 negotiating secrets that are both easy to use and very effective for real estate investors. They also work well in all areas of your life."

"Well, I hope they're as simple and easy as all the rest of the things you've taught me!"

"I think so; let's get to it! Most, if not all, successful real estate investors are successful negotiators, whether they have any formal training or not. In real estate, we are continually negotiating all aspects of a deal—from purchasing, to renovating, to managing, to selling—and each and every step of the way requires a certain level of negotiating skill."

"See, I knew there were some secrets behind the curtain. I wish you would have told me before I bought my last car!" Rich chuckled.

I smiled when I pictured Richard using the following strategies on his next car purchase. I urge you to pay very close attention to all 18 of these secrets as you can use them in all aspects of your life.

• • • •

THE TRUTH ABOUT NEGOTIATING

Some people consider themselves good negotiators because they can, at times, get the proverbial "blood out of a stone." Such people are focused on the short term and enjoy scooping the very last dollar off the table. However, if you plan on investing in real estate over a long term, this win–lose strategy will definitely slow down your progress. As discussed earlier, solid relationships are the key to creating long-term wealth, and if you enter each negotiation with a war mentality, you will destroy potential relationships before they have a chance to begin.

The occasional triumphs you can create with a confrontational attitude do not qualify as mastery of negotiations and, most important, they do not bring the long-term profits you should be looking for. By learning these simple strategies you will develop more long-term relationships, thus allowing you the time to go on to new challenges instead of dealing with yesterday's problems.

As a real estate investor, your negotiations will range from the small dollar amounts in a contract right through to the millions of dollars it takes to buy a major building. It is important to know that no matter what the dollar amount, the process is the same. These strategies have been tested and documented over the last 20 years and each is designed with one goal—to help you maximize long-term profits and build your reputation so people will bring you the easy deals as well as the tough ones.

There is human psychology behind a lot of the negotiation secrets you're going to discover, but the underlying foundation is building relationships while still getting what you need. It's human nature to work with people you like and who treat you well. If you follow these strategies, you'll be well respected by bankers, realtors, investors and family members. Business people will feel good about working with you and will often give you first right-of-refusal on opportunities.

To reach the level of success you want, and to achieve your Personal Belize, it is imperative that you practise the art of negotiating. You need to understand the "poetry" of negotiating, and you need to take negotiating finesse to a whole new level. This will ensure that the next time you're putting together a complex but profitable real estate transaction, you will have the tools to get what you want and at the same time give others what they want.

Although the saying "Money makes the world go 'round!" may be true in a very general sense, if you look behind the curtain and analyze what really happens, you'll see that it's negotiations that make the world go around. Without negotiations, either simple or complex, money does not change hands. So before money moves, negotiations must take place.

For example, the last time you went to a movie, you entered into a short negotiation. The theatre offered a price for a movie and you accepted that price. You probably didn't get into a huge discussion over the price with the manager, because you thought that the market price was set and you could afford it. You probably participated in this negotiation unconsciously.

Many people don't understand that without some sort of negotiation (a dialogue between someone who has something and someone who wants it), deals would not be signed, contracts wouldn't exist and the engine of the economy would seize up. Hence, money would stop flowing.

 **KEY INSIGHT**

> By understanding that *negotiations make the world go 'round,* the better you'll master the art of negotiation and the easier life will become.

What Exactly Are Negotiations?

Negotiations can be as significant as those that surround the Israeli/Palestinian peace accord, or they can be as relatively unimportant as buying a used record at a flea market. Negotiations occur every day in both our business and personal lives. To be successful in either arena, it is vital that you learn how to negotiate. The secret to your success will come from finding a way to make each and every one of the following negotiation strategies fit every situation.

Nothing is either as simple or as complex as negotiating. Every desire that demands satisfaction and every want or need that is required to be fulfilled is a potential situation for negotiation. Whenever people exchange ideas with the intention of creating relationships, whenever they confer for agreement, whenever money changes hands—each case is a matter of negotiating.

Consider these more obvious negotiating situations: buying a piece of property, buying or selling a car or haggling with the street vendors in Mexico. In these situations, you know you are negotiating, and you can simply apply the secrets you're about to learn.

This principle becomes a little more complex when you enter situations that you may not perceive as negotiations. These include situations such as going grocery shopping (the store offers food at a price and you accept it), buying season's tickets for a musical series or sporting team (you're offered a discount if you buy the whole season, and you either accept it or ask for further reduction), deciding where to go to dinner with your group of friends (you try to fulfill everyone's wants and needs) or driving your car (you trust in other drivers, making positive assumptions about their actions and knowledge). Negotiations even occur at home with your family.

There are very clear rules to successful negotiations. You should use all of them in every negotiation. Use your highlighter to mark the points you feel are key to your situation.

PROCEED WITH CAUTION!

In this chapter the word *opponent* is sometimes used to describe the other party in the negotiations. It is not intended to mean *adversary*. I do not condone adversarial negotiations. In fact, if negotiations become adversarial, it is much more productive just to walk away.

The Eighteen Rules of Negotiation

Rule 1: Set Goals and Write Them Down

Before negotiations start, make sure you have specific goals. When you are setting your goals, make them realistic. Include the absolute worst outcome you will accept as well as the best you could possibly get. If you are negotiating on a piece of property, know your bottom and top price. Don't just set goals on price; set them for the terms of the deal, including the date you want possession, the list of items in the house you must have and any other key item you require. Write these points down in advance of the negotiation.

In real estate investment, often it is more profitable to give in on price—if you get the terms you want. In over 90 percent of transactions, you will find a vendor's main focus is the selling price. However, if you are employing the ACRE system, price is not as critical as the terms of the deal. For instance, in real estate it often makes sense to give the vendor his or her full asking price if you get an extra long closing date and special financing conditions.

The clearer your goals are, the more powerful you will feel in the negotiation. Keep your goals in mind while negotiating and do not stray from them.

Rule 2: Have an Agenda and a Plan

In addition to setting goals, it is imperative that you have an agenda. You cannot negotiate by the seat of your pants and expect to win. In fact, planning is the most important step in any negotiation. Be sure to plan your meeting in advance! Think through how you want the discussion to progress. How do you plan to open the negotiation? What will your opening offer be? What do you expect the other party to open with? What compromises will you offer? What won't you compromise on? As you write down these steps, you will see the weak areas in your argument. Be prepared with responses to these weaknesses, because the person you're negotiating with will surely question them.

If you have a strong agenda, you will come across as prepared and professional, which puts you in a much better bargaining position. The physical act of writing out your agenda will bring items to the surface you hadn't initially thought of. As you create your agenda, use these 18 negotiating rules as your guide. Make sure you address all of them in your agenda, thus ensuring you are ready for all situations that may develop during the discussions.

KEY INSIGHT

> The number one reason people do poorly in a negotiation is their failure to prepare an agenda.

RULE 3: CREATE A RELATIONSHIP, NOT AN ARMED CAMP

In creating a relationship, you will ensure that you get what you want, while providing the other party with wins too. To create a relationship, minimize the differences between you and the other party. To do that, you need to search for common ground. For example: I was involved in a real estate deal where the seller had received two offers on his property. The realtor who had brought one of the offers mentioned that the buyer was an airline pilot. The seller perked up and started asking questions: how long had he been flying, what kinds of planes? It turned out that the seller had been a pilot in the Korean War. The seller ended up accepting the offer from the pilot even though it was $2,500 less than the other offer because he felt an affinity to the buyer. Never manipulate a relationship for financial gain; just make sure that you are looking for common ground where both parties can relate.

RULE 4: SEEK THE WIN–WIN DEAL

One key to productive business relationships is discovering how to create situations that benefit all parties involved. Although you enter the negotiations with the intent of getting the ultimate deal, it would be detrimental if you leave little or no profit in it for the other party. The skilful negotiator moves his or her business ahead to success while helping the other parties do the same.

Many people think that the hard-nosed, take-it-or-leave-it nego-tiator who squeezes every last nickel out of the other side is the best negotiator. In fact, nothing could be further from the truth. Great negotiators always try to ensure that they win, while giving the other side something that they need or want. Always think win–win. In a win–win negotiation, both sides achieve what they want and the discussions are more fun and often more profitable. In a win–lose negotiation, the loser feels dejected and demoralized—and if asked if they would do another deal with the purchaser, the answer would be *no*! And if the other party ever did have to negotiate with the individual again, they would be playing to get even.

How can both sides of a negotiation win, you might ask? The answer lies in your attitude and in your problem-solving skills. In order for both sides to win, you can't subscribe to the limited-pie theory, based on the assumption that the pie is only so big and there is no more to divide up. The pie, in fact, is only limited if you both want exactly the same thing. Different people want different things. In negotiating you cannot assume the other person wants the same thing as you. To do so is a serious mistake. Find out what the other person would like to accomplish and figure out how that fits with what you want; then negotiate a win for both sides.

As you grow your real estate business, you'll find you're willing to pay a little extra to people you trust to perform what they promise, who always produce quality work and who understand your needs. You'll also find this street goes both ways. If people know and trust you, they will gladly pay you more or bring you the best deals first.

Rule 5: Separate People from the Problem

In order to succeed at the game of negotiations, you must discover how to focus on the facts at hand and not let the other person's personality affect your decisions. Just like in analyzing a piece of real estate, it is imperative to remove your emotions from the transaction and focus on the facts. Always view the situation from the other person's perspective. Put yourself in his or her shoes and figure out how the situation looks from both sides. You'll then have a clearer view of the problem and can focus on the solution.

If you are in a long and protracted negotiation, try a little role reversal. After you have ended for the day, play the part of your opponent and have someone you know and trust play your part. The insights you gain from this short exercise will prove to be invaluable the next time you meet face to face with your opponent. Make notes of these insights; they often will prove to be the breakthrough you are looking for.

Rule 6: Focus on Motivations, Not Taking Positions

The key motivators for you could be many: the purchase price, your requirement for early access to show the property to potential renters or even a specific closing date. The key is to try and determine what the other party's motivators are. A very powerful way to unlock a deadlocked situation is to figure out the other party's motivations and then figure out how to fulfill them without jeopardizing your own position.

Once you've identified the other person's motivations, use this information to your advantage. Look for areas where you can accept a compromise. Start by giving in on positions that are important to the other party but not to you. For example, you might give the vendor the exact possession date he or she needs while getting a break on the price in exchange. Or, if the vendor is in financial trouble, solve his or her problem by explaining how selling quickly to you will save his or her credit rating. By proposing to complete the deal quickly, speed becomes the important factor, not the price.

The way to discover a vendor's motivation is to ask thoughtful questions and listen very carefully to the answers. Take notes while the vendor responds. This is a powerful listening strategy that makes the other party feel that his or her point is important. Then read the concerns back to the vendor. Use the phrase, "This is what I heard you say were your biggest concerns" and go on to list them.

By conceding early on the points that are not that important to you, you'll establish an atmosphere of cooperation. You have then created a situation where the other party will feel obligated to give in on concerns that are important to you. For instance, in a real estate deal, if you discovered that the seller was pressed for a quick sale and you wanted to get a good price, you might say, "I understand that getting the house sold and moving to your new city in 30 days is very important for you. If I were to give you the exact possession date that you require, what kind of a price would you be willing to sell for?"

Notice how you have filled a need and have provided the other party with a situation wherein he or she can return the favour. And you did it all without compromising your position.

Rule 7: Search for Agreement

The words "Do you agree?" are a powerful tool. Use them often and use them early to encourage the other party to keep repeating the word *yes*! Tie this tactic in with Rule 6. Wherever possible, create empathy as you look for room to negotiate by trying to discover the areas where both sides agree or share interests. Get agreement on small points. It's like putting small weights on one side of a balance scale; eventually you'll get enough weight on your side that it will carry the big negotiating point. For example, you might reach small agreements on the possession date, the amount of the deposit, the financial terms, which appliances stay with the property, etc. You've come so far in the negotiations; now all you have to do is settle on the price!

Rule 8: Listen Only to Reason, Not Pressure

Unskilled negotiators will often use pressure tactics such as "We have another buyer looking at the property tomorrow," or "This offer is good today only," or worst of all, "That's the deal ... take it or leave it!" These high-pressure tactics are designed to manipulate you into making a decision. Do not allow yourself to be pulled into the trap.

In negotiating, use only reason and logic to state your position, and be open only to reason and logic from the other party. Yielding to pressure sets a bad precedent; this is true when dealing with a vendor, a tenant or a contractor. Responding to pressure tactics will set you up for additional pressure tactics later on. If you feel yourself coming under undue pressure, it is important to invite the other party to state the reasoning behind his or her stand or be ready to call his or her bluff (see Rule 9).

Rule 9: Be Willing to Walk Away from the Table

This is one of the most powerful cards you have in your hand as you play the negotiating game. It gives you the ultimate power. You must be willing to walk away from a deal if things are heading to a conclusion that does not fit your goals. Just because the negotiations have gone on for a while doesn't mean you have to continue them.

I'll reiterate: real estate is like a good transit system. If this property goes by, another one will come your way soon. So there is no need to buy in a panic; knowing that puts you in a position of power.

When you do walk away, however, leave the relationship on a high. Use a "more in sorrow than in anger" approach. In other words, leave the door open for the negotiation to continue if the other party chooses. You might say something like, "I'm sorry, but that's far more than I want to pay. I really would like to do business with you, but I can't under these terms. If you can come up with another way we can do this deal, I'd be glad to listen. Call me."

This proves that you're serious and shows the other party that you won't be manipulated into making a bad decision. Once you've made the other party aware that it doesn't matter if you buy it, you have transferred more power in your hands. This approach will also stop the vendor from trying other tactics. As an aside, the first time you do walk away, you'll be pleasantly surprised at how good it feels. Walking away from what could have been a bad deal is very self-empowering. Learn to do this and you'll never get caught in a bad deal.

One critical thing to remember: only walk away if you haven't completed an agreement. If you have come to an agreement, both parties have negotiated well and the deal has been confirmed from both sides—the door to walk away has closed. That is why it's critical that you do your homework before you finalize a deal (see Rule 13).

Rule 10: Silence Is Golden

Or, perhaps more appropriately, "When in doubt, say nothing!" When you encounter an opponent who won't budge from his or her position, sometimes the best tactic is to say nothing! This is especially effective if you are in a purchasing position. Silence creates an air of stalemate and 99.5 percent of the time the other party feels obliged to break it. An old rule of thumb is, "He who talks first, loses!" Great salespeople know this. They ask you a question such as, "Would a possession date of 30 days fit your plans?" and then they keep their mouth shut!

Sometimes this silence can last for what feels like an eternity. Some people call this a pregnant pause, and it truly can be! During this silence, your opponent is probably conceiving (pun intended) what to give in on to make you happy and close the deal. If you have to, bite your lip to keep from talking, but keep silent. Leave the ball in your opponent's court.

Rule 11: He or She Who Mentions a Number Loses First

This is a truism when negotiating not only price but also possession date, access to the property, terms, etc. Your preparation has helped you decide your top and bottom prices, and you also know the payment terms and closing dates you need. With this preparatory work done, you have an advantage. However, just because you know your game plan, there is no need to be in a hurry to reveal it. Sit back and wait for the appropriate time. Sometimes the other party may need a little prodding and, if it comes to that, just outright ask for his or her price, terms or delivery schedule.

A few techniques to get the other party to put their price on the table first include:

- **Trial balloon.** You say something like, "Would there be any sense in looking at an offer of $xxxx?" If it is a good price, the other party will say *yes*. If not, he or she may divulge a number or just say *no*. If he or she says *no*, you can say, "I didn't think so, but what would be a good number for you?" This will usually get the other party to put his or her price out.

- **Disinterest.** Don't show a lot of interest in what the other party is selling. You might say, "This isn't really the type of property I was looking for. Although, I suppose, if the price were right I might be interested. What would you let it go for?"
- **Kick start.** Make an offer that is crazily low. It usually brings a startled response from the other party. You then say, "Well, what did you have in mind?" Psychologically, the vendor will choose a figure closer to his or her bottom line because he or she will try to minimize the difference between the two numbers. A word of caution: don't use this technique unless your relationship is quite strong. This tactic can cause anger in the other party; you could lose face in the negotiation and the vendor may outright refuse to negotiate with you.

Implementing rule 11—not mentioning a price—usually puts the onus on the other party to do so. In addition, when the vendor does mention the price, he or she may state terms that are better than those for which you were prepared to ask. Also, on a surprising number of occasions, the vendor will even start off with a price already lower than what you were prepared to pay. So, silence can truly prove to be golden.

RULE 12: NEGOTIATE ONLY WITH THE DECISION-MAKER

Always negotiate only with the person who has decision-making authority. You can waste hours of your time negotiating with people who pretend they have authority, only to learn that you have to start the process all over again with their superior or their partner. In a real estate deal, especially involving a "For Sale by Owner," always ask the party you're talking to if that party can make the deal or if there is a partner involved, too, who will be part of the decision-making process. Otherwise, whenever it comes down to the crunch, after hours of discussions, the person will refer to the other party, as in "I'll have to talk to my spouse first."

The vendors may even try to use a tactic called "good cop, bad cop," so named because you see it used on TV detective shows. One person takes a likeable, easygoing approach with you, while the other takes a tough stand. The tough guy (or bad cop) will usually be absent. The good cop will say he or she would like to make the deal but knows the bad cop will never go for it. When this tactic is used well, the good cop also plays on your emotions by saying something like, "I took your offer to my wife (bad cop) and she is really ticked at me for even bringing it up. I'm in real trouble now. Can you help me out? Could you give me $xxxx?" Don't fall for this obvious tactic. Remember, you should only negotiate with reason, not by responding to pressure. If the vendor tries this tactic, ask him or her to bring along the other party so that everyone concerned can discuss the deal.

Rule 13: Do Your Homework and Know Your Options

I know it sounds like a lot of work, but would you turn down an opportunity that can return huge rewards? I didn't think so. Before you enter any serious negotiations, you must know your stuff! You should at least have background information and pricing references for the industry or product you are about to discuss. You wouldn't buy a digital camera without doing some comparison shopping for models, prices, warrantees, etc. Why would you enter into a real estate negotiation without at least a minimal amount of pertinent information? Without reliable background information, you cannot make good business decisions. In addition, if you enter any negotiations without doing your homework, your chances of being caught in a bad deal increase exponentially.

During your research, pricing knowledge is important and is easy to find. But don't stop there. A little more homework will present you with options you may not have even considered, such as the knowledge of a number of similar properties that have all come for sale at the same time and automatically increase the seller's competition.

Talk to other people who are selling in the area. An innocuous question about "the house down the street" will often give you a lot of useful information. Keep your eyes and ears open at all times, and opportunities will reveal themselves. If the property has been a "grow op" in the past, the neighbours will know and you can confirm this because you'll have done the police checks. This knowledge will be very useful when negotiating for the property.

If you enter negotiations lacking knowledge of your options, you'll be forced into single-issue bargaining—usually over price. By focusing on just one issue, you will end up settling for a mediocre deal. The person with the best information in a negotiation is usually in the stronger position.

SOPHISTICATED INVESTOR STRATEGIES:
EXTRA TIPS FOR NEGOTIATING ON THE PHONE

Due to the busy schedules we all have, there comes a time when negotiating over the telephone is unavoidable. Here are some common pitfalls that you must keep in mind:

- The caller always has the advantage of surprise and is the best prepared.
- Important points are easily omitted or assumed.
- It is impossible to read the other person's body language.
- It is much easier for the other party to say *no* when they don't have to look you in the eye.

Avoid negotiating over the phone whenever possible. But when using the phone is unavoidable, take it seriously! Here are some quick Do's and Don'ts:

Do's
1. Talk less! The less you talk, the more your opponent will feel the need to fill the space (see also rules 9, 10, 11 and 16).
2. If your opponent calls you, just listen and take notes. Then call him or her back with your side of the story. This will allow you time to prepare a proper response.
3. If you have to initiate the call, develop a checklist to avoid omissions and assumptions.
4. Re-state agreements in your own words and confirm the terms upon which you both have agreed.
5. Have an excuse ready to break off the discussion. This will allow you to bow out gracefully if needed.
6. *Be prepared!* Don't ignore rules 2 and 13 just because this is a phone call instead of an eye-to-eye meeting. Telephone negotiating can work, but only if you are prepared!

Don'ts
1. Don't push yourself into a quick decision. Telephone negotiating can create a false sense of urgency where parties feel pressured to close the deal.
2. Don't negotiate an issue to conclusion until both parties understand the process for solidifying the deal. For example, how will things be put into writing? By a lawyer, a letter of confirmation, notations on a faxed order form, etc.?
3. Don't negotiate when you are involved in another activity, e.g., during a meeting or staff review, as you will not be completely focused on the negotiating process.

*Source: The Training Company

Rule 14: Find Your Point of Power

Generally, the power in negotiations lies with the person holding the chequebook. But as you'll see, power grows from several different sources. Find the one that fits your role in each negotiation.

- **The power of risk-taking.** How risky is this venture to you? If you feel that you must have this deal no matter what, then you're working from a very limited power base. On the other hand, if you're willing to walk away from the deal, the power is all in your corner. Desperation does not make for a strong negotiating position.

- **The power of information.** People tend to defer to those who seem to be experts. If you gather enough information, you can position yourself as an expert and create a power base for yourself. Your opponents don't have to know that you only started to research the situation last month.

- **The power of past performance.** A track record in real estate can be a trump card when dealing with suppliers. Take, for example, how professional you can look in negotiations with a vendor when you state that you've bought five properties this year, every one of them closed on time and in each case the vendors left happy. As you legitimize your company as a "player," your comments and requirements will be taken much more seriously. When you're able to offer evidence of a positive track record of your past purchases, you will move your power rating up a couple of notches.

- **The power of a good reason.** The first thing to do when looking for the best price on anything is to find a reason why you should be able to buy it for less. Does it need work? Is the area considered tough? Has it been for sale a long time? Did a comparable property just sell for less than what the vendor wants? Be imaginative. Be outrageous. You don't necessarily have to be logical.

- **The power of approach.** The way you approach the other party can influence the outcome. If you approach the vendor with a hard-nosed, take-it-or-leave-it approach, the other party is likely to leave it. If your approach is genuine, as in, "I'd really like to do business with you if we can come to an agreement," the other party is more likely to try to come to an agreement with you.

- **The power of emotion.** Sometimes it isn't the money that's important in a negotiation—it's what the money represents. When looking to sweeten a deal, always look for the things that have a high emotional value. A vendor may not want to give up that last $1,000 on the deal, but often the pot can be sweetened with something with higher emotional value. Hockey tickets, for instance. Help the vendor picture himself sitting with his son on the blue line at tomorrow night's hockey game and he may just forget about that last $1,000. Human responses can be quite illogical. Why do you think so many companies buy those outrageously expensive season's tickets? Once again, both parties leave happy having received satisfaction from the deal!

RULE 15: BE PATIENT
Whenever possible, don't negotiate under any type of time constraints. The old "80/20 rule" applies in negotiations as well: 80 percent of the concessions happen in the final 20 percent of the negotiating time. Act as if you have all the time in the world, even if you don't. Keep most of your concessions to the end. As in poker, play your hand slowly and deliberately. If you do find yourself under time constraints, negotiate the major items first.

RULE 16: BE CONFIDENT
People have a tendency to attack weakness. Your best defence is to show only strength. After some preliminary discussions, start the real negotiations by saying something like, "Well, when we do this, we usually …" The other party will perceive you as a veteran at this type of deal. It also legitimizes any further statements you make regarding past performance.

Once you become very practised, you can feign signs of vulnerability in areas where you want to direct your opponent. Much like the hockey goaltender, show the other party the corner, knowing full well that he or she will shoot there. What the other party doesn't know is that you want him or her to shoot for the corner, as that's where you excel at stopping the puck! It isn't difficult to make the other party perceive they're in control, even though it is still you who is directing the pace of the negotiating process.

RULE 17: NEVER ABUSE; ALWAYS AMUSE

Never abuse your opponent! The old adage of catching more flies with honey than vinegar is very true in constructive negotiations and the building of long-term business relationships. You'll get much farther by using the line, "I simply could not afford to pay you what you think this property is worth," instead of using the adversarial line, "You must be kidding! You want *that much* for this piece of junk?"

RULE 18: FOLLOW THROUGH

Last, but not least, it is imperative that you live up to your end of the agreement. If you've negotiated a deal, you probably promised something (money, action), so you must complete your end of the contract.

Weaseling on a deal creates a precedent for the other party to renege on their responsibilities. This results in a very awkward, time-wasting and non-productive relationship. In addition, the other party in the deal probably has friends and business contacts, who are sure to hear about your inability to live up to your commitments. Bad reputations are easy to get and hard to lose!

• • • •

Trying to remember all of these tactics may seem a little daunting at the beginning, but after using them for a while, you'll discover they become second nature. I urge you to use these negotiating tools in all aspects of your life, not just in real estate. You will soon be positively surprised with the results and the confidence your successes will provide you.

SOPHISTICATED INVESTOR ACTION STEP

Keep a summary list of the 18 Rules for Street-Smart Negotiating close at hand. As a registered reader of this book, you can download a full copy from www.reincanada.com.

Post it on your bulletin board or put it on your desk. Commit the rules to memory. Make the secrets become second nature and use them at every opportunity you get.

The big secret in life is that there is no big secret. Whatever your goal, you can get there if you're willing to work.

—Oprah Winfrey

Richard looked up from his negotiations notes with a smile. "Boy, these negotiating strategies are filled with a lot of common sense. These ACRE system checklists and rules make it easy."

"That's what they're designed to do. All right, when are you going to try out these tactics?"

"I've already thought of that. I completed the due diligence on a duplex in that transition neighbourhood I told you about and the numbers look great. I found it in a for-sale-by-owner ad in the newspaper while I was waiting to meet my banker to talk about the first deal. So I'll be sitting down with the vendor tomorrow after work. I can hardly wait to try this approach. Emma didn't get to see the first property, but she's excited about being involved with the second one. Wait until she sees me in action with these negotiations!"

I nodded in agreement. "I think that's a great strategy. Make sure only one of you negotiates with the vendor over price and terms; that way the vendor won't feel ganged-up on. And you know what might happen? Emma might end up finding more properties than you because she can devote more time to it now that her work hours have been cut back. That's a huge opportunity for both of you!"

"The second part of the plan," Richard continued, "is to go out and celebrate with a nice dinner right after we submit our offer, whether the vendor accepts it or not. I now understand why you're so positive and upbeat all the time; you have a family and a team that supports what you do and you celebrate with them. Now that's success!"

"Okay, Richard, go and get your offer accepted. Remember everything we discussed about presenting offers, including attaching a cover letter and giving the vendor at least two options to choose from. I think you'll be pleasantly surprised with your results on this one."

"All right! I'll phone you as soon as I have a deal," Richard said confidently.

"Wait! Before you run out, I must warn you about something. Many investors get caught up in the excitement of making the deal and they forget about finishing what they've already started. Don't let this property distract you from closing on your first deal. You still have bankers, lawyers and inspectors to deal with."

"I've got it under control. Emma has already ordered the inspection, and we have already sat down with the banker for our initial discussions," Rich called out as he checked his watch and headed towards the door. "I'll call you as soon as I have news. I can't wait to try out these negotiating tactics."

• • • •

Two weeks passed and during this time I hadn't heard much from Richard and Emma. I knew that pulling the deal together would be time-consuming, but he had sent me e-mail updates on their progress.

Emma arranged a professional property inspection that had gone very well. The inspector noted a few minor issues with the downspouts and the furnace needed servicing, neither of which caused any major concern.

At the same time, Richard and Emma were working with their banker, building a strong relationship. They had decided to work with a banker they'd known a few years, and the results were quite amusing. They were nervous when they presented their Sophisticated Investor Binder and box of donuts. The first words out of the banker's mouth were, "So, when did you start using the ACRE system?" Obviously this banker had dealt with investors before.

The bank arranged a conservative market appraisal of the property, and the property was assessed at slightly above what they were paying for it. That was good news. Finally I received the call.

"We got it!" were the first words I heard as I picked up the phone. No "hello" or "how are you"—just "We got it!" Both Richard and Emma were on the line, and both sounded very excited.

"That's fantastic," I enthused.

"The bank has just given us a written confirmation letter. There are no additional conditions we have to meet. In other words, the property is going to be ours. We take possession in just over a month."

"Great! What have you been doing since finding out?" I inquired, as sometimes a month can be a short time to get all the paperwork registered, especially in some jurisdictions in Canada.

"The lawyer you recommended already has the paperwork. We followed your system and gave him the details and the contracts at the same time we gave them to the bank, so he could get started. He's already up to speed. The bank says they will have no problem getting their lawyers to have the paperwork in time. You're right, it's great dealing with a bank that understands the value of relationships! So right now it's out of our hands."

"Sounds like you've got this all under control. It really is easy when you follow a system, isn't it?"

"Sure is. And you know what else? Remember that duplex we were looking at as a possible second property? Well, our offers were rejected two weeks ago, but we decided to do our due diligence on it anyway, just for practice."

"How would the numbers have turned out, if you had got it?" I asked.

"That's the funny part. The numbers would have worked great. In fact, we were going to buy it and make the one unit our home and rent out the other. This would have allowed us to live for half of what we're paying today, and the building is located near a great school. We planned on using the ACRE system to buy our own home.

"We were disappointed that we didn't get it. And then the telephone rang. We were expecting a call from our banker and answered with, "Did we get it?" The voice on the other end of the phone hesitated for a moment and then said, "Yes." But it wasn't our banker. It was the owner of the duplex saying he was accepting one of our offers. He said the whole time he had it listed, we were the only ones who treated him with respect and confidence. He said he had a couple of other offers, for roughly the same price, but he always felt those purchasers were pushing him. So that's why he accepted our offer—we gave him a choice and never pressured him."

I said, "This won't be the last time this happens to you, using multiple offers."

"If the inspection goes well, it looks as if we'll soon have our second investment property and our own house to live in. You have no idea how much this ACRE system has brought our family together and opened our eyes to opportunities," Emma said with a real sparkle in her voice.

"Remember, this is just the beginning of a fun and profitable three-year journey. But at this stage, you should definitely go out, all four of you, and celebrate all that you've accomplished in such a short time.

Most investors will take a little longer than you have to get their first couple of properties. The added bonus for you is that you also are getting a house you'll live in—giving you even more control of your life."

"Don," Emma said, "you have no idea how much we are looking forward to owning our own home. We never, in our wildest dreams, thought we ever would. Our banker even told us about ways in which we can get this property for very little down payment because it will be our residence. That's exciting."

"Yes, these ACRE strategies work for rental properties as well as buying a personal residence.

"Obviously, the next thing you will be learning about is being a landlord. I can't wait to teach you all of the secrets and systems that make this easy as well. Suffice it to say that, in real estate investments, the relationship you develop with your tenants is the most important business relationship you'll have. We'll talk about how to choose and keep long-term tenants and how to reduce your maintenance and operations costs."

Richard piped in, "I bet there will be systems and checklists to follow."

Emma chuckled at this remark.

"Of course! It wouldn't be a very good system without that, now would it?" I said wryly. "But we'll leave that for another day as your first property already has a good tenant in it, and your second one doesn't close for a couple of months. Congratulations and get out there and celebrate!"

Note to the Reader

You will discover, along with Richard and Emma, the secrets of landlording. As a registered user of this book you will also have access to further information. Make sure you register at www.reincanada.com

True success lies in having the will to take the steps required to make your Personal Belize come true.

—Don R. Campbell

At the start of this book, Richard and Emma began a journey that will lead them increasingly closer to their Personal Belize. As I write this chapter, it is now just over three years since Richard and I met on that flight from nowhere, and the difference in his and his family's life today is remarkable.

Yes, he still has a job. Real estate hasn't provided him with complete financial freedom in just three years. The good news is his job has changed for the better. About one year after Richard bought his first two properties (yes, Richard and Emma bought the duplex, where they live), one of the suppliers he'd been dealing with for years through his day job noticed a remarkable change in Richard's attitude. He was more pleasant to be around, his negotiation skills had become honed and there was a spark that the supplier had never seen in Richard before.

One day, he took Richard for lunch and offered him a new job. It pays a little more, but more important, it provides Richard with much more flexibility in managing his time. In his new job, Richard meets with clients out of the office. Driving around town is a bonus for Richard as it gives him the opportunity to visit different neighbourhoods and to see more properties.

But perhaps the best news to come out of his job change is that Richard's new boss is investing with Richard. Richard provides the real estate expertise, and his boss provides some investment capital. A true win–win relationship. Richard's boss is too busy to find good pieces of real estate and therefore loves this opportunity to take advantage of the real estate market through Richard.

With Richard's new job and freedom, he and Emma now own five revenue-generating properties in their target area. These properties, which have a total of nine suites, are all creating positive cash flow, which has allowed Emma to leave her part-time job to focus on her mom, her family and, of course, real estate. Richard and Emma began with nothing more than a dream, a small amount of cash and some determination, and already they are seeing amazing results.

Because they bought in an area that fit the Goldmine Score Card, and due to Richard's increasing talents as a negotiator, many of their properties have already dramatically increased in value, making their personal net worth grow right along with it. What they don't know is this is just the beginning. Soon they will be learning advanced real estate techniques, techniques that build on the foundation they have already created. Although we can't call Richard "rich" yet, it's obvious that he will live up to his name not too far down the road—all because he's followed a proven system and does not allow excuses or distractions to get in his way.

Richard and I continue to converse via e-mail as he and Emma ask for assistance in reviewing their due diligence and offer-to-buy options. On one property, we exchanged e-mails for 12 days. In their last e-mail, they stated that they had finally walked away from the deal, despite their enthusiasm for the property. The deal didn't fit the system well enough. This was a huge success story.

You may ask, how can walking away from a deal be a success story? It's really rather simple: Richard and Emma have learned to remove their emotions from the process and wait for the right property, a sign of a potentially great investor. If the system says no, successful investors listen and walk away from the deal. There are lots of properties out there; your job as an ACRE system user is to invest only in properties that fit the system.

Richard's e-mail detailed how, one day after they had walked away from the property, they found another property only two blocks away. It not only fit the system by providing them a positive cash flow, it was below market value.

The ACRE system works, if you allow it to. Here are two real-life stories from investors who have been using the ACRE system. I've included them to illustrate how you, no matter what your age or financial level, can create amazing results of your own. In the stories you will find additional lessons, not mentioned elsewhere in the book. Read these stories with your highlighter in hand, and mark the areas and ideas you can use in your life. Then, when you're finished, make a commitment to yourself to create a success story of your own. For additional success stories, make sure you visit the Real Estate Investment Network™ (REIN™) website at www.reincanada.com and click on the Success Stories link. Many have used these stories to inspire them to take action and create results. You'll be amazed at how easy it is to create success using a combination of the ACRE system and a little persistence.

Sharon and Amy Join Forces—with Amazing Results

Amy's Story

I grew up in a household where we believed your home was your castle. At that time I didn't really understand what that meant, but I sure do now. My family moved to Calgary in 1972 and my parents purchased a home in the middle-class neighbourhood of Dalhousie. They paid a whopping $32,000 for a three-bedroom, four-level split with a single attached garage. At the time, the price was outrageous! I mean, people were only earning $7,000 a year and to pay that much for a house was insane. Little did my parents know that Calgary's real estate market was about to take off—and so were interest rates.

In 1980, my parents and I were out for a Sunday afternoon drive and we came across a few new houses being built on the Bow River in a community called Bowness. The next thing I knew, we were moving. My parents put our Dalhousie home on the market and it sold in a matter of weeks for over $130,000. In less than eight years, my parents had increased their net worth by $100,000 without even trying! Once again, I really didn't understand what that meant other than the fact I had to pack my room in preparation for the move.

I completed a Bachelor of Commerce degree at the University of Calgary and started my first real job with Petro-Canada. I was immediately transferred to Vancouver. I became a first-time renter and after three years of shelling out $740 a month on rent, I thought it would be a good time to buy my own place. But there was one thing that got in my way. No, it wasn't money—it was *fear*! But I was quickly convinced by everyone that owning your own home was the only way to go. I had almost enough for the down payment on a brand new, two-bedroom condo in Burnaby. My dad loaned me the rest, and I bought my first piece of real estate for $103,500. I was 25 years old. The asking price was $108,900, so I thought I had negotiated myself a pretty good deal.

As luck would have it, I was transferred back to Calgary six months after purchasing my new home. But the real estate market in Vancouver had changed considerably. There was a boom happening and I was about to cash in. My condo sold for over $30,000 more than I had paid for it. In just six short months, my return on investment was 86 percent! I realized that I had made more in six months on my real estate investment than I had earned working all year. I think this is when I first started to understand the financial power of owning real estate.

Sharon's Story

My introduction to real estate is similar to Amy's. I knew from a very early age that I did not want to be a renter. I grew up in a small fruit-growing town on the River Murray in South Australia. My parents rented until I was 12 years old. They then bought their first home in which my dad still lives at the age of 85.

I moved to Adelaide for work and after renting for a couple of years I had saved nothing and gained nothing. I purchased a townhouse with the help of other people's money for the down payment. After a year, I decided it was time to upgrade to a bungalow. I placed an ad in the local paper and my townhouse sold in less than a week for double what I had paid for it. Buying in the right town at the right time proved to be a big payoff.

My next purchase was a bungalow in a seaside suburb that I recognized had amazing potential for growth. Seven years later, I sold this home for triple the price I had paid for it. This sale once again proved that having patience as a real estate investor pays off handsomely. My return on investment (ROI) was 1,060 percent on this property! At that time, I decided to move to Calgary, Alberta to stay with my Canadian friends.

Within a year, I recognized that Calgary's real estate market had all the signs of taking off, so I purchased a half-duplex as an investment property. By this time I had made a few friends. One of them owned five houses. As I'm a little competitive, I immediately set a goal to own six. During this time, I worked full-time as a squash professional and coach at the Calgary Winter Club and as the Junior Women's National coach; due to time restraints, my real estate passion took a back seat to my coaching.

Through squash I met Amy and we discovered that we had a mutual interest other than squash. We both had a secret desire to own real estate. It's no longer a secret. As she will tell you, our lives were transformed after attending a real estate evening hosted by Don Campbell and the Real Estate Investment Network where a very successful investor was the guest speaker.

AMY AND SHARON'S SUCCESS TAKES OFF WHEN THEY FORM A TEAM

At this event, the guest speaker, spoke passionately about real estate as he shared his success story. He talked about real estate winter, spring, summer and fall, and the value of surrounding yourself with like-minded people. This resonated so much with where we were at that we decided to go into real estate investing with a passion.

Since making that decision, we have accumulated substantial wealth through real estate. We would not have been able to do this without the simple strategies laid out in the ACRE system. We now follow a system based on access to vital information and statistics, and we surround ourselves with like-minded people, who have the same passion for real estate that we do.

We own property in Calgary, Red Deer, Edmonton and Fort McMurray. Up until now, most of our investments have been single-family homes, duplexes, four-plexes and a six-plex. One we are particularly proud of is a six-plex. We responded to a three-line classified ad advertising a six-plex in Edmonton (three hours from where we live). We followed the ACRE system and decided that the location of the property and the motivation of the vendor perfectly matched what we were looking for. We bought the property, after completing our due diligence. We could not believe the deal we were getting, and this was in a super hot market. We kept the property for 27 months and made a 1,700 percent return on our investment!

The four-plex came from another motivated vendor. The property had been on the market for several months. We viewed it one weekend and could not figure out why another investor had not purchased it. Maybe they hadn't seen the potential of the area; however, we did. We purchased the property. It still has the original tenants, one of whom manages it for us. Oh yes, it also creates positive cash flow of $800 per month after all expenses!

Sure, we could have done okay in real estate by ourselves; however, following this system and being a member of REIN has allowed us to exceed even our wildest real estate dreams. We have a Personal Belize and we are working towards it every day.

• • • •

Mark and Carol Garrett Turn Unexpected Unemployment into Opportunity

We were married on a hot, sunny day in September of 2000; we were like many other Canadian newlyweds—focused on our future, in love and in debt. We started off life together sharing a house with Carol's childhood friend where we paid rent and two-thirds of the utilities. Our original idea was to rent for a year, save money and buy our first house. The year turned into four as we let "life" take precedence over our goals. Carol had a successful career in a local building-supply company and was working her way through the management ranks. I had taken a job at a startup software company with the hopes of learning how to run a business.

During the first three years of our marriage, we, like many young couples, struggled through financial issues—some investments, lots of debt and high hopes. Financially, we were not very responsible and did not manage our savings. By the end of our first year, we were carrying a massive loan for an investment gone bad, student loans, a high-interest line of credit and irresponsible credit-card debt. We knew better, but it just kept happening. We went into debt counselling offered through Carol's work in the fall of 2001, and soon we were looking at a bright future again.

But the plan the debt counsellors gave us was one we had heard many times before, and obviously hadn't worked for us before. We felt as if we were still back on the starting line. In October 2002, I read the book *Rich Dad, Poor Dad*, which I insisted Carol read. As a result, we embarked on a one-year mission to learn about investing in real estate. During this journey we discovered many educational programs; unfortunately, they were all expensive and/or designed for the American market. It was at this frustrating point in June 2003 that we learned of Don Campbell and the Canadian Quick Start Program, where he taught the ACRE system. Finally, a Canadian-based system that was by Canadians, for Canadians! No hype, just fundamentals.

Upon receiving the Quick Start package, we devoured the information and even fought over the audio portion. Carol took it to the gym and listened to it while she worked out on the treadmill, and I listened to it when I could get my hands on it. After learning all about how the ACRE system worked, we realized where we were going wrong, what we needed to do and the necessary steps to get there.

In September 2003, my co-workers at the software company and I were called into our company boardroom and greeted by a man we didn't know wearing a designer suit, Rolex watch and Italian leather shoes. "I'm actually surprised to see everyone here at the office today. I was told by the CEO of the company that everyone was terminated on Friday. I guess you weren't ... but you are now," the mystery man announced. While everyone looked around at each other with dumbfounded expressions, a co-worker, whose wife was expecting his second child, worriedly asked, "What am I going to do?" Interestingly, I was surprised at my reaction. I was shocked at losing my job, yet very excited knowing that now I had the time to go on a real estate journey based on the ACRE system.

Quickly, and with the support of Carol, I started up a consulting company and began to support a few of the clients, who were now in turmoil from the closing of the software company. This new company created the freedom, the courage and the opportunity for us to put into practice what the clients were learning and working towards.

Only days after becoming unemployed, I had the good fortune to have dinner with Don Campbell. It was at this face-to-face meeting where I saw the real possibilities of real estate as a vehicle to success. At that dinner I also met a veteran investor named Arlen Dahlin. That night I learned that Arlen had amassed an incredible amount of properties using the principle of OPM—Other People's Money. Arlen was developing joint venture relationships that help others create success alongside of him. He worked with partners who wanted to invest in real estate, but didn't have the time or the interest to do the hard work of finding and managing the properties. This sounded exactly like what Carol and I could do using the ACRE system to choose quality properties. It was not long after that we found people willing to form a joint venture with us on these properties.

Carol and I closed on our next three properties in March of 2004, and then began to perfect the process. One of the key lessons we learned through the ACRE system is the importance of investing ethically. Many mortgage brokers we met asked us to sign gift letters, falsify income statements and take part in other "common practices." Carol and I took a stand against this type of practice; we only work with full disclosure.

Soon after this Carol began to look at leaving her job and moving into full-time real estate investing.

Creating Our Personal Belize

We had always been goal-setters but this time it was different. After creating our Personal Belize, we could literally see and hear our goals. This made them much more real and substantially more compelling—I attribute a lot of our success and drive to our Personal Belize.

Originally, our idea was to help ourselves finally get a place to call home. Yes, initially we wanted to use the ACRE system just to buy our own home. Then we saw a way to augment our finances through investing in real estate, and now we earn our living by investing in real estate. It started out as an idea to help ourselves, and now we are helping others reach their dreams by creating an opportunity to invest in real estate through joint venturing.

It's amazing what an idea can create. We just wanted to move out of our friend's house into our own place. Now we have purchased 23 properties. I am so excited about the future and all the new people we've met as a result of our new-found goals. We have new people in our lives, who are more important than any amount of money. Now, the question I have for you is: what are you going to do to make your goals a reality? Just think of the possibilities that an idea can create!

Best Moves
- Both of us married the best business partner in the world.
- Mark lost his job.
- We surrounded ourselves with like-minded, positive, focused people at REIN Canada.
- We built a support network of professionals and fellow investors who continue to help, guide and inspire us.

Worst Moves
- We started investing without a system.
- We did not complete all of the due diligence on our first few properties.
- We put emotion into investment.

Personal Philosophy
- "You can get everything in life you want if you will just help enough other people get what they want."—Zig Ziglar
- Follow a system and stay focused.
- Buy what works for your investors, not always what works for you.

- Keep it simple, consistent, ethical.
- Pay for what you need, don't be greedy, and provide a warm, comfortable home to the most important people in the game—your tenants.
- In the beginning, equity appreciation is the goal; positive cash flow is an added bonus. Five to seven years from now this will change; cash flow will become much stronger.

THE NUMBER-ONE KEY STEP TO BECOMING SUCCESSFUL OVER THE LONG TERM
- Stay focused on your goal and take consistent, daily action toward that goal, even as life gets in the way.

THE NUMBER-TWO KEY STEP TO BECOMING SUCCESSFUL OVER THE LONG TERM
- Be ethical and help others get where they want to be.

• • • •

At the printing of this book, Mark and Carol have purchased 27 properties, with several more in progress. You can read about their success at the Cashflow Portal, a website with over 900 members that is dedicated to bringing together like-minded individuals who are ready to take control of their financial future.

If you have a success story you would like to share, please send it directly to success@reincanada.com. Your story may be considered for inclusion in a future book.

Don R. Campbell's Canadian Quickstart ACRE System Home Study Program

The ACRE system is taught through a nine-CD home study program titled "The Real Estate Investment Networks' Quick Start System." It is 100 percent Canadian and has been developed by the author of this book, Don R. Campbell, and special guest Tim Johnson.

This is a must-have for all Canadian real estate investors. Registered readers of this book can receive a special discount. For more details visit www.realestateinvestingincanada.com and click on the Quick Start Button or call 1–888–824–7346 and we will send you a detailed package.

Knowledge without action leads to mediocrity.
—Don R. Campbell

"What's next? Where do I start?"

The above are the two most common questions I hear when I share the ACRE system, and I completely understand where these questions come from. Although the ACRE system is a simple step-by-step program, it can feel a little overwhelming at the beginning. Simply put, action brings results. At the start of this book, you'll remember that the goal is to provide you with a system that you can put into action and break through the insanity of doing the same thing over and over again—expecting different results. I trust you marked up your book, made notes in the margins, worked through the exercises and really began to create the success mindset. This is just the beginning.

CREATING LONG-TERM WEALTH—NOT A GET-RICH-QUICK SCHEME

As you already know, the real world is very different from the "book world." Your real estate portfolio is built one step at a time (sometimes the steps are giant and sometimes they are small). It's impossible to know exactly what steps you're going to take three or four days down the road until you take today's step. The reason is this: each time you move forward, your view changes and your options change—often for the better!

It doesn't matter how low or how high you're feeling about your real estate each day, you need to take a step forward towards your ultimate goal, your Personal Belize. Devote time to yourself. Devote the time it takes to make your vision come true. When you do that, the rest will take care of itself; it always does.

KEY INSIGHT

Start creating your future life—today.

The ACRE system is all about taking action in real estate investment—action that is focused on results using proven systems. You may have already taken some action in real estate. It could be that you've just completed your Personal Belize assignment, or maybe you've just placed your first offer, or maybe you've bought your 100th property. Congratulations.

If you're just ready to get started, congratulations on that choice as well. Deciding to take action is a very important step; however, results only come from actually following through on this decision. Whether you're a veteran or a rookie, if you begin to feel frustrated with your performance, or start to make excuses why the ACRE system won't work in your life, I urge you to ask yourself: "What's holding me back? Why aren't I taking advantage of the opportunities out there?"

Two Common Reasons You're Being Held Back

The most common reason is that you've put your Personal Belize to the side or it is just not compelling enough. This happens to all of us. But remember, no matter how busy your life is, nothing, or nobody, should shake you off your chosen path to your vision. If you feel yourself get distracted from the important steps that lead to your vision, then your vision is simply not compelling enough. If it is truly motivating, your Personal Belize won't let distractions get in your way. The simple fix is to continually refine and embellish your vision so you can't help but get excited and motivated by it.

The second reason is even more common with real estate investors (both veteran and rookie) and that is the feeling of being overwhelmed, of not knowing where to turn or in which direction to go. I understand; we've all been there. But let me be brutally honest: you are the master of your success. Without you on board, who's steering your ship?

Putting It into Action

Every week (this will quickly change to every day when you see how much impact it has on your life) put aside one hour with no phones, no distractions, no employees, no boss, no e-mail—nothing. I urge you to take out your daytimer or calendar right now and book this time for the next four weeks (you and I both know that if you don't book it, other "emergencies" will get in the way). These one-hour time slots will be reserved for you alone—alone with your thoughts. Scary!

During each of these hours, spend 15 minutes of this time focused solely on drawing the big picture in your mind, reviewing, updating and clarifying your Personal Belize. Now, use the remaining 45 minutes to focus solely on actions you can take (both large and small) over the next seven days that are totally focused on getting you closer to your vision. Break your large goals and actions into smaller steps you can complete in a week. Without this plan, a week will fly by and you'll be no closer to your goal than at the beginning. Life has a way of distracting everyone from what's really important.

Your focus for the coming week may be on practising your ACRE due diligence system or defining your Personal Belize. You may focus on strengthening key relationships or your time may be best spent negotiating and buying properties. Whatever you work out during this one-hour meeting with yourself, write your action steps down. They are completely your choice. Then make sure you make a commitment to yourself to use your time available for real estate to the maximum.

SOPHISTICATED INVESTOR

Even if you have already created amazing results in real estate, I urge you not to stop there. Book your one-hour weekly sessions and focus on taking your results to the next level. You will be truly amazed at what this simple one hour per week will do to your business!

Book your one-hour session with yourself right now!

What I Choose to Do in the Next Seven Days		
Your Action Step	Deadline	Completed
1.		
2.		
3.		
4.		
5.		
6.		
7.		

YOUR NINE STEP ACTION PLAN

After interviewing thousands of investors over the years, I discovered a distinct pattern. I asked both rookie and veteran investors what steps they took to ensure that they started to create success more quickly. Here are the key steps investors have used over the last 12 years to get on the road to success. They provide you with a clear road map to follow. You will note that there are three blank lines provided for you to write in your additional action steps, which are often created when you have completed the exercises in this book.

Road Map to Success

Your Name: _____

     Date: _____

- ❑ Clearly define what you want real estate to provide you by completing your Personal Belize.
- ❑ Review and re-write the notes you made during the reading of this book. Look for insights you learned and action steps to take.
- ❑ Complete your Goldmine Score Card on at least two areas in which you're thinking of investing. Spend some time looking around areas that score well to get a feel for them.
- ❑ Surround yourself with successful, like-minded and supportive investors. Make sure you do "What's behind the curtain?" investigations before you join a group, so you know that the organization and the people are there to support your vision, not just to take your money. To find groups endorsed by the ACRE system, visit www.reincanada.com.
- ❑ Practise your due diligence on at least five properties listed in the local classified ads.
- ❑ Place at least one offer to purchase within seven days. Make sure you use a recommended real estate lawyer and that you insert the key clauses discussed in the ACRE system in the offer.
- ❑ Create business cards with *Real Estate Investor* as your title. You will be amazed at how handy they will be and how many doors they open.
- ❑ Develop your Sophisticated Investor Binder and sit down, face to face, with a real estate-specific banker or broker. Create a relationship. Follow the steps in this book related to working with a banker.
- ❑ Eliminate excuses from your life. Excuses are the tell-tale signs of mediocrity.
- ❑ Visit the Canadian Real Estate Investors' resource site at www.realestateinvestingincanada.com to tap into Canadian-specific support systems and strategies that you can start using immediately and with confidence.

- ❑ _____

- ❑ _____

REAL ESTATE
INVESTMENT
NETWORK™

#1018, 105 – 150 Crowfoot Cres. NW, Calgary, Alberta T3G 3T2
phone (403) 208-2722 fax (403) 241-6685 www.reincanada.com

Property Goldmine Score Card

Property Address: _____

Town: _____ Prov: _____

Source: _____ Tel:_____

Property Specific Questions

☐ Can your **change the use** of the property?
☐ Can you buy it <u>substantially</u> **below retail market value**?
☐ Can you <u>substantially</u> **increase the current rents**?
☐ Can you do small **renovations** to <u>substantially</u> increase the value?

Area's Economic Influences

☐ Is there an **overall increase in demand** in the area?
☐ Are there currently **sales over list price** in the area?
☐ Is there a noted **increase in labour and materials cost** in the area?
☐ Is there a lot of **speculative investment** in the area?
☐ Is it **an area in transition** – moving upwards in quality?
☐ Is there a major **transportation improvement** occurring nearby?
☐ Is it in an area that is going to benefit from the **Ripple Effect**?
☐ Is the property's area in **"Real Estate Spring or Summer?"**
☐ Has the **political leadership** created a 'growth atmosphere?'
☐ Is area's **average income increasing** faster than provincial average?
☐ Is it an area that is attractive to the **'Baby Boomers?'**
☐ Is the area **growing faster** than the provincial 'average?'
☐ Are **interest rates** at historic lows and/or moving downward?

_____ = Total ✓'s

Does This Property Fit Your System?   ☐ yes ☐ no
Does It Take You Closer To Your Goal?   ☐ yes ☐ no

ALL PROPERTIES
Due Diligence Checklist

Due diligence is critical for ANY property you are considering investing in. Whether you are a silent partner or the actual person finding and investigating a property, you must do your own independent due diligence. This checklist will provide you a foundation from which to work, and will assist you in asking the critical questions. Remember, it does all come down to the accuracy of numbers. DO NOT SKIP ANY STEPS! (If you are purchasing a condo, use this form PLUS the Condo Due Diligence Checklist together)

Location:

❑ How many check marks does the area get using the **Property Goldmine Scorecard**?

    (6 checks or more is best)

❑ What is the nature of the local economy?

    Diverse   or   Single Industry

❑ In what area of town is the property located?

    Older   Newer   Transitional

❑ What is the type and quality of the surrounding properties?

    Type: _____

    Quality vs rest of neighbourhood: _____

❑ What amenities and services are nearby?

❑ Transit   ❑ Shopping   ❑ Schools

❑ University/College   ❑ Major Employer

Building:

❑ What is the overall Curb Appeal? (scale 1 to 10)   ____

❑ What is the overall Interior Appeal? (scale 1 to 10)   ____

❑ How well has the property been maintained? (scale 1 to 10) ____

❑ Is there any deferred maintenance repairs required in the next 12 months?

        If YES, list it: _____

        If YES, Estimate cost of repair: $_____

❑ Are there any appliances you need to purchase? YES / NO
❑ Has a complete professional inspection been completed? YES / NO
       If NO, when are you scheduling it for? _____
❑ Is a Real Property Report (site survey certificate)
   available from vendor? YES / NO
If YES, is it acceptable to your lawyer for closing? YES / NO

Financial:

❑ Have you completed a **Property Analysis Form**? YES / NO
       (You must complete the form for EVERY property before you
       make your offer)
❑ Do the results of the **Property Analysis Form** fit your
   investment system? YES / NO
       (if NO, look for a different property)
❑ If currently a rental—are financial statements
   available for the property? YES / NO
       What is the expense to income ratio?
       (35 – 45% is workable)
       Are the numbers believable?
       Do they fit market norms? YES / NO

❑ What is the current rent on the property? _____
       (If not currently rented, what should it
       rent for when analyzing the market?)
❑ What are rents for similar properties in the area? $_____
❑ What is the vacancy rate history of the property? _____%
When vacant, does it seem difficult to re-rent? _____
What is the vacancy rate history for the area? _____%
How does that compare with the property's history? _____

Additional Critical Due Diligence:

Check the following items to ensure you're not buying unknown trouble:
- ❑ Confirm taxes and other charges are current (city hall).
- ❑ Confirm no outstanding workorders or compliance orders (city hall—health Department).
- ❑ Open or past complaints registered to the address. Known as a problem property (police).

❑ Who will be managing the property?   _____
If YOU—is there a reliable company when you get
tired of managing?   YES / NO

❑ What banker/broker has a program to assist you with the
financing on this property?   _____

❑ What is the vendor's REAL motivation level?
(0 = none, 10 = extremely)   _____

❑ Do you plan on keeping the current tenant—do they fit YOUR
tenant profile?   YES / NO

❑ Do you need vacant possession to make it fit your system?   YES / NO

CONDOMINIUM PURCHASE
Due Diligence Checklist
In addition to completing your Property Analysis Form,
when purchasing a condo or group of condos you need to take a very
close look at the following:

1. Building:

❑ How many units in the building?   (25+ *is best*)   _____

❑ What is the ratio of owner occupied to rentals?   _____
   (Looking for potential "anti-renter" situation)

❑ What is the age of the building?   _____
   *(Age important for financing, condition of building's
   maintenance important for costs)*

❑ Are there any Deferred Maintenance issues pending?
   *(See Condo Reserve Fund Study & Last 24 months of condo
   board minutes)*

   If YES, review and estimate total cost of:
   *(Remember each unit will be responsible for
   their portion of these costs)*

   A. Roof replacement or repair $_____
   B. Mechanical
       (Does it need engineer inspection report?) $_____
   C. Interior or exterior refurbishment $_____
   D. Post Tension deterioration $_____
   E. Parking Lot Resurfacing $_____
   F. Intercom system repair/replace $_____
   G. Other $_____

❑ Is the parking area of adequate size?
       (Important to your tenants & your exit strategy)
   A. What is the ratio of stalls to suites?   _____/_____
   (A minimum 1 stall per unit advised)
   B. Can you rent additional stalls?   YES / NO
   C. Is there adequate on-site visitor parking?   YES / NO

❑ What is the typical rent for the property? $_____

❑ Does the opportunity to increase the rent exist?   YES / NO

       A. If YES by how much? $_____

❑ What is the building's previous year's vacancy rate?   _____%

       A. How does that compare

          to area average?   _____%

❑ What is the typical renter profile in building?
(Eg., age 25-40, SM/F etc.) _____

    ❑ Does this fit your desired renter profile?   YES / NO

2. Legal:

❑ Is there pending litigation against the condominium
corporation?   YES / NO

      (The Condo Board must reveal this to you—also check board minutes)

❑ Is there a recent Phase 1 Environmental Study available?   YES / NO

❑ Is the property approved for CMHC financing?   YES / NO

3. Condominium Corporation:

❑ Talk with representatives of the Condo Board to get a feel for
the atmosphere.

❑ Review 2 years of Condo Board meeting minutes for potential
problems.

❑ Review the Annual Condo Budget.

       A. Compare last year's budget for accuracy with actual
          operating costs.

       B. Review the upcoming year's budget to see if appropriate
          adjustments have been made.

❑ Review the Condominium bylaws.

       A. Do they hold any penalties towards renter units?
          (Eg., renter restrictions, large damage deposit to condo corp, etc.)

       B. Define whether there is an easy grievance arbitration
          procedure.

❑ What are the monthly Condo Fees
   and what do they include? $_____
        A. If they seem high do they include heat and/or power?
        B. If they seem low, is there an adequate amount allocated
           to the Reserve Fund for future repairs, or will a condo
           fee increase be needed?

❑ Read the Rental Management Contract *(and rental pool agreement
   if in place)*.
        A. Are the contracts coming due for negotiations?   YES / NO
        B. Are management costs slated to increase in
           near future?   YES / NO
        C. Speak with management company
           representative AND on-site manager to get
           a feel for their thoughts on the building

❑ Is there a rental pool in place?
        A. What is the unit factor for distribution
           of pooled rents?   _____
        B. Who manages the pool? What is their fee? _____%
        C. Read the guidelines—can you participate?   YES / NO

❑ Is the Building Insurance Policy adequate?   YES / NO
        ❑ Review the condominium's financial statements
           for an adequate reserve fund vs upcoming
           required repairs

❑ Are there any pending or current cash calls to be paid by
   the owners?   YES / NO

❑ Ensure you complete a **Property Analyzer Form** with accurate
   market numbers.

R.E.I.N.™ Property Analyzer

Property Data:

Address:_____ City/Area: _____ Date Viewed: _____

Asking Price: _____ Size (sq ft): _____ Age:_____

Major Repairs:_____ Est Repair Cost $ _____

Owner: _____ Tel: _____ Fax: _____

Source: _____ Tel: _____ Fax: _____

Overall Condition: 1 2 3 4 5

Income & Inspection

Suite # or Desc	# of Bedrooms	Current Rent	Projected Rent	Increase Date	Inspection Comments

Total Monthly Rent $ _____ $ _____

Total Annual Rent $ _____ $ _____

Expenses:

	Current Annual	Current Monthly	Projected Monthly	Comments
Heat (gas, oil, elect, hot water, other _____)				Paid By Tenant / Landlord
Electricity				Paid By Tenant / Landlord
Water/Sewer				Paid By Tenant / Landlord / Condo
Taxes				Included in Mortgage Payment?
Condo Fee				Last Increase date:
Insurance				
Property Management	%			Current Management Rating 1 2 3 4 5
Vacancy Allowance	%			Current Vacancy _____%
Rental Pool Mgmt	%			
Repairs & Maintenance	%			Overall Condition 1 2 3 4 5
Resident Manager				Current On-site Impression 1 2 3 4 5
Other:				
TOTAL MONTHLY	$ _____	$ _____		

TOTAL MONTHLY INCOME less TOTAL MONTHLY EXPENSES (Before Debt Service)=

Current: $ _____   Projected: $ _____

TOTAL PROJECTED INCOME $_____

Mortgaging/Debt Service:

	Balance	Interest Rate	Expiry Date	Monthly Payment
1st Mortgage		%		P I T
2nd Mortgage		%		P I T
Vendor Take Back		%		P I T
Other		%		P I T

TOTAL DEBT SERVICE $_____

NET CASH FLOW $_____

Purchase Details:

PROJECTED PURCHASE PRICE $ _____

1st Mortgage Funding ($ _____)
2nd Mortgage Funding ($ _____)
Vendor Take Back ($ _____)
Other Funding ($ _____)

TOTAL DEBT FUNDING ($ _____)
DOWN PAYMENT REQUIRED $ _____

Purchase Costs:

Professional Inspection $_____
Value Appraisal $_____
Real Property Report (Survey) $_____
Mortgage Set-Up Costs $_____
Mortgage Broker Fees $_____
Legal Costs (incl disbursements) $_____
Staying Power Fund $_____
Immediate Repairs $_____
Immediate Renovations $_____
Other _____ $_____
Other _____ $_____

TOTAL PURCHASE COSTS $ _____

TOTAL CASH REQUIRED TO CLOSE (Down payment + Purchase costs) $ _____

1. Does this property take me closer to my goal or farther away? ❑ Closer ❑ Farther
2. Does this property fit my system? ❑ Yes ❑ No
3. Will this property be impeccably property managed? ❑ Yes ❑ No
4. Who will manage the property? _____

A

ABSTRACT OF TITLE
A written history of the title to a parcel of real estate as recorded in a Land Registry Office.

ACCELERATION CLAUSE
A clause in the mortgage document that accelerates the maturity date and states that upon default, the principal sum of the mortgage and accrued interest falls due.

ACCRUED INTEREST
Interest that has accumulated unpaid since the last payment date.

ADD-ON INTEREST
An interest amount added to the principal of a debt and made payable as part of the debt, usually in equal periodic installments (also called pre-calculated interest).

ADJUSTABLE RATE MORTGAGE (ARM)
A mortgage for which the interest rate is adjusted periodically according to movements in a pre-selected index.

ADJUSTMENT DATE
The date regarded as the official beginning of a mortgage.

AFFIDAVIT
A statement of declaration in writing and sworn or affirmed before an authorized individual, such as a notary public.

AGENCY
A relationship that arises out of a contract, where an agent is authorized by a principal to engage in certain acts, usually in dealing with one or more third parties.

AGREEMENT OF PURCHASE AND SALE
A written contract to buy property in which the purchaser and vendor agree to sell upon terms and conditions as set forth in the agreement.

ALIENATION CLAUSE
This is a clause that enables the mortgagee to demand payment of the outstanding balance including interest upon sale or transfer of title (also known as a "due-on-sale" clause).

AMORTIZATION
The gradual retirement of a debt by means of partial payments of the principal at regular intervals.

AMORTIZATION OF A MORTGAGE
The arrangement for paying off a mortgage by installments over a period of time.

AMORTIZATION PERIOD
The time period required to completely retire a debt through scheduled payments of principal.

ANNIVERSARY DATE
The occasion of one year from an event pertaining to a mortgage, e.g., the registration date.

ANNUAL BUDGET
Now required by the Condominium Property Act, this budget is the basis upon which contributions are levied and funds collected.

ANNUAL GENERAL MEETING (AGM)
Once per year, within 15 months of the last one, a condominium board is required to convene an Annual General Meeting of unit owners.

ANNUAL PERCENTAGE RATE (APR)
The yearly interest percentage of a mortgage as expressed by the actual rate of interest paid, given the term, rate, amount and cost of arrangement.

APPRAISED VALUE
An estimate of property value written by a qualified individual (AACI). Appraisals performed for mortgage lending purposes may not reflect the market value of the property, or the purchase price.

APPROVED LENDER
Lending institution authorized by the government of Canada through Canada Mortgage and Housing Corporation (CMHC) to make loans under the terms of the National Housing Act; only approved lenders can negotiate mortgages that require mortgage loan insurance.

APPURTENANCE
Something that is outside the property itself, but belongs to the land and is joined thereto; e.g., a road over another's land providing an access (right-of-way) is an appurtenance.

ARREARS
To be "in arrears" is to be behind in the payments called for under a mortgage agreement.

ASSESSED VALUE
An amount assigned to a taxable property for the purpose of equalizing the burden of taxation.

ASSIGNEE
One who takes the rights or title of another by assignment.

ASSIGNMENT
The method by which a purchase and sale contract is transferred between two parties (for a consideration or fee).

ASSIGNMENT OF MORTGAGE
The assigning of a mortgagee's interest in the mortgage to a new mortgagee. The legal sale of the mortgage with or without an agreement to repurchase.

ASSIGNMENT OF RENTALS
The enforceable diversion of income from a mortgaged property to the mortgagee.

ASSIGNOR
One who transfers or assigns the rights or title to another.

ASSUMABILITY
A feature of a mortgage that allows the buyer to take over the seller's mortgage on the property.

ASSUMPTION AGREEMENT
A document that binds someone other than the mortgagor to perform mortgage obligations.

ASSUMPTION OF MORTGAGE
The action of a purchaser taking responsibility for a mortgage debt by way of a legal agreement. The original covenanter(s)' responsibility pursuant to the mortgage obligation remains intact in such arrangement, so long as the existing documentation remains registered.

ATTORNMENT OF RENT
The redirection of rental income to a mortgagee, usually in the event of default.

AUTHORITY
The legal right given by a principal to an agent to act on the principal's behalf in performing specific acts or negotiations.

AVERAGING
Sometimes called "leveling." This is the calculation made to determine the interest when a second mortgage is taken out; averaging determines the average interest rate of the two mortgages.

B

BALANCE DUE ON COMPLETION
The amount of money a purchaser will be required to pay to the vendor to complete the purchase after all adjustments have been made.

BALLOON PAYMENT
This is a final mortgage payment at the end of the term that pays off the outstanding loan in full. The amount of money (principal) required to discharge a mortgage at maturity.

BARELAND CONDOMINIUM
In traditional condominiums, both the master lot and the walls and roofs of the buildings are common property. In bareland condominiums, only the land is condominiumized, and the structures are the responsibility of the owners.

BIRD DOG
A person who looks for properties that fit your guidelines and brings them to you for a fee.

BLANKET MORTGAGE
A single registered document that encumbers more than one property.

BLENDED PAYMENT
Equal payments consisting of both principal and interest, paid regularly during the term of the mortgage.

BOARD OF DIRECTORS
Every Condominium Corporation must have a board of directors, which is responsible for the proper administration of the condominium and the by-laws.

BREACH OF CONTRACT
Failure to fulfill an obligation under a contract. Breach confers a right of action on the offended party.

BRIDGE OR INTERIM LOANS (MORTGAGES)
Interim loans are used to bridge the gap between the initial construction and the first advances available under the terms of the construction mortgage.

Interim loans can also be used for financing between phases of construction, until the construction is completed to a stage whereby the mortgagee lender will advance funds to pay for the phase of the construction. Usually, when the mortgage is advanced, the proceeds of the mortgage are used to return the bridge or interim financing. Bridge financing is also used when a sale closes after a purchaser takes possession on a purchase.

BROKER
A person licensed by the provincial or territorial government to trade in real estate. Brokers may form companies of offices that appoint sales representatives to provide services to the seller or buyer, or they may provide the same services themselves; also referred to as agents.

BUILDING CODES
Regulations established by government providing for structural requirements.

BUILDING PERMIT
Certificate that must be obtained from the municipality by the property owner or contractor before a building can be erected or repaired; it must be posted in a conspicuous place until the job is completed and passed as satisfactory by a municipal building inspector.

BUYDOWN
A payment to the lender from the seller, buyer or third party causing the lender to reduce the interest rate during the term of the mortgage.

BUYER BROKERAGE AGREEMENT
Written agreement between the buyer and the buyer's agent, outlining the agency relationship between the two parties, and the manner in which the buyer's agent will be compensated.

BUYER'S AGENT
Person or firm representing the buyer; primary allegiance is to the buyer.

BY-LAWS
A set of rules and procedures adopted by a special resolution of unit-owners for the administration of the condominium corporation. Each condominium corporation has its own special by-laws.

C

CANADA MORTGAGE AND HOUSING CORPORATION (CMHC)
A Canadian Crown Corporation that administers the National Housing Act. CMHC services include the insuring of high-ratio mortgage loans for lenders.

CAP
Refers to a maximum interest rate increase for a mortgage.

CAPITAL GAIN or LOSS
The difference between the base price (cost plus purchase expenses) and the sale price of a capital asset.

CAPITALIZATION RATE
The rate of return anticipated by an investor in a property.

CAPITALIZED VALUE
The value of a property based on the net income.

CAVEAT EMPTOR
"Let the buyer beware." A buyer must fully examine the product or service he or she is buying before making the purchase.

CERTIFICATE OF CHARGE
A mortgage document in the Land Titles System.

CESSATION OF CHARGE
A discharge of a mortgage in the Land Titles System.

CHAIN OF TITLE
The sequence of conveyances and encumbrances affecting a title to land from the time that the original patent was granted or as far back as records are available.

CHARGE
The name given to a mortgage document when title is registered under the Land Titles Act.

CHATTEL MORTGAGE
An encumbrance against moveable possessions or personal property that may be removed without damage to the property, e.g., appliances.

CHATTELS
Moveable possessions and personal property that may be removed without damage to the property, e.g., appliances.

CLOSED MORTGAGE
A reference to the absence of the privilege to accelerate repayment during the term of a mortgage either by bulk payment(s) or increase to scheduled remittances. A penalty applies if you repay the loan in full before the end of a closed term.

CLOSING
See "Date of Completion"; the day the legal title to the property changes hands.

CLOSING COSTS
Costs in addition to the purchase price of the home, such as legal fees, transfer fees and disbursements, that are payable on the closing date; they typically range from 1.5–4 percent of a home's selling price.

CLOSING DATE
The date on which the buyer takes over the property.

CLOUD ON TITLE
Any encumbrance or claim that affects title to property.

COLLATERAL MORTGAGE
A mortgage that secures a loan given by way of a promissory note; the money that is borrowed can be used to buy a property or for another purpose such as home renovation or a vacation.

COLLATERAL SECURITY
An additional form of security, pledged to reduce the risk of a mortgagee.

COMMISSION
Amount agreed to by the seller and the real estate broker/agent and stated in the listing agreement and payable to the broker/agent on closing.

COMMITMENT
A written notice from a lender who advises of approval to advance a specified amount of funds under certain conditions.

COMMON LAW
That part of the law formulated, developed and administered by the old common law courts, based originally on unwritten common customs.

COMMON PROPERTY
Every part of the condominium plan that is not a unit is common property. The condominium corporation is responsible for the maintenance and service of the common property.

COMPLETION LOAN
A mortgage loan disbursed following the satisfactory completion of construction.

COMPOUND INTEREST
Interest on both the principal and on interest that has accrued.

COMPONENT FINANCING
A device by which lending is split into separate parts and treated individually.

COMPS (comparables)
A listing of comparable properties used to value a similar property. Often used in appraisals.

CONDITION PRECEDENT
An event or action necessary before an agreement becomes binding.

CONDITION SUBSEQUENT
A condition referring to a future event upon the happening of which the contract becomes no longer binding on the parties.

CONDITIONAL OFFER
Offer to purchase that is subject to specified conditions; usually a stipulated time limit within which the specified conditions must be met.

CONDOMINIUM
The ownership of a separate amount of space in a multiple dwelling or other multiple-ownership of common elements used jointly with other owners.

CONDOMINIUM FEE
A monthly common payment among owners that is allocated to pay expenses.

CONSIDERATION
Something of value given to make a promise of repayment enforceable.

CONSTANT ANNUAL PERCENT
The percentage required to pay the principal and interest to amortize a loan.

CONSTANT PAYMENT MORTGAGE
A mortgage that is paid by equal periodic amounts consisting of principal and interest payments. It may be self-liquidating, which means the mortgage is entirely paid off at maturity (fully amortized), partially amortized, at the end of which there remains a principal balance due at maturity (also known as balloon mortgage).

CONSTRUCTION ADVANCE
Moneys advanced to the borrower under a construction loan.

CONSTRUCTION LIEN
A claim against property pursuant to labour, services or materials supplied.

CONSTRUCTION LOAN
A short-term loan made to a builder for construction of buildings, usually to be paid out by another mortgage upon final completion. Also, a description used in reference to a mortgage that is advanced in pre-determined stages, according to the amount of work completed.

CONSTRUCTION LOAN AGREEMENT
An agreement between a lender and a builder setting out terms of an agreement—loan amount, rate, method of drawing funds and conditions for advancing.

CONTRACT
An agreement between two or more parties given receipt of lawful consideration to do or refrain from doing some act.

CONVENTIONAL MORTGAGE
A mortgage loan that does not exceed 75 percent of the lending value of the property. Mortgages that exceed this limit must be insured by CMHC (or similar insurance provider).

CONVEYANCE
The transfer of property ownership. Also, the written instrument whereby such transfer is effected. Conveyance includes a mortgage, charge, and lease, etc.

CO-OPERATIVE
The ownership of a separate amount of space in a multiple dwelling or multiple-occupancy building with proportioned tenancy in common ownership of common elements. It's used jointly with other owners; however, the owner does not have clear title to a specific unit but becomes a shareholder of the corporation, which owns all of the property and occupies by way of a tenancy agreement subject to shareholders agreement administered by an elected board of directors.

COVENANT
An agreement contained in an instrument creating an obligation. It may be positive, stipulating the performance of some act. It may be negative or restrictive, forbidding the commission of some act. A clause in a legal document which, in the case of a mortgage, gives the parties to the mortgage a right or an obligation; for example, a covenant can impose the obligation on a borrower to make mortgage payments in certain amounts on certain dates; a mortgage document consists of covenants agreed to by the borrower and the lender.

CROSS-COLLATERALIZATION
A reference to security involving various liens held in support of one or more advances made by a lender to a borrower.

D

DAMAGES
Compensation or indemnity for loss owing to breach of contract.

DATE OF COMPLETION
The date specified by an agreement of purchase and sale, when the purchaser is to deliver the balance of money due and the vendor to deliver a duly executed deed.

DEBT SERVICE
The amount of principal and interest payments made under a mortgage.

DEBT-SERVICE RATIO
Measurement of debt payments to gross household income.

DEFAULT
Failure to abide by the terms of a mortgage loan agreement. Failure to make mortgage payments (defaulting) may give cause to the mortgagor to take legal action to possess (foreclose on) the mortgaged property.

DEFERRED INCOME
An accounting method of dealing with income that is received but not included in a statement of earnings as normal earnings.

DEFICIENCY
An insufficient payment, often relating to an amount recovered under a power of sale or foreclosure action.

DEFLATION
A decline in the general level of prices; or an increase in the value of money; or an increase in the amount of money in circulation.

DELAYED PARTICIPATION LOAN
Where a lender disposes of a loan to several other participants putting up their respective shares later.

DEMAND NOTE
Payment is made on demand, usually within a few days' notice to the borrower.

DEPOSIT
Payment of money or other valuable consideration as a pledge for fulfillment of contract. Money placed in trust by the purchaser when an offer to purchase is made; the sum is held by the real estate representative or lawyer until the sale is closed, then paid to the vendor.

DEPRECIATED REPRODUCTION COST
Appraisal method by which the cost of replacing a structure, minus depreciation, gives the depreciation reproduction cost.

DEPRECIATION
A loss in value due to any cause.

DISCHARGE OF MORTGAGE
A document executed by the mortgagee, and given to the mortgagor when a mortgage loan has been repaid in full before, at or after the maturity date.

DISCLOSURE STATEMENT
A statement contained in a consumer credit transaction in order to disclose complete credit terms and interest rates.

DISCOUNT
Reduction in product price or cost of a service. A discount is the difference between the nominal face value of a loan and the actual cash received by the borrower, because interest is paid at the beginning of a loan based on the sum to be repaid at maturity.

DISCOUNTED CASH-FLOW ANALYSIS
This is a method of analysis that calculates the true value of an investment in terms of the present value, i.e., what the investment is worth now, although it is spread over a number of years. To compensate for future earnings a discount factor is added in so that a real comparison can be made between an investment with quick return and one that is placed over a number of years.

DISCOUNTED LOAN
The face value of the loan minus the interest or discount charged by the lender is the amount actually advanced to a borrower.

DOMINANT TENEMENT
The estate that derives benefit from an easement over a subservient estate, as in a right-of-way.

DOWER INTEREST
A wife's interest in the lands of her husband accruing to her by virtue of the marriage.

DOWN PAYMENT
The portion of the house price the buyer must pay upfront from personal resources before securing a mortgage; it usually ranges from 5–25 percent of the purchase price.

DOWNSIDE LEVERAGE
Occurs where the debt service on a mortgage exceeds the yield on an investor's property, thereby reducing cash flow.

DRAWEE
The person, bank or corporation from whom a bill, note or cheque is drawn and from whom payment is expected by the payee or his assignee.

DRAWER
The person or corporation who writes a cheque or note for payment to a third party. In the case of a bill of exchange, the drawer is the creditor and is usually the payee.

DUAL AGENT
A real estate broker/agent who acts as agent for both buyer and seller in the same transaction.

DUE ON SALE CLAUSE
A mortgage clause that states that if the property is sold, the mortgage cannot be assumed by the new purchaser without qualification. The mortgage becomes immediately due and payable upon the sale of the property.

E

EASEMENT
The right acquired for access over another person's land for a specific purpose, such as for a driveway or public utilities.

ECONOMIC DEPRECIATION
Loss in value of property due to external influences related to the property, i.e., not controlled by the owner.

EFFECTIVE GROSS INCOME
The estimated gross income less allowances for vacancies and rent losses.

EFFECTIVE INTEREST RATE
The actual interest rate on investment where a debt or loan was bought at a discount or at a premium.

ENCROACHMENT
A fixture, such as a wall or fence, which illegally intrudes into or invades on public or private property, thus diminishing the size and value of the invaded property.

ENCUMBRANCE
Outstanding claim or lien recorded against a property, e.g., a mortgage, or any legal right to the use of the property by another person who is not the owner.

END LOAN
The mortgage loan to the final customer, such as a purchaser of a condominium unit.

EQUITABLE MORTGAGE
The transfer of equity in property as security for a debt. Any mortgage registered after the first mortgage.

EQUITY
The value of real estate over and above the mortgage(s) against it.

EQUITY OF REDEMPTION
The right of the mortgagor to reclaim clear title to the real property upon full repayment of the debt.

ESCROW ACCOUNT (American term)
An account held by an agent on behalf of his principal for the payment of money due to a third party on the event of specified incidents, e.g. a vendor's solicitor will hold funds on his behalf until title deeds to a property have been delivered and the property has been registered and the keys delivered to the purchaser; or an account maintained by a mortgagee for the payment of property taxes or life insurance premiums.

ESTATE
The degree, quantity, nature and extent of interest that a person has in real property.

ESTOPPEL CERTIFICATE (renter confirmation)
A written statement or certificate that states certain facts upon which the receiver of the statement or a third party may rely, e.g., a lender's estoppel statement as to a purchaser or property. The lender cannot later deny the truth of these statements because a third party has relied and acted upon them.

EXACT DAY INTEREST
Interest calculated on the basis of 365 days per year or 366 days in a leap year.

EXCULPATORY CLAUSE
A clause that excuses one party from personal liability in the event of a default.

EXPROPRIATION
The act of forcefully taking private property for public use.

EXTENSION AGREEMENT
The lengthening of a term on a contract to extend the maturity date; or to permit more time for the performance of an obligation or condition; or the extension of the coverage of a lien to include more property.

F

FEASIBILITY ANALYSIS
An analysis to determine the feasibility of a project. Details of construction costs, projected income from the project plus location and economic factors affecting the project will be required. Similar to a feasibility study by a developer conducted to decide whether to proceed with plans and required by the lender to decide whether to provide funds.

FEE SIMPLE
The highest estate or absolute right in real property. In common law, the most common way real estate is owned. The most complete ownership interest one can have in real property.

FINAL ORDER OF CLOSURE
Judgment taken against a mortgagor, extinguishing the equity of redemption.

FINANCING STATEMENT
A statement filed by a creditor in a public records office identifying the parties, giving their addresses and describing the collateral.

FIRST MORTGAGE
The mortgage agreement that has first claim on the property in the event of default.

FIRST MORTGAGE BOND
Bonds issued by a corporation secured upon the property and earnings of the issuing corporation.

FIXED-RATE MORTGAGE
This is the usual form of mortgage where the interest rate remains the same during the entire life of the term.

FIXTURES
Permanent improvements to property that may not be removed at the expiration of the term of lease or tenure.

FLAT PAYMENT
An all-inclusive monthly payment that is calculated to include principal, interest and taxes. Under this system there is no specific breakdown as to the amounts of the principal, interest and taxes.

FLOATING RATE OF INTEREST
Rate of interest that fluctuates according to prime lending rates, e.g. 2 percent above prime rate is usually chargeable on short-term loans such as construction loans.

FLOOR TO CEILING LOAN
A permanent loan or advance made in two stages, (a) on completion of construction according to agreed upon terms and conditions and (b) the balance advanced upon occupancy or upon cash flow requirements.

FORECLOSURE
Remedial court action taken by a mortgagee when default occurs on a mortgage, to cause forfeiture of the equity of redemption of the mortgagor.

FORWARD COMMITMENT
Lender's commitment to make or assume a future loan.

FREEHOLD
The ownership of a tract of land on which the building(s) are located. The oldest and most common type of ownership of real estate.

FULLY AMORTIZED LOAN
A mortgage loan wherein the stipulated payments repay the loan in full by its maturity date.

FURTHER CHARGE
A second or subsequent loan of money to a mortgagor by a mortgagee, either on the same or on an additional security.

G

G/E CAPITAL
The General Electric Capital Corporation insures high-ratio mortgages for lenders.

GALE DATE
The dates on which interest is charged or compounded on the mortgage loan.

GAP FINANCING
A loan required by a builder to obtain funds during the period between a permanent take out commitment and a construction loan. The construction lender will usually require permanent mortgage commitment to the full amount of the construction loan plus a holdback provision that only the "floor" amount will be funded at the completion of construction.

GENERAL CREDITOR
A creditor who has no security other than the promise of the debtor.

GRADUATED AMORTIZATION MORTGAGE
A special method of repayment on a mortgage whereby repayments in the initial period are low and are gradually stepped up at a higher rate. Graduated payment mortgages were devised to enable lower income families to become home owners.

GRANT
A technical term used in deeds of conveyance to indicate a transfer of an interest or estate in land.

GRANTEE
The party to whom an interest in real property is conveyed (the buyer).

GRANTOR
The person who conveys an interest in real estate by deed (the seller).

GROSS RENT MULTIPLIER
Method of appraising the fair market value of property by multiplying the gross rents by a factor that varies according to the type and location of the property.

GROSS DEBT SERVICE (GDS)
The percentage of gross annual income required to cover payments associated with housing. If the dwelling unit is a condo, all or a portion of common fees are included, depending on what expenses are covered.

GROSS DEBT SERVICE RATIO
Allowable ration of payments for principal, interest and taxes to gross income.

GROSS INCOME
The scheduled income from the operation of the business of management of the property, customarily stated on an annual basis.

GUARANTEED INCOME MORTGAGE
A guarantee included in a purchase money mortgage by a seller-mortgagee that there will be a minimum cash flow or net operating income to the purchaser-mortgagee. The guarantee is limited to a short period and may be combined with a management contract whereby the seller, as manager, will operate the property.

GUARANTOR
A third party without interest in the property who agrees to assume responsibility for a debt in the event of default by the mortgagor.

H

HIGH-RATIO MORTGAGE
A mortgage loan that exceeds 75 percent of the lending value of the property and must be insured against default of payment.

HIGHEST AND BEST USE
This refers to the use of land that would most likely produce the greatest net return over a given time.

HOLDBACK
An amount of money retained by a construction lender or owner until satisfactory completion of the work performed by a contractor; a standard holdback is 10 percent of the cost of the building project.

HYPOTHECATE
To use something as security without giving up possession of it.

I

IMMEDIATE PARTICIPATION LOAN
A loan in which all of the partners contribute their share immediately.

INCOME BOND
Bonds that pay a fixed rate of interest contingent upon earnings. These bonds may originate from reorganiza-

tion because of a default on mortgage bonds.

INCOME/EXPENSE RATIO
Ratio of operation expenses to gross income and expressed as a percentage (also known as operating ratio).

INCOME PROPERTY LOAN
A loan that is secured on property that already has a source of income, e.g., rents that will cover the debt service payments on the loan.

INDENTURE
A document of deed, usually in duplicate, expressing certain objects between the parties.

INFLATION
A general increase in consumer prices, most often expressed as an annual percentage rate.

INJUNCTION
A judicial process or order requiring the person to whom it is directed to do or refrain from doing a particular act.

INSTRUMENT
A form of written legal document.

INSURABLE VALUE
The term is used conventionally to designate the amount of insurance that may be carried on destructible portions of a property to indemnify the owner in the event of loss.

INTEREST ADJUSTMENT
A date from which interest on the mortgage advanced is calculated for your regular payments. This date is usually one payment period before regular mortgage payments begin, as interest payable is due from the date the mortgage is advanced.

INTEREST ESCALATION
Rate of interest on a loan is raised periodically during the term of the loan so as to encourage early repayment.

INTEREST-ONLY LOAN
Borrower pays back interest only on the loan and there is no amortization until later or until the end of the term. This may occur when a purchaser wishes to re-sell a property after a short period or if he or she wishes to build up enough income from the property before locking into a set amortization.

INTEREST RATE
The cost of a loan expressed as a percentage.

INTERIM FINANCING
Interim loans are used to bridge the gap between the construction loan and the permanent loan (hence "bridge" loans) lasting from one to three years.

INTERMEDIATE TERM LOAN
A short-term loan from three to five years with partial or no amortization (balloon loan).

IRREVOCABLE
Incapable of being recalled or revoked; unchangeable, unalterable.

J

JOINT AND SEVERAL NOTE
Promissory note on which there are two or more promisors who are jointly and severally liable.

JOINT TENANCY
Ownership of land by two or more persons whereby, on the death of one, the survivor or survivors take the whole estate.

JUNIOR FINANCING
This is a subordinate mortgage or loan very often given by a seller of property, second in priority to an existing loan.

K

KICKER
An extra bonus or additional payment over and above the fixed interest already paid to an investor, e.g., a percentage of gross profits or cash flow.

L

LAND ACQUISITION LOAN
Loan advanced to acquire land as opposed to improving land or buildings.

LAND CONTRACT
A contract drawn between a buyer and seller for the sale of property.

LAND DEVELOPMENT LOAN
Loan advanced for the purpose of developing raw land for residential and related uses.

LAND TRANSFER TAX
A fee paid to the government for the transferring of property from seller to buyer.

LEASEHOLD
A type of interest in a property that is certain only for a specified period of time granted by contract.

LEASEHOLD APPRAISAL
A method of estimating the value of a leasehold property.

LEASEHOLD MORTGAGE
A mortgage given by a lessee on the security of the leasehold interest in the land.

LEGAL DESCRIPTION
A written description by which a property can be definitely located and which is acceptable for registration in a land registry system.

LENDING VALUE
An independent appraiser's value interpreted by the lender as to the worth of a property in the current market, given a reasonable time period to sell the property.

LESSEE
Tenant under a lease.

LESSEE'S INTEREST
The market value of a property less the value of the lessor's interest. The present worth of the annual advantage, if any, accruing to the lessee by reason of the contract rent being less than the economic rent.

LESSOR
The person who grants use of the property under lease to a tenant.

LETTER OF COMMITMENT
Letter written by the lender stating the amount of the loan, specified interest rate, term of loan and specific conditions.

LETTER OF CREDIT
Letter issued by a bank or other lending institution promising payment to a third party in accordance with the terms of the agreement. Letters of credit may be used in situations where a deposit or security is required, e.g., a builder who is about to

sign a contract and has to put up security that the job will be finished, or a security deposit under a long-term lease.

LEVERAGE
Upside leverage in real estate occurs when the yield or net return on property exceeds debt service for a loan. Downside or reverse leverage occurs when the debt service is greater than the net return on investment.

LIEN
A legal claim against a property for money owed; a lien may be filed by a supplier or a subcontractor who has provided labour or materials but has not been paid; a lien must be properly filed by a claimant; it has limited life, prescribed by statute that varies from province to province; if the lien holder takes action within the prescribed time, the owner may be obliged to pay the amount claimed by the lien holder; the lien holder may force the sale of a property to pay off the debt.

LIEN HOLD BACK
A percentage of the contract price or estimated cost of work to be done, which is held back from the mortgage advance.

LINE OF CREDIT
A maximum credit limit allowed by a bank to a borrower, as long as the borrower maintains an acceptable balance on account or has a good credit rating. The terms of the credit line will vary from time to time according to the changing circumstances of the borrower or the bank.

LIS PENDENS
A legal document giving notice that an action or proceeding is pending in the courts, which affects the title to the designated property.

LIST (ASKING) PRICE
The price placed on a property for sale by the seller.

LISTING AGREEMENT
A legal agreement between the listing broker and seller, setting out the services to be rendered, describing the property for sale and stating the terms of payment; a commission is generally payable to the broker upon closing.

LOAN COVERAGE
The ratio of net operating income to debt service; in general, loan coverage of 1.3 is considered adequate for a loan to value ratio of 75 percent.

LOAN FEE
A charge for making a loan in addition to the interest charged to the borrower.

LOAN LOSS RESERVE
A reserve shown on a balance sheet of a real estate company as provision for any future losses in assets.

LOAN ORIGINATION
Analysis of loan applications from prospective purchasers to determine if they meet with requirements. Upon approval, the lender will issue a commitment letter.

LOAN PORTFOLIO TURNOVER
The average length of time required for the turnover of mortgage loans, i.e., until maturity.

LOAN PROCESSING
Upon application and approval of a loan, the lender has to go through a fairly standard procedure to finalize and disburse the loan such as the setting up of files, ordering of credit reports, verification of employment and bank accounts, etc.

LOAN-TO-VALUE RATIO
The ratio of the loan to the lending value of a property expressed as a percentage.

LOCK-IN CLAUSE
A clause that restricts prepayment of a loan during a specified period of the whole term of the mortgage. This ensures that the lender receives a stipulated return on his investment and discourages "shopping around" for another loan.

M

MARGIN OF SAFETY
A measure of the extent to which a loan is protected by property values or operating income. In the case of a mortgage, the margin of safety is the excess of equity (at fair market value) above the outstanding amount of the loan.

MARKET VALUE
The highest price estimated in terms of money that a property will bring if exposed for sale in the open market.

MARKETABLE TITLE
A title that a court of equity considers to be so free from defect that it will enforce acceptance by a purchaser.

MATURITY DATE
The last day of the term of the mortgage agreement. A mortgage loan must then be paid in full or the agreement renewed.

MECHANICS LIEN
A claim against the interest of the owner in a property for labour, services or materials supplied to it.

MIXED-USE DEVELOPMENT
A large scale real estate project that is developed for a number of uses. An example of mixed-use development is a shopping centre complex.

MORATORIUM
Legislation enacted to assist debtors by postponing or suspending their contractual payments.

MORE OR LESS
Term often found in a property description intended to cover slight, unimportant or insubstantial inaccuracies to which both parties are willing to assume risk.

MORTGAGE
The legal pledge of real estate as security for a loan. Lenders consider both the property (security) and the financial worth of the borrower (covenant) in deciding on a mortgage loan.

MORTGAGE BANKER
By legislation a chartered bank authorized under the BANK ACT of Canada to take deposits from individuals for placement in mortgages, by pooling these deposits and funding mortgages. The security for the depositor is an interest in the mortgage through the bank. A mortgage broker cannot by law pool money from individual depositors and fund mortgages, unless licensed to do so under other legislation.

MORTGAGE BOND
A bond issued by corporations and secured by a mortgage on their property.

MORTGAGE BROKER
A person who originates real estate loans and allocates mortgage funds. These funds are placed on behalf of others, through negotiation of lenders and borrowers for the best possible arrangement and satisfaction of all concerned. Licensed in Ontario by the Ministry of Financial Institutions. Could also be known as an underwriter, correspondent or investment dealer in a mortgage transaction.

The mortgagor pays the broker a fee for arranging the mortgage.

MORTGAGE COMMITMENT
A formal indication by a lending institution that it will grant a mortgage loan on property, in a certain specified amount and on certain specified terms.

MORTGAGE DEBENTURE
Synonymous with mortgage bond.

MORTGAGE INSURANCE
Applies to high-ratio mortgage; the borrower arranges and pays for the insurance, which protects the lender against default, if the borrower is unable to repay the mortgage.

MORTGAGE LIFE INSURANCE
Pays off the mortgage if the borrower dies.

MORTGAGE LOAN
An agreement by which a sum of money is borrowed and a promise to repay is given, wherein as a further security the borrower gives to the lender a conveyance or charge on property that he owns.

MORTGAGE NOTE
A promissory note executed in favour of the lender giving him an encumbrance or lien on the borrower's property. A mortgagor is usually personally liable on the note.

MORTGAGE PORTFOLIO
Several mortgages held by a mortgagee, lender or broker en bloc.

MORTGAGE POSTPONEMENT
The process whereby a mortgagee may permit the borrower to renew or replace an existing mortgage that falls due prior to the maturity date of the subject mortgage.

MORTGAGEE
The lender.

MORTGAGEE IN POSSESSION
A mortgagee goes into possession by entering into actual occupation of, or by obtaining the receipt of, the rents of the mortgaged premises.

MORTGAGING OUT
Term applied to a mortgage that exceeds the current value of the property on which it is secured. This type of mortgage may be obtained on improvable

property where the security is based on future value and future earnings that are expected to exceed construction costs.

MORTGAGOR
The borrower.

MULTI-FAMILY DWELLING
A property in which more than one suite is rentable.

MULTIPLE LISTING SERVICE (MLS)
Trademark owned by the Canadian Real Estate Association. Used in conjunction with a real estate database service operated by local real estate boards under which properties may be listed, purchased and sold.

N

NATIONAL HOUSING ACT (NHA)
The National Housing Act (1954) provides for insuring loans made by approved lenders and for direct mortgage lending under a variety of programs by Canada Mortgage and Housing Corporation (CMHC) to improve housing conditions in Canada.

NATIONAL HOUSING ACT MORTGAGE
A first mortgage, originated by an approved lender, granted under the terms of, and insured under, the National Housing Act of 1954.

NEGATIVE CASH FLOW
Where operating costs exceed gross rental income or debts.

NET OPERATING INCOME (NOI)
The balance remaining after deduction of operating expenses from gross receipts and gross rental, but not including the deducting of debt service on mortgages. Free and clear return on property is calculated by the ratio of NOI to total investment, including mortgages and equity. This gives a direct means of comparing the return on different properties.

NET RATE OF INTEREST
The interest rate received by a mortgage lender net of the servicing fee deducted by a loan correspondent.

NET WORTH
A person's total financial worth, determined by subtracting total liabilities from total assets.

NOMINAL INTEREST RATE
Often referred to as "effective rate." The interest rate stated on the face of a loan document. However, if the loan amount is discounted or sold at premium, the effective rate of interest will either be higher or lower.

NON-RECOURSE LOAN
A loan clause that waives personal liability of the borrower on the loan.

NOTICE DOR
Notice filed in court by mortgagor under foreclosure proceedings that he desires an opportunity to redeem and make good on past due balances

O

OAC
On approved credit.

OBLATORY ADVANCE
An advance made according to terms of a pre-existing construction loan agreement or mortgage.

OFFER TO PURCHASE
A written proposal to purchase real estate that becomes binding upon acceptance of the vendor.

OPEN OR CLOSED
The restriction or denial of repayment rights until the maturity of the mortgage is a "closed" mortgage. If specified on the document as "open," then the mortgagor can pay extra payments of principal sums at any time or at specified times, with or without repayment penalty.

OPEN-END MORTGAGE
A mortgage under which the lender has the option of advancing more funds where, for example, the value of the property is anticipated to increase.

OPERATING EXPENSES
Generally speaking, all expenses, occurring periodically, which are necessary to produce net income before depreciation. Under some conditions these expenses are placed in two categories, namely, operating expenses and fixed charges.

OPTION
A right given by the owner of a property to another (for valuable consideration) to buy a certain property within a limited time at an agreed price; an option holder who does not buy at or within the

specified period loses the deposit and the agreement is cancelled.

OWNER
The lawful possessor of the title to real property.

P

PACKAGE LOAN
A combination of two types of loans, e.g., a construction loan and permanent financing. The borrower benefits by having to negotiate with a single lender and having to pay a single set of closing costs.

PARTIAL DISCHARGE
A discharge of a definite portion of the mortgage lands usually given after the mortgagor has prepaid a specific portion of the mortgage debt.

PARTICIPATION LOAN
An agreement whereby two or more lenders share in advancing a portion of a loan made by the originating or "lead" bank. Terms of the agreement set out a method of apportionment and interest rates. The lead lender generally services the loan for which it receives a fee.

PERCENT PAID OFF
The percent of principal that is paid off at a given time under an amortization schedule, i.e., equity build-up.

PERCENTAGE RENTAL AGAINST MINIMUM
A rental paid under a percentage lease whereby rent paid by a tenant varies according to the volume of business, e.g., a percentage of gross receipts, sales or revenue is paid to the extent that it exceeds a minimum rental.

PERCENTAGE RENT PLUS MINIMUM
A percentage rental that must be paid in addition to the minimum; minimum rent is not credited against percentage rent payable.

PERMANENT FINANCING
A long-term mortgage usually intended to finance both land and improvements after completion of construction; it is used to pay off a construction loan.

PERSONAL LIABILITY
A person is liable on a debt to the full extent of his or her entire assets, as opposed to limited liability where a maximum or ceiling is fixed on the amount of assets that can be drawn upon to satisfy a debt.

Joint and several liability fixes the liability of each individual borrower for the total debt; joint liability binds all the borrowers together in one action; and several liability fixes the liability of each borrower to the extent of his or her share of the debt.

PERSONAL PROPERTY
All property except land and the improvements thereon.

POINTS
Discount charges imposed by lenders to raise the yield of their loan. One point equals 1 percent.

POLARIS
The Province of Ontario Land Registration Improvement System's new simplified method of registration of transfer, charge, discharge, etc.

PORTABILITY
A mortgage option that enables borrowers to take their mortgage with them to another property without penalty. A transfer fee may apply.

POSTPONEMENT CLAUSE
A junior mortgage may contain a postponement clause, by which the mortgagee permits the borrower to renew or replace an existing first mortgage that falls due prior to the maturity date of the junior mortgage.

POWER OF SALE
The right of a mortgagee to force the sale of the property without judicial proceedings should default occur.

PREPAYMENT CLAUSE
A clause inserted in a mortgage that gives the mortgagor the privilege of paying off all or part of the mortgage debt in advance of the maturity date.

PREPAYMENT PENALTY
The sum of money (the amount of extra interest as set out in the mortgage document) a mortgagee may require from a mortgagor to exercise the option in a mortgage to prepay any outstanding principal.

PRE-QUALIFICATION
An interview with a client (usually) prior to the writing of an offer to purchase real estate in order to determine the applicant's qualifications for a mortgage.

PRIME RATE
The rate charged by banks to their most credit-worthy borrowers. Sometimes referred to as the rate of interest paid on government bonds.

PRINCIPAL
The amount actually borrowed or still owing on a mortgage. Interest is paid on the principal amount.

PRIOR CHARGE
An encumbrance ranking in priority to the mortgage in question.

PRIOR ENCUMBRANCE
A claim on the property with priority ranking to the mortgage in question.

PRO FORMA STATEMENT
A financial statement of the gross income, operating costs, net operating costs and net operating income for a specified financial period, e.g., one year, using specified assumptions.

PROGRESS ADVANCES
Loan advances made on a property under construction whereby the lender makes advances on the basis of the retention at all times of an amount of the loan that in his/her opinion will be sufficient to complete the building, should the borrower fail to complete it.

PROJECTED INCOME
Estimated income from a property.

PROMISSORY NOTE
A written document acknowledging a debt and promising payment.

PROPERTY
Refers to the rights that an individual enjoys by virtue of his/her ownership.

PURCHASE-MONEY MORTGAGE (Vendor take back)
A mortgage loan taken back by the vendor of a property in lieu of purchase money in order to help provide financing to the purchaser.

Q

QUALIFYING
The process of qualifying the borrower and/or lender to ensure they respectively have the financial ability and inclination to undertake the mortgage.

QUANTUM MERUIT
The amount that should be paid as merited by the service performed.

QUIT CLAIM DEED
A general release of all claims or rights to a parcel of land.

R

REAL ESTATE
Land, buildings and other fixed improvements, including items that are not moveable.

REAL ESTATE BOARD
Non-profit organization representing local real estate brokers/agents/salespeople. Provides services to its members and maintains and operates an MLS system in the community.

REALTOR
A real estate broker holding active membership in a local real estate board.

REDEMPTION
The buying back of a mortgage estate by payment of the sum due on the mortgage.

REDEMPTION PERIOD
A period of time allowed by law during which a mortgagor may redeem his or her property by paying off the entire debt in arrears.

REFINANCE
To pay off (discharge) a mortgage and other registered encumbrances by arranging a new mortgage.

REGISTRATION AND DISCHARGE DATES
Dates of registration by number in the local Registry Office and/or Land Titles Office, which are then given to the mortgagee. When the loan has been paid in full at or after maturity date, the mortgagee executes the "discharge" or cessation of charge and registers same to liquidate the mortgage and allow the mortgagor to redeem the mortgage.

RELEASE OF COVENANT
A release given to the mortgagor of a property that has been sold to a new purchaser, who is acceptable to the mortgagee. This release is usually given after the new mortgagor has signed an assumption agreement.

RENEWAL AGREEMENT
An agreement whereby the lender may agree to extend the loan, but possibly on revised terms as to principal repayments and interest rate.

RENT CONTRACT

Rental received by the real estate owner under any lease contract.

RENTAL HOLDBACK STANDBY LOAN

A holdback is an amount withheld from the borrower under permanent financing until a certain occupancy rate is achieved. As this deprives the construction lender of full takeout protection, the developer may obtain a standby loan commitment to supplement the holdback.

RENTAL REQUIREMENTS

This is the "ceiling" portion of a permanent loan commitment that is advanced upon reaching a minimum rental or occupancy rate.

RENTAL VALUE

The monetary amount reasonably expectable for the right to the agreed use of real estate. It may be expressed as an amount per month or other period of time, or per room, per frontal foot or other unit of property.

RENT ECONOMIC

The income that real estate can command in the open market at any given time for its highest and best use.

REPRODUCTION COST

The cost of reproducing a new replica property on the basis of current prices with the same or very similar materials.

RESTRICTION

A limitation placed upon the use of property contained in the deed or other written instrument in the chain of title.

RESTS

The periodical balancing of an account made for the purpose of converting interest into principal and charging the party liable thereon with compound interest.

RETURN ON INVESTMENT (ROI)

(a) Free and clear return is calculated as the percentage of net operating income to total investment in the property; (b) Cash flow return is the ratio of cash flow to equity investment (also known as return on equity and cash-on-cash return); (c) Total return is cash flow, including loan amortization as a percentage of the total invested.

REVERSION

The right to repossess and resume the full and sole use and proprietorship of real property that tem-porarily has been alienated by lease, easement or otherwise. According to the terms of the controlling instrument, the reversionary right becomes effective at a stated time or under certain conditions, such as the termination of a leasehold, abandonment of a right-of-way or at the end of the stimulated economic life of the improvements. It is the present or discounted value of something to be collected at some future date.

RIGHT

The interest one has in a piece of property, i.e., a claim or title enforceable by law.

RIGHT OF SURVIVORSHIP

The distinguishing feature of joint tenancies that provides that, where land is held in undivided portions by co-owners, upon the death of any joint owner, his/her interest in the land will pass to the surviving co-owner, rather than to his/her estate.

RIGHT OF WAY

The right to pass over another's land, more or less frequently, according to the nature of an easement.

RIPARIAN RIGHTS

The rights of owners of land on the banks of watercourses to take advantageous use of the water on, under or adjacent to their land, including the right to acquire wharf slips and fish from them.

RUNNING WITH THE LAND

A covenant is said to run with the land when it extends beyond the original parties to the agreement and binds all subsequent owners to either liability to perform it or the right to take advantage of it.

S

SALE AND LEASEBACK

A method of financing where a property is sold to a purchaser who simultaneously enters into a long-term lease of the property with the vendor. The vendor (now lessee) remains in possession for the specified term of the lease and agrees to pay the rental to this purchaser (now lesser) as well as all operation expenses. This enables the user to free his or her cash investment in the real property for some other use.

SALES HOLDBACK

A percentage of the principal amount of the mortgage held back by the mortgagee until the property in question has been sold to a party satisfactory to the mortgagee.

SANDWICH LEASE
A lease in which the "sandwich party" is the lessee of one party and the lesser to another. Usually, the owner of the sandwich lease is neither the fee owner nor the user of the property.

SEALED AND DELIVERED
A term indicating that a conveyor has received adequate consideration as evidenced by his/her voluntary delivery. The word "sealed" adds more strength, since under old conveyance law an official seal was used as a substitute for consideration.

SECOND MORTGAGE
A mortgage loan granted (and registered) when there is already a first mortgage registered against the property, usually with shorter terms and a higher interest rate than the first mortgage.

SECURED CREDITOR
A creditor who has one or more forms of security that gives a prior claim on the security in case of default.

SELLER FINANCING
When an owner of a property provides the purchaser with a mortgage (or other financing) so that the buyer does not have to obtain any or all of the financing from another source.

SELLER'S AGENT
Represents the seller as a listing agent under the listing agreement with the seller, or by cooperating as a sub-agent, typically through the MLS system.

SERVIENT TENEMENT
An estate or land over which an easement or some other service exists in favour of the dominant tenement.

SETBACK
The distance from the curb or other established line within which no buildings may be erected.

SHORT-FORM MORTGAGE
A mortgage document that follows the exact language of the long form prescribed by law but is abbreviated, using shortened terminology. It has the identical legal effect of a long-form mortgage.

SINGLE-FAMILY DWELLING
A residential property designed for occupancy by one family and situated on land zoned specifically for that purpose.

SPECIFIC PERFORMANCE
A remedy in a court of equity compelling a defendant to carry out the terms of an agreement or contract. It is available only where the remedy of damages cannot afford adequate relief to the plaintiff.

SPECULATIVE BUILDER OR DEVELOPER
One who builds without having a commitment to buy or lease from a purchaser or tenant.

STANDBY COMMITMENT
A commitment from a lender to make a loan in a specified period of time, on specified terms, with the understanding that the borrower will not likely draw down the funds.

STATEMENT OF ADJUSTMENTS
A balance statement prepared by lawyers setting out the details of a mortgage transaction. It indicates credits to the vendor, such as the purchase price and any prepaid taxes, and credits to the buyer, such as the deposit and the balance due on closing.

STATUS CERTIFICATE (also called an ESTOPPEL CERTIFICATE)
A written statement or certificate that states certain facts upon which the receiver of the statement or a third party may rely, e.g., a lender's estoppel statement as to a purchaser or property. The lender cannot later deny the truth of these statements because a third party has relied and acted upon them.

STATUTE
A law established by an act of the legislature.

STATUTE OF FRAUDS
A law that provides that certain contracts must be in writing in order to be enforceable by law. It includes real estate contracts.

STATUTE OF LIMITATIONS
That period of time specified by statute within which an action at law must be brought or else be forfeited.

STEP-DOWN LEASE
A lease providing for decreases in rental payment at specified dates.

STEP-UP LEASE
A lease providing for increases in rental payment at specified dates.

SUBORDINATION CLAUSE
A mortgage clause that gives priority to a mortgage taken out at a later date.

SURVEY
A document that illustrates a property's boundaries and measurements, the position of major structures on that property and any registered or viable easements.

SURVIVORSHIP
The right of a person to secure ownership by reason of his/her outliving someone with whom he/she shared undivided interest in the land.

T

TAKEOUT MORTGAGE LOAN
A long-term mortgage loan that is advanced to a borrower on completion of construction or in compliance with any other conditions in the loan commitment. The funds are normally used to pay off or take out the construction lender.

TAX LIEN
A lien imposed by a taxing authority on real estate for failure to pay taxes within the time required by law.

TENANCY AT WILL
A licence to use or occupy lands and buildings at the will of the owner.

TENANCY IN COMMON
Ownership of and by two or more persons. Unlike joint tenancy, the interest of the deceased does not pass to the survivor but is treated as an asset of the deceased's estate.

TENURE
A system of land holdings for a temporary time period.

TERM (OF LOAN)
The length of time that a mortgage agreement covers. Payments made may not repay the outstanding principal by the end of the term because of a longer amortization period. Also indicates when the principal balance becomes due and payable to the lender.

TIME IS OF THE ESSENCE
Requires punctual performance of a contract on closing date and is indicated by so stating, as in an Agreement of Purchase and Sale.

TITLE
The means of evidence by which the owner of land has lawful ownership thereof. A freehold title gives the holder full and exclusive ownership of land and buildings for an indefinite period of time; in condominium ownership, land and common elements of buildings are owned collectively by all unit owners, while the residential units belong exclusively to the individual owners; a leasehold title gives the holder a right to use and occupy land and buildings for a defined period of time.

TITLE INSURANCE
A policy that insures the lender and purchaser against loss due to a flaw in the title of property held as collateral for a mortgage.

TITLE RESTRICTION
A restriction in a deed to limit or govern the use of the land.

TITLE SEARCH
An examination of the chain of title to real property as indicated in the public records in order to determine the ownership of the property and the existence of any encumbrances or defects.

TORRENS SYSTEM
Also known as the "Land Titles System." System of recording titles provided by provincial law. It is a system for the registration of land title, indicating the state of the title, including ownership and encumbrances without the necessity of an additional search of the public records.

TOTAL DEBT SERVICE (TDS)
The percentage of gross annual income required to cover payments associated with housing and all other debts and obligations.

TRANSFER
To convey from one person to another.

TRANSFER OF CHARGE
Assignment of a mortgage under the Land Titles System.

U

UMBRELLA MORTGAGE
Also referred to as a "wrap-around mortgage." A special arrangement whereby one document encompasses one or more already existing mortgages registered on

the same property. The mortgagee is responsible for remission of payment(s) to lender(s), while the mortgagor makes one payment to the mortgagee.

UNDERWRITER (MORTGAGE)
A person employed by a mortgage lender or mortgage broker who approves or turns down loan applications based upon the quality of the real property, the creditworthiness and ability of the applicant to pay, as well as guidelines of the lender with regard to the ratio of the mortgage loan to the value of the property.

V

VALID
Having force or binding force that is legally sufficient and authorized by law.

VALUABLE CONSIDERATION
The granting of some beneficial right, interest or profit for suffering of some detrimental forbearance, loss or default by one party in exchange for the performance of another.

VARIABLE INTEREST MORTGAGE
A loan where the interest rate may vary during the term of the mortgage. The variance is usually tied to some specific factor such as the prime bank rate or the guaranteed investment certificate rate for a designated lender.

VENDOR
A seller of real property.

VENDOR TAKEBACK MORTGAGE
A mortgage that a vendor of real property takes from the purchaser, usually as part payment of the purchase price for that property.

VOID
Of no legal effect; a nullity.

VOIDABLE
Where one party to a contract is entitled to rescind the contract at his or her option.

W

WAIVER
An international relinquishment of some right or interest; the renunciation, abandonment or surrender of some claim.

WITNESS
To subscribe one's name to a deed, will or other document for the purpose of attesting its authenticity and proving its execution by testifying, if required.

WRAP-AROUND MORTGAGE
Sometimes erroneously called a blanket mortgage. A new mortgage that is registered on title and that includes a prior existing mortgage. The new mortgagee undertakes the responsibility as mortgagor under the original mortgage.

Y – Z

YIELD
The return on an investment expressed as a percentage per annum of the amount invested.

ZONING
The public regulation of the character and intensity of the use of real estate through the employment of police power. This is accomplished by the establishment of districts in each of which uniform holding restrictions related to use, height, area, bulk and density of population are imposed upon the private property.

Note to Reader: These terms are intended as quick references only. Be sure to seek legal or accounting advice for all of your real estate transactions.

APPENDIX 3: SUPPORT TOOLS AND KEY CONTACTS

Real estate is a team game and the strength of your team will help determine how quickly you achieve success. In addition, keeping on top of key economic trends as well as changes to laws that affect real estate investors is absolutely critical.

With this in mind, here are some additional support tools, websites and education materials that can greatly assist you.

Landlord and Tenant Government Websites

The following is a list of government websites that outline landlord and tenant laws. Many of them provide shortened versions of their acts in plain English. It is important for you to review information for your areas.

British Columbia http://www.pssg.gov.bc.ca/rto/

Alberta http://www3.gov.ab.ca/gs/information/landlord/

Saskatchewan http://www.saskjustice.gov.sk.ca/legislation/summaries/landilordtenantact.shtml

Manitoba http://www.gov.mb.ca/finance/cca/rtb/resource.html

Ontario http://www.orht.gov.on.ca/scripts/index_.asp

Quebec http://www.educaloi.qc.ca/TLR_Law/F01_ResumeCapsules/index.php3?no=19&noCat=6

New Brunswick http://www.legal-info-legale.nb.ca/pub-landlord-tenant.asp

Nova Scotia http://www.gov.ns.ca/snsmr/consumer/resten/

Prince Edward Island http://www.irac.pe.ca/rental/

Newfoundland and Labrador http://www.gov.nf.ca/gs/cca/rt/

Northwest Territories http://www.justice.gov.nt.ca/RentalOffice/rentalofficer.htm

Yukon http://www.gov.yk.ca/depts/community/consumer/landtact.html

Nunavut http://www.gov.nu.ca/Nunavut/index.shtml

Don R. Campbell's ACRE System Nine-CD Home Study Program

The ACRE system is taught through a nine-CD home study program titled "The Real Estate Investment Networks' Quick Start System." It is 100 percent Canadian and has been developed by the author of this book, Don R. Campbell, and special guest Tim Johnson.

This 100% money-back guaranteed program is a must-have for all Canadian investors, both veteran and rookie alike. Registered readers of this book can receive a special discount. For more details visit www.realestateinvestingincanada. com and click on the Quickstart button, or call Don's office directly at 1-888-824-7346 and they can rush it to you.

Tim Johnson

Tim Johnson is now a full-time dad and real estate investor. He lives in a spectacular area in Southern Alberta where he continues to use real estate to create wealth and cash flow. He was instrumental in introducing the Real Estate Investing Network™ (REIN™) program to Alberta and developing the foundation from which the ACRE system grew. His financial insights have impacted thousands of Albertans. Tim has also written a very moving and insightful book titled *Searching for Sam*, which describes his emotional journey after his young son tragically drowned. Read more about *Searching for Sam* at www.searchingforsam.com.

Alan Jacques

Due to Alan Jacques' success in business and real estate, he is now able to focus his attention on three key areas: his family, his photography and his writing. He brings his unique talents to all three. Alan as founder of REIN™, has helped change thousands of people's financial lives across the country and continues to do so today. He is now completing his latest book, *The Q Solution*, in which he provides insights into producing breakthrough results in your business and personal life.

Les Hewitt

Les Hewitt, who graciously wrote the foreword for this book, is the best selling co-author of many books including *The Power of Focus, The Power of Focus for Women* and *The Power of Faithful Focus*. He also offers business-coaching programs.

REAL ESTATE INVESTMENT NETWORK — REIN™

The Real Estate Investment Network™ (REIN™) is a group dedicated to providing real estate investors unbiased research and strategies for the Canadian marketplace. Members of REIN meet monthly in select cities across the country. Some of its members live outside Canada. It is now entering its 13th year of operation and has assisted members in riding the upward swings in the market while avoiding the downturns. Members have safely and securely purchased close to $1 billion of residential real estate. REIN's members focus on long-term wealth as opposed to getting rich quick. This success comes from focusing on real life economic fundamentals and putting the ACRE system into action. This system takes the hype out of the marketplace so you can focus on what works right in your back yard.

REIN is an exclusive paid-membership program, which is dedicated to educating its members about how, where and when to buy Canadian real estate. From networking with other active investors, to providing direct access to leading-edge experts, it is the most complete program of its kind anywhere in North America. You will never have to buy from, invest with or put money into any real estate deal with anyone in, or associated with REIN. However, REIN offers many opportunities to do joint ventures or purchase properties with other members. You are always in control!

REIN's single objective is to help *you* become an experienced, confident and wealthy real estate investor. There are no huge upfront fees; REIN believes that money is best spent investing in real estate—not on seminars.

To receive a FREE 12-page package on the benefits of being a member of Canada's most successful real estate investment program, with over $1 billion dollars purchased and 13 years of market experience, call 1-888-824-7346 today or e-mail your mailing address and telephone number to Don R. Campbell's office at info@reincanada.com or visit www.realestateinvestingincanada.com and click on the REIN button. We look forward to helping you achieve your own Personal Belize.

INDEX

retirees affect on, 41
vendors
    assessing, 83–84
vision. *See* Goals

W
WestJet Airlines, 47
Winter, Real Estate, 74
workforce, 46. *See also* Jobs
working capital, 108

Z
zoning, 50